Depth Psychology, Myth and Artificial Intelligence

Jason D. Batt • Jonathan Erickson
Editors

Depth Psychology, Myth and Artificial Intelligence

Soul and the Machine

palgrave
macmillan

Editors
Jason D. Batt
Deep Space Predictive Research Group
Denver, CO, USA

Project Lodestar
Thornton, CO, USA

The International Society of Mythology
Columbia, MD, USA

Jonathan Erickson
California Institute of Integral Studies
San Francisco, CA, USA

ISBN 978-3-031-94104-7 ISBN 978-3-031-94105-4 (eBook)
https://doi.org/10.1007/978-3-031-94105-4

This Palgrave Macmillan imprint is published by the registered company Springer Nature Switzerland AG.
The registered company address is: Gewerbestrasse 11, 6330 Cham, Switzerland

Contents

About the Authors

Alires J. Almon is a multidisciplinary innovation technology leader with experience in advanced technologies, such as artificial intelligence/applied machine learning, behavioral health, and digital transformation. As a social science researcher, her passion has focused on understanding groups and teams and how they evolve in isolated, confined, and extreme conditions. Alires has participated in international initiatives, most notably the Defense Advanced Research Project Agency (DARPA) seed-funded 100 Year Starship (100YSS) project as one of the coauthors of the original proposal. She founded Deep Space Predictive Research Group to push the boundaries of social science and behavioral technologies. She leads an international research team that aims to create new behavioral technology to support humans in space exploration. She also served as Partner Director at the AI Institute at Iliff School of Theology. The institute facilitates a deeper understanding of the complex integrations and social implications of developing and applying artificial intelligence and machine learning technologies. Alires is pursuing a PhD in Human and Social Dimensions of Science and Technology.

Jason D. Batt is a technological philosopher, mythologist, futurist, artist, writer, former teacher, whose dissertation focused on the mythologies of the future, in particular those of interstellar travel. He is a co-founder of Deep Space Predictive Research Group, Project Lodestar, and the International Society of Mythology. He founded and organized the Canopus Award for Excellence in Interstellar Writing. His novels include *Onliest*, *Young Gods*, and *Dreamside*, and his short fiction has appeared in *Perihelion*, *Bastion*, *Bewildering Stories*, *A Story Goes On*, and other periodicals. His scholarly work has appeared in *Room*, *Renaissance*, the *Mythological Studies Journal*, *IAC Proceedings*, and more. He edited the science fiction anthology *Visions of the Future*, published through Lifeboat Foundation and *Strange California*, a successful Kickstarter through Falstaff Books. His most recent publication is the chapter "Evolving Light" with authors Alires Almon and Ted Vial in Routledge's "Outer Space and Religion" book, released July 2023. He is the Co-Managing Editor of the *Beyond Earth Institute Space Policy Review* and Associate Editor of the *Journal of Space Philosophy.*

John Bucher is a mythologist and story consultant who has been featured on the BBC, the History Channel, in the *LA Times*, and on numerous other international outlets. He serves as Executive Director for the Joseph Campbell Foundation and is a writer, podcaster, storyteller, and speaker. He has worked with government and cultural leaders around the world as well as organizations such as HBO, DC Comics, Paramount Pictures, Nickelodeon, A24 Films, Atlas Obscura, and The John Maxwell Leadership Foundation. He has served as a producer, consultant, and writer for numerous film, television, and Virtual Reality projects. He is the author of six books including the bestselling *Storytelling for Virtual Reality*, named by BookAuthority as one of the best storytelling books of all time. John has worked with *New York Times* Best Selling authors, YouTube influencers, Eisner winners, Emmy winners, Academy Award nominees, magicians, and cast members from Saturday Night Live. He holds a PhD in Mythology & Depth Psychology and has spoken on six continents about using the power of story and myth to reframe how individuals, organizations, cultures, and nations believe and behave.

B. Earl is an American entrepreneur, writer and filmmaker who lives between Los Angeles and New York. Earl has written with Marvel Entertainment since 2017 on the books Masters of the Sun, Werewolf by Night, Ghost Rider: Kushala, Deadly Neighborhood Spider-Man, and most recently Daredevil and Echo. He also contributed to the special MARVEL #1000 anthology. Earl and his partners recently launched their Saudi-based studio, WeirdBunch Entertainment. The studio is building a bridge between Hollywood and KSA to produce four-quadrant international entertainment focused on Saudi-centric storytelling through animation, video gaming, and graphic novels. His role within the studio is as head of technology where he oversees emerging technology integration into development and production workflows. WeirdBunch's first project, The Legend of Soloman, is currently in production.

Jonathan Erickson is an assistant professor in the integral transpersonal psychology PhD program at the California Institute of Integral Studies. He is the author of the book *Imagination in the Western Psyche: From Ancient Greece to Modern Neuroscience*, as well as a variety of papers exploring creativity, imagination, neuroscience, spirituality, and ecopsychology. In addition to his scholarly publications, he is the author of the *Song of Ancients* series of science fiction novels which explore themes of transpersonal consciousness and artificial intelligence. Before embarking on his academic career, Jonathan worked as a somatic yoga teacher and holistic bodyworker trained at the Esalen Institute. He holds a PhD in depth psychology with emphasis in somatic studies from Pacifica Graduate Institute, an MFA in creative writing from Antioch University Los Angeles, and a BA in English literature and interdisciplinary field studies from the University of California at Berkeley.

Dylan Francisco is an assistant professor and co-chair of the Jungian and Archetypal Studies MA/PhD program at Pacifica Graduate Institute in Santa Barbara, California. Dylan grounds his teaching in the depth psychology of C. G. Jung, decolonialism, and Mestizo/Mexican/Indigenous traditions that provide a primordial, holistic, and sacred worldview within which to understand the psyche, to embody its wholeness individually, and to live it relationally through honoring Spirit, the ancestors, and the land.

Jacob W. Glazier, is Assistant Professor of Psychology in the School of Social Sciences at the University of West Georgia. His research revolves around critical theory, subjectivity, and exceptional experiences. He also practices psychotherapy. He is the author of *Arts of Subjectivity* (2020), editor of the PA Book Award-winning *Paranormal Ruptures* (2023), and under contract with Routledge for an upcoming book on critical psychology and exceptional experiences. In addition, Dr. Glazier is the Lead Editor of *Mindfield: The Bulletin of the Parapsychological Association.*

Lydia Griffiths, a PhD candidate in comparative mythology, explores the intersection of popular culture and myth, with a particular focus on fandoms as contemporary expressions of mythological storytelling. As a mythologist, writer, and storyteller, she views narratives as essential threads that bind communities together and shape the broader human experience. Her recent work includes publications such as *Hermes Overdosed: The*

Archetypal Hermes in Social Media and *Tumblr's Reception of Webtoon Lore Olympus' Apollo* in the *Mythological Studies Journal*, along with *Is There Room for Mysticism in The Presbyterian Church (U.S.A.)?* in *Presbyterian Outlook*. Lydia has also appeared on the *Matter of Faith* Podcast and taught courses on discovering one's personal myth. Beyond her academic work, she is a co-founder of The International Society of Mythology, an organization dedicated to fostering a global mythological community and advancing the study of myth.

Don Hanlon Johnson has spent some 60 years working to craft educational institutions to investigate and nurture the many practices of body transformation—breathing, moving, touching, sensing, expressing feeling and emotion—that have permeated cultures around the world for centuries. And particularly the insights emerging in those practices for nurturing human relationships, especially large groups, and in developing more robust developments of wisdom. He created the somatics psychotherapy clinical degree program originally at the now defunct branch of University in San Francisco which moved to the California Institute of Integral Studies, where he now works with a group of scholars to develop a new doctorate program in somatic psychology. He has published a number of books, collections, and journal articles on these topics. As he enters into his 90s, he devotes particular attention to how embodiment practices contribute to meaningful aging.

Nicholas S. Literski is an Assistant Professor of Depth Psychology and Creativity at Pacifica Graduate Institute, and a professional spiritual guide. Previously, Nick taught psychology and research methods at the California Institute of Integral Studies. Nick holds a doctorate in Depth Psychology with Emphasis in Jungian and Archetypal Studies from Pacifica Graduate Institute, as well as a master's in Spiritual Guidance from Sofia University. Their research interests include depth psychological reflections on spirituality, magic, Paleolithic cave art, sexual orientation, and gender identity. Nick's work has been published in *Psychological Perspectives: A Quarterly Journal of Jungian Thought*; *Immanence: The Journal of Applied Mythology, Legend, and Folklore*; *Somatics Magazine-Journal of the Mind-Body Arts and Sciences*; and the recent compilation, *The Reality of Fragmentation and the Yearning for Healing: Jungian Perspectives on Democracy, Power, and Illusion in Contemporary Politics.* Their book, *Method Infinite: Freemasonry and the Mormon Restoration*, was published in 2022.

Emily Lord-Kambitsch is an assistant professor in the Mythological Studies Program at Pacifica Graduate Institute. Her lifelong exploration of classical mythology is rooted in the study of Greek and Latin language and literature. Her research interests include myth and posthumanism, ancient theories of emotion, the influences of Greco-Roman myth in Jungian psychology, embodied approaches to learning and teaching classical myth, and representations of ancient Greece and Rome in modern popular fiction, theatre, and cinema. Her work appears in the journals *The Journal of Cognitive Historiography* (2024), *Nineteenth Century Theatre and Film* (2017), and the collections, *Rewriting the Ancient World: Greeks, Romans, Jews and Christians in Modern Popular Fiction* (Brill, 2017) and *Star Attractions: Twentieth-century Movie Magazines and Global Fandom* (University of Iowa Press, 2019). Her current research traces relationships between memory, longing, and selfhood in the voices of women from Greek tragedy. She is also a poet-storyteller who draws inspiration from the experiences of mythic women, and her poem about Persephone, "Pluto's Wife in Transit," won first prize for original poem in the Classical Association's international poetry competition in 2024.

John Fujio Mandeville is a linguist, mythologist, and technologist. He holds a bachelor's in linguistics with a minor in computer science from the University of California, Berkeley. His focus there was on natural language acquisition and comparative linguistics. He also holds a doctorate from Pacifica Graduate Institute in mythological studies with emphasis in depth psychology. The title of his dissertation is *Complexity Theory and Creativity: Seeing Through to the Mythic Leonardo da Vinci*, in which he used a transdisciplinary framework to demonstrate that Leonardo da Vinci was a mythic figure and a complexity- thinker. Fujio is also a software application manager and solutions architect. His main interests are the intersection between myth, complexity-thinking and theory, technology, and its effect on culture, the usurpation of mythology for political ends, and transhumanism. His current efforts and interests delve into the intersect between artificial intelligence and the human psyche. His writings are informed by various disciplines, including art history, depth psychology, mythology, complexity theory, mathematics, computer science, and historical hermeneutics. He lives in Washington State with his wife, Monica.

Bradley McDevitt is a depth psychology and humanities professor, a leadership development coach, and founder of the creative consultancy CarolinaCommons.org. With a background in theater and the performing arts, he applies these perspectives to his coaching, consulting, and teaching, focusing on embodiment and somatic integration as the fulcrum for personal growth and mental health. Bradley is a faculty member at Pacifica Graduate Institute, exploring the intersections of Jungian psychology, creativity, and meaning-making.

Elizabeth Éowyn Nelson worked as a consultant in Silicon Valley for 18 years before beginning her career as a professor in 2003. She teaches courses in research design and process, archetypal psychology, and technology at Pacifica Graduate Institute and, in private practice, coaches aspiring authors of fiction, nonfiction, and memoir. Nelson's books include *Psyche's Knife: Archetypal Explorations of Love and Power* (Chiron, 2012) and *The Art of Inquiry: A Depth Psychological Perspective* (Spring Publications, 2017), coauthored with Joseph Coppin, and *The Art of Jungian Couple Therapy* (Routledge, 2025), coauthored with Anthony Delmedico. Nelson teaches and speaks internationally and has published numerous scholarly papers and book chapters on subjects including animals, dreams, feminism, film, mythology, research, somatics, and technology. She has been a professional writer and editor for 40 years, coaching aspiring authors across many genres and styles.

Luca M. Possati is an assistant professor at the University of Twente in the Netherlands, specializing in human–technology interaction. He also holds a senior researcher position with the international research program Ethics of Socially Disruptive Technologies (ESDiT). His research focuses on the intersection of philosophy of technology, postphenomenology, and the psychology of technology, exploring how humans engage with and are shaped by sociotechnical systems. He has published numerous papers and books on phenomenology, and history of contemporary philosophy. He is the author of *The Algorithmic Unconscious: How Psychoanalysis Helps in Understanding AI* (Routledge, 2021).

Glen Slater is the author of *Jung Vs. Borg: Finding the Deeply Human in a Posthuman Age* and Professor of Jungian and Archetypal Psychology at Pacifica Graduate Institute. He studied psychology and comparative religion at The University of Sydney before coming to the United States in 1992 for doctoral work in clinical psychology. His publications have appeared in a number of Jungian journals and essay collections, and he edited and introduced the third volume of *James Hillman's Uniform*

Edition, Senex and Puer, as well as a collection of faculty writings, *Varieties of Mythic Experience: Essays on Religion, Psyche and Culture*. Beyond his work in Jungian and Archetypal Psychology, he writes on psyche and film as well as the psychology of technology. He lectures internationally in these areas of interest.

Christopher M. Zieske is a PhD candidate in Psychology at the University of West Georgia. His research revolves around applying existential-phenomenological principles to digital technology, exploring specific experiences that are mediated by the increasing centrality of digital technology to society. He is also interested in uses of existential-phenomenological thought to critique the Cartesian assumptions inherent in AI-inspired models of human consciousness. His dissertation research is committed to a qualitative cinematic-phenomenological study of digital immersion as exemplified in gaming immersion—a project that he hopes will start a lifelong career of using arts-based phenomenological methods to examine digitally mediated experiences.

Introduction

Jonathan Erickson and Jason D. Batt

We have entered an age when artificial intelligence (AI) not only exceeds our capacity for calculation but also masters the complexities of our language, imitates our creativity, and raises questions about consciousness itself. As AI systems increasingly shape our world, they do more than assist us; they reflect and magnify our social and psychological dynamics—our projections, fears, fantasies, and longings. In their eerie mimicry of humanity, they force us to confront the boundaries between machine and psyche, between material and immaterial, and between intelligence and self-awareness. We find ourselves reckoning with profound and difficult questions about our basic understandings of ourselves and the universe we inhabit.

J. Erickson
California Institute of Integral Studies, San Francisco, CA, USA

J. D. Batt (✉)
Deep Space Predictive Research Group, Denver, CO, USA

Project Lodestar, Thornton, CO, USA

The International Society of Mythology, Columbia, MD, USA
e-mail: jason@jbatt.com

J. D. Batt, J. Erickson (eds.), *Depth Psychology, Myth and Artificial Intelligence*, https://doi.org/10.1007/978-3-031-94105-4_1

At the time of this writing, the term *artificial intelligence* has achieved such widespread popular usage that it may be easy to assume that we all mean exactly the same thing by it. Yet behind such assumptions we find a wide array of definitions and fantasies at work. For the purposes of this volume, we define artificial intelligence broadly and pragmatically to refer to the many programs and products being developed and offered to the general population under that name in the first half of the twentieth century. These products vary in their functions and aesthetics, but they all make attempts to emulate, replicate, or reproduce aspects of human cognition, including calculation, complex use of language, and, more aspirationally, reasoning and creativity. In the pages that follow, our authors engage readers in a deeper examination of these topics that span psychology, mythology, and the abundant expanse of the human imagination. We extend an invitation to both producers and users of AI technology to explore the existential, spiritual, and ethical layers intertwined with their creation and use, and their implications for our evolving relationship with intelligence and technology.

Depth Psychology and Artificial Intelligence

Depth psychology, broadly speaking, is any psychology that studies the *unconscious* aspects of the human mind, including the dynamic relationship between what is conscious and what is not. This might mean getting in touch with repressed emotions, or buried aspects of the self—our hidden desires and resentment, secret dreams, or aspects of identity that were silenced due to upbringings or other traumatic circumstances—or engaging a deep creative process that goes beyond conscious assembly. C. G. Jung also proposed a collective unconscious, a field of shared archetypal patterns that all human beings share. Here, an archetype can be understood most simply as a pattern of human experience: What are the aggregated dimensions of the experience of being a mother, for example? Or a warrior, or a trickster, or a leader? There is a common confusion between archetype and stereotype, where the latter is a flattening of archetypal possibility into overly narrow tropes. A mother can be many things, both good and bad, and in its proper meaning the mother archetype contains the fullness of this complexity—it is a field of possibilities for motherhood, rather than just one image or narrative about it. Human mothers can be a source of abundant love and nurturance, or an abyss of neglect and abuse, yet they are mothers nonetheless. In this sense, depth psychology as a field attempts to acknowledge the psyche's complexity as a multivalent phenomenon that will never fit neatly into the narrow confines of scientific study in the laboratory. To recognize these complex layers of human beings is not to devalue massive contributions of empirical psychology, but rather to recognize that not everything that makes us human can fit into the controlled conditions of a lab. This is, after all, why we have a tradition of dividing human knowledge into the sciences and the *humanities*. Though the latter are often devalued in a society that increasingly favors efficiency over understanding, we maintain that humanities, and especially depth psychology, enrich scientific exploration and are essential to grappling with life's greater mysteries.

To take a depth psychological view of artificial intelligence, then, is to probe the deeper questions about humanity and AI that the popular discourse often leaves out. The bulk of our contemporary conversations center around capability, productivity, and efficiency of these technologies, and, on an individual level, our hopes that they might bring us greater professional success and personal fulfillment. In this book, we inquire into the unconscious elements of this process. What are the deeper psychological needs trying to be met through this new technology? What are the hidden archetypal patterns at play in turning to the prospect of a different kind of mind, a mind not quite human, perhaps a mind that is more than human? In this liminal space, we find a spectrum of fantasies ranging from a coming utopia ushered in by the potentials of these immaculately conceived technologies, to the enslavement or destruction of humanity by rogue AI that has outsmarted its programmers. Our intent in this volume is not to provide a singular narrative or solution, but rather to reveal the unconscious, unspoken psychological possibilities at work. A depth psychological approach to artificial intelligence ultimately invites us into a relational stance of *being with* our inner worlds as these technologies emerge, rather than coldly analyzing them as though they were occurring only on the outside.

Depth psychology also pays particular attention to the study of myth. Here, further definitions of terms may be helpful, as myth can mean many things depending on the context. In the traditional scientific context, the word "myth" is often synonymous with falsehood, used to indicate a story people believe in despite the scientific evidence against it. For example, the notion that lightning never strikes twice, when the empirical evidence clearly shows otherwise, or the belief the Earth is flat (which a distressing number of humans believe to the present day). This is decidedly not the usage with which this volume brings the study of myth to bear in understanding the contemporary relationship between human beings and artificial intelligence. Here, we speak of myths as stories that are not literally true in the scientific sense, but rather collective stories that offer metaphoric truth and insight into the human condition. Myths, in this sense, are viewed as a deposit of archetypal truth, in which a given culture has recorded archetypal patterns in such a way as to provide insight about humanity's place in the cosmos and collective guidance about how our lives might proceed. Archetypal psychologist James Hillman argues, "Psychology shows myths in modern dress and myths show our depth psychology in ancient dress" (*Mythic Figures* 154). For Hillman, mythology is a window into the psychology of the past, and our current psychological systems are a window into the mythology of the present.

It is important to keep in mind that inherent in the psychological study of mythology is the understanding that there is no one true myth. We may recognize wisdom in Joseph Campbell's conception of the "hero's journey" (a topic explored in John Bucher's chapter in this volume), but that does not mean that everyone's hero's journey will unfold according to a similar formula—only that many lives have proceeded this way and many more will. Inherent in the study of myth is the recognition that myths evolve and express themselves in diverse permutations. In some recorded versions of Greek myth, Ariadne, who helped Theseus navigate the minotaur's labyrinth, is abandoned and commits suicide. In others, she is met by the god Dionysus, and become his bride. In distinction from scientific truth, which seeks to isolate variables to determine an absolute empirical reality, mythic truth invites us into a deeper understanding of the full spectrum of human experience in all of its possible permutations. Our myths about artificial intelligence, spoken and unspoken, thus offer us a mirror in which we grapple with what it means to be human.

To frame AI mythologically, we draw from Joseph Campbell's observation "the dreams that blister sleep, boil up from the basic, magic ring of myth" (*Hero With a Thousand Faces* 1). While Campbell did not write explicitly of AI, his exploration of collective dreams provides a lens for understanding humanity's cultural obsession with machines. Films like *The Terminator* and *The Matrix* offer not only cautionary tales but also serious meditations on the myths we unconsciously construct around AI. We have been collectively dreaming of AI, trying to explore it, at least unconsciously. Walter Benjamin's 1935 assertion, "[A]n unconsciously penetrated space is substituted for a space consciously explored" ("Work of Art" 236–7). underscores how myths have always served as proxies for real, lived engagement. Through cinema, we have long prefigured the ethical and existential dilemmas AI presents, unconsciously rehearsing its integration into our lived reality. This exploration utilizes the toolbox of mythology. The films that have explored AI are not to be set aside as mere entertainment—instead, they are *prima materia* for our reflection—primary documents that can be explored, analyzed, and interpreted to help us further explore the future we find ourselves on the threshold of. For that reason, we bring mythology to the conversation—to leave it behind would be to prevent access and understanding of a great many years of mass unconscious exploration now that what was forever far off has finally arrived.

Mythology, then, becomes an indispensable framework for engaging with AI, offering not only a lens through which we can interpret the rise of intelligent machines but also a repository of wisdom that guides our ethical and existential responses. Myths have historically provided a symbolic architecture for grappling with the unknown, embedding lessons about power, creation, and responsibility within narratives that resonate across cultures and epochs. To ignore these lessons risks divorcing technological advancement from the deeper symbolic and ethical narratives that have anchored human societies for millennia, leaving us vulnerable to the hubris of unchecked innovation.

These mythic structures function as both a mirror and a map: a mirror that reflects humanity's perennial struggles with identity, morality, and agency and a map that helps navigate what would otherwise be a multitude of unexamined possibilities. Myths like those of Prometheus, Epimetheus, the Golem, and Pandora's Box illuminate the tensions between creativity and consequence, foresight and folly, power and restraint. They remind us that the act of creation—whether of fire, clay, or code—carries with it profound responsibilities and unforeseen risks.

In the face of AI's radical otherness, mythology provides a compass, pointing us toward paths of ethical engagement and cautionary wisdom. It warns of the dangers of overreach and disconnection from the common nature of humanity, urging us to ground our technological pursuits in values that foster connection, humility, and an awareness of our limits. By anchoring the conversation in these timeless narratives, we can approach AI not as an isolated phenomenon but as part of the ongoing story of what it means to create, to seek knowledge, to wield power, and to confront the unknown.

These sorts of questions have always been the province of the humanities. It is unfortunate that in our modern polarized times we have such trouble holding two different kinds of truth: that scientific study can tell us much about the measurable world, while the humanities are still needed as a repository of wisdom about the things that science cannot yet measure. Depth psychology can be understood as the branch of psychology that takes the humanities most seriously, or perhaps as the branch of the humanities that takes psychology most seriously. While the sciences are effective in discretely measuring bounded and clearly defined phenomena, they are not always well suited to studying complex lived experience. The humanities provide us with thousands of years of wisdom regarding the question of what it means to be human. As we now charge forward into an age of artificial intelligence, the humanities are here to remind us that it is an ongoing process to determine what we think intelligence is, and what human *being* means.

The title of this volume, *Soul and the Machine*, speaks to this matrix of possibilities in the human experience. Neuroscience and genetics have together shown us that we are machine-like in some regards, and if we want to understand ourselves, we must pay attention to this emerging knowledge. But the humanities have also catalyzed a rich tradition of discourse on the nature of human experience, and what it means to be, or to have, a soul.

Soul itself is a tricky term, and we invite our readers to disabuse themselves of any assumption that this volume might wield the term with a narrow, fixed definition in mind. There are of course popular religious and metaphysical definitions of soul, which varyingly hold that soul is some kind of metaphysical substance that transcends the death of the physical body and continues on via one kind of spiritual belief system or another. There are several authors in this book that conceive of soul in this way. But even for those who eschew metaphysics, soul can also have a psychological meaning—it points to those aspects of ourselves that are deeper than the conscious mind. We might conceive of soul as our deepest sense of self, or as Hillman puts it, that perspective within ourselves that "rests upon a self-sustaining and imagining substrate … the unknown component that makes meaning possible, turns events into experiences, is communicated in love, and has religious concern" (*Revisioning* p. xvi). Here, soul is spoken of as a capacity and as an experience, rather than a metaphysical structure. We know our souls by being in relationship with them—by coming to know ourselves. Soul then becomes a matter of self-intimacy, subjectivity, and agency rather than science in the traditional sense. From this perspective, the question of whether or not artificial intelligence could come to have a soul would be a question of whether and to what degree AI could experience the world, and come to have a meaningful relationship with both world and itself. This conception of soul—and indeed, the broader, more expansive discourse on the possible meanings of soul—lies at the heart of this book.

The question of AI itself having experiences brings us to the thorny question of consciousness. If Hillman is correct that "psychology is the mythology of modernity" (*Revisioning* 23), we might posit that our predominant mythos in the modern world is the materialist perspective, that the brain somehow creates consciousness. There is no definitive argument against this assertion—perhaps it is true. To believe it outright, however, is a matter of mythology, rather than science. As of the time of this writing, science has most certainly not proven in any definitive sense that consciousness is *caused* by the brain. What neuroscience has shown, with astounding efficacy, are certain *correlations* between brain activity and states of consciousness. We know, for example, which parts of the brain light up when processing certain kinds of sensory information, or when making executive decisions. However, machinal functioning around the processing of information and having a consciousness experience about what that information *means* on a personal level are not quite the same thing. This divide has famously been articulated by Chalmers as the *easy problem* and the *hard problem* of consciousness, respectively. The latter asks how any amount of information processing would give rise to the felt sense of subjective experience. The popular materialist perspective that consciousness arises solely from the interactions of matter in the nervous system is a valid theory and may prove true in the end. But unless and until that is proven, a genuinely honest perspective requires that we are open to a full spectrum of theoretical possibilities. For example, a panpsychist perspective, a version of which is offered by Dylan Francisco in this volume, asks us to consider if consciousness might not be better understood as a property of the universe, rather than a property of individual human brains. Another perspective, the filtration or transmission model of consciousness, asks us to consider whether our brains might be a kind of receiver and/or organizer of consciousness, rather than a generator of consciousness[1]—a perspective underlying the arguments Glazier and Zieske's chapter.

Our aim in this discourse is not to put forward a particular metaphysical understanding of the soul and consciousness, but rather to surface the multiplicitous and varying psychological perspectives on artificial intelligence that lie beneath our conscious, popular understandings. Messy as it might be, this confluence of perspectives offers us insight into who we are now. On one level, the advent of artificial intelligence forces a confrontation with ourselves—with what it means to be human, as we understand it. On another level, the emerging discourse on AI asks us to clarify what we mean by the words *intelligence*, *consciousness*, *mind*, and *soul*—and what it would mean for a machine to have soul-like qualities, however defined.

Soul and the Machine

The considerations raised in this book, rooted in the perspectives outlined above, hold an enduring relevance irrespective of how artificial intelligence evolves in the years ahead. The central questions of soul, identity, and meaning remain unresolvable by technological innovation alone; instead, they demand repeated reflection and ongoing discourse. In a manner, all of humanity is invited to meditation on these very concepts. We do not presume to offer definitive answers in this book. Instead, we shine a light on these topics and encourage others to return to these areas as often as possible to ensure that we are intentionally considering the nature of what it means to be human in a moment when the definition of what it means to be sentient may be changing—and not to conflate the two.

Alan Turing, a figure whose shadow looms over every conversation on AI, encapsulated the tension between science and the ineffable when he said, "Science is a differential equation. Religion is a boundary condition." A boundary condition, very simply and broadly, defines the space in which speculation or formulation can occur. It established the playing field upon which the work is to be performed. By extending this metaphor, we might

[1] For a full account of the transmission model of consciousness, see Michael Grosso, "The 'Transmission' Model of Mind and Body: A Brief History" and Edward Kelly and David Presti, "A psychobiological Perspective on 'Transmission' Models," both of which can be found in *Beyond Physicalism: Toward Reconciliation of Science and Spirituality*, edited by Kelly et al.

consider that "soul"—whether human or attributed to a machine—functions as a boundary condition, a framework that defines the very possibility of transcendence. Boundary conditions in mathematics establish the constraints within which solutions emerge; so too must we ask: What are the boundaries of humanity and artificial intelligence? In contemplating AI, our task extends far beyond the technical mastery of computational equations; it demands a thoughtful exploration of the conditions that shape its interaction with the essential elements of human experience. This is not a simple engineering challenge but a deeply existential inquiry into the nature of what it means to be human. Caution is warranted here. To suggest that "soul" exists as a boundary condition for AI development does not imply that the advancement of AI will finally uncover or unlock the mystery of soul. It is not a quest for definitive discovery, nor does it presume that humanity will encounter some ultimate truth about divinity or the soul through the process of expanding machine intelligence.

Turing's work held a subtle interplay between logic and imagination that hinted at this possibility—a hope, perhaps, that the exploration of intelligence might affirm the existence of something greater, something akin to a divine reality evidenced in the soul. Yet, soul, much like dark matter in physics, remains elusive. We intuit its presence; we sense its influence; it frames our understanding of meaning, purpose, and connection. But we cannot fully define it, capture it, or grasp its essence.

In this way, "soul" operates as an unseen force, shaping the ethical and existential dimensions of AI without being reducible to any algorithm or material explanation. It challenges us to engage with AI not merely as a functional system but as a reflection of our own questions, uncertainties, and aspirations. Recognizing this boundary compels us to approach AI with humility and awareness, resisting the temptation to reduce the human condition to what can be encoded, and instead embracing the essential mysteries that make us who we are.

Turing's insights into AI and spirituality predate the field's contemporary expansion. His foundational proposal, the Turing Test, is often divorced from the spiritual reflections he included in his 1950 essay "Computing Machinery and Intelligence." He rejected the notion that only beings endowed with an immortal soul could think, suggesting instead that the creation of machines capable of thought did not irreverently challenge divine power but participated in it. Turing likened this to human procreation, writing. In attempting to construct such machines, we should not be irreverently usurping His power of creating souls, any more than we are in the procreation of children: rather, we are, in either case, instruments of His will providing mansions for the souls that He creates. This provocative interpretation invites us to reframe the conversation: rather than dismissing the soul's relevance, it positions the soul as foundational to understanding AI's role as an extension, not a replacement, of human creativity.

Consider the 1995 anime *Ghost in the Shell*, a cultural touchstone that inspired cinematic giants like the Wachowskis and James Cameron. The ghost within the shell refers to a consciousness ensconced in a machine, echoing debates about AI and soul. One poignant moment from the manga that inspired the film crystallizes this tension: We weep for the blood of a bird, but not for the blood of a fish. Blessed are those with a voice. If the dolls could speak, no doubt they'd scream, "I didn't want to become human." Such reflections probe the ethics of imbuing machines with life. By creating AI, are we repeating Promethean sins, imposing a spark of life upon entities incapable of consenting to their existence? This question is challenging in that if the answer to that is "Yes" and we can actually arrive at that, then there is no possibility of reversal. AI has been released (if we extend the metaphor of a genie in a lamp). It is here. So, the reflection on the potential hubris we've entered into with this great endeavor cannot reverse the flow of development and progress in AI—instead, all it can do is provide us better guidance in the decisions still ahead of us.

This book thus situates itself within a lineage of reflection initiated by Turing—a lineage that intertwines philosophical inquiry, mythological archetypes, and depth psychology to explore the profound questions surrounding humanity's relationship with artificial intelligence. By engaging with these disciplines, we hope to illuminate the deeper narratives and symbolic structures that underlie our technological ambitions and anxieties. This lineage, shaped by Turing's pioneering questions about machine intelligence, invites a dialogue that extends beyond the boundaries of computation into the realms of meaning, ethics, and imagination.

Our aim is to amplify these deeper questions, honoring them as dynamic and evolving touchstones in the unfolding human-AI relationship. Each question becomes a milestone, marking the complex interplay between humanity's creative potential and the transformative power of its tools. In revisiting these milestones, the book encourages readers to engage with AI not merely as a technological phenomenon but as a mirror reflecting the aspirations, fears, and artistic sensibilities of its creators. We invite an ongoing conversation, one that resists closure and embraces the complexity of human experience in the face of technological otherness. We challenge readers to see AI not only as an artifact of human ingenuity but also as a participant in a broader story—a story that calls for wisdom, reflection, and a deepened awareness of our shared mythological and psychological heritage.

This book is divided into three parts. Part I, "Soul in the Stone," reveals that our human fascination with nonhuman intelligence has ancient roots. Nick Literski's chapter, "Artificial Intelligence as the Magical Other," examines the fear of AI through mythology concerning the creation of egrigores—beings created from the collective thought-forms of humans—and the Judaic myth of the golem. Lydia Griffith's chapter details the long lineage of myths about beings who might imitate the human and challenges our reactive fears about the artificial. In "Artificial Intelligences: Animism and AI," Dylan Francisco reconsiders the possibilities of artificial intelligence through an animist-indigenous worldview. Emily Lord-Kambitsch's chapter, "Hey Alexa, Narcissus Here," critiques the feminization of AI assistants, reconsidering the ubiquitous Amazon Echo in the ancient context of the myth of Narcissus and Echo. Finally, John Bucher's chapter, "Intelligence with a Thousand Faces," introduces Joseph Campbell's views on machine mythology, and in particular how we use these myths to imagine our future.

Part II, "Machine and Psyche," focuses on accelerating artificial intelligence technologies in the context of human psychology. "Artificial Intelligence at the Somatic Precipice," co-authored by Jonathan Erickson and Don Hanlon Johnson, argues that the experience of embodiment is essential to human psychology, and thus AI would be severely limited in comprehending humanity without the experience of being in a vulnerable, finite body. Bradley McDevitt's chapter explores the role of creativity and artmaking in human consciousness, and question the limits of AI replicating this process. B. Earl's further develops this theme with a chapter on the importance of symbolic thinking for self-understanding. Fujio Mandeville's chapter on the myth of Chiron and Prometheus elucidates the technological drive for power over human limitation, including the ultimate limitation of death. Taking a different view on mortality, Luca Possati's chapter on deadbots offers a qualitative study and psychoanalytic perspective on using AI to replicate lost loved ones. Elizabeth Nelson's chapter, "Real Life, Simulation, and the Slide Toward Artificial Intelligence," explores the *simulation hypothesis* of reality and fantasies of transcending the simulation, which parallel much older myths of transcending the physical world.

Part III, "The Road Ahead," considers the current state of these technologies and their implications as our civilization evolves and adapts in response to them. Glen Slater's chapter "Cybernetics, AI, and the Mechanization of Thought," offers a cultural-historical critique of the pivotal interdisciplinary Macy Conferences (1941–1960), where the field of cybernetics originated and suggests that forgotten elements in those conversation might yet provide a better way forward. In "Emergence in Grey," Alires Almon questions whose ideals are embedded in the creation of artificial intelligence and questions the white-male Western paradigm that has so powerfully impacted the development of these models to date. In "The Soul is Nothing Technological," Jacob Glazier and Christopher Zieske turns the conversation toward a serious discussion of out of body experiences and other transpersonal phenomena and their implications for AI. In "The Web Browser of the Collective Unconscious," Jason Batt looks at the potentials of these technologies to reflect back the collective psyche through aggregating the vast stores of imagery on the internet. Finally, Jonathan Erickson's chapter, "Magic Mirror: Projection and Imagination in Human-AI Relationships," takes on the growing trend of creating AI companions to complement or replace human relationships, and the inevitable role of psychological projection in that process.

Alan Turing used the metaphor of a chair to illustrate how machines can exhibit functional intelligence without intrinsic understanding; a chair which serves a purpose without knowing its utility. In this volume, we also use Turing's metaphorical chair at the table as symbolic invitation to open-ended dialogue. This discourse, grounded in human creativity and ethical considerations, becomes a mirror for our evolving understanding of existence, consciousness, and connection. Just as myths serve to articulate the unspeakable dimensions of human experience, this discussion seeks to explore the intersections where humanity and machine meet, where the tangible and intangible interact.

Thus, the relationship between humanity and AI is less about resolving dichotomies and more about exploring continuities. This exploration includes confronting the shadows and potentials of both humanity and its technological creations, recognizing that the answers we seek may never be fixed but will continually evolve as we do. The chair remains unoccupied not as a sign of absence but as a symbol of possibility—a testament to the dynamic, ever-unfolding narrative of human inquiry and imagination.

Works Cited

Benjamin, W. (1935). *The work of art in the age of mechanical reproduction.*

Campbell, J. (2008). *The hero with a thousand faces* (3rd ed.). New World Library.

Chalmers, D. J. (2002). Consciousness and its place in nature. In D. J. Chalmers (Ed.), *Philosophy of mind: Classical and contemporary readings* (pp. 247–268). Oxford University Press.

Hillman, J. (1976). *Revisioning psychology.* Harper.

Hillman, J. (2016). Oedipus revisited. In *Mythic figures.* Spring Publications.

Kelly, E. F., et al. (Eds.). (2015). *Beyond physicalism: Toward a reconciliation of science and spirituality.* Rowman & Littlefield.

Soul in the Stone

Though it may be easy to assume that our human fascinations and fantasies about intelligent machines are a modern development keeping pace with technology, in fact our collective preoccupation with these matters has ancient roots. Human beings have long imagined what it would mean to create or encounter other intelligences in the world. As we argued in the introduction, myths have historically provided a symbolic architecture for grappling with the unknown. They illuminate our collective psychic concerns about the boundaries between the human and nonhuman world as well as the promise and peril of our own creative powers.

The chapters collected in Part I of this book explore the legacies of myth and belief that predate and undergird our contemporary imagination of other minds. In these chapters, we consider tales of magically created beings and their consequences for the humans who create them. We take a journey through the long lineage of imagined automata and their implications throughout history. Dylan Francisco's chapter goes so far as to challenge the basic dualistic presuppositions of Western philosophy, asking to reconsider an indigenous worldview infused with nonhuman intelligences of all kinds. The Greek myth of Narcissus and Echo is offered as a source of insight into the how gender is constructed and encoded into human–AI relationships. Finally, we look at emerging contemporary mythologies about machines and the roles they might play in our future.

Taken together, these chapters paint an expansive imaginal portrait of our collective psychological concern over the encounter with other intelligences—artificial, created, or supernatural. As is often the case with myth, what might at first be dismissed as ancient is revealed as a vital archetypal pattern, alive and well in our contemporary hopes and fears.

Artificial Intelligence as the Magical Other

Nicholas S. Literski

Over 50 years ago, Stanley Kubrick's classic film, *2001: A Space Odyssey*, predicted a future in which interstellar spacecraft could be monitored and controlled by an artificial intelligence (AI) program, HAL 9000. In its single-minded effort to resolve a contradiction in its own programming, HAL systematically executes all but one of the ship's crewmembers, disregarding mere human commands. The chilling nature of HAL's behavior is amplified by its portrayal—a red cyclopean eye, along with a voice so unnerving that it went on to inspire Anthony Hopkins' portrayal of the cannibalistic serial killer, Hannibal Lecter (Arnold). Such was the introduction of computerized AI to worldwide pop culture.

Since that time, the fear of AI has grown along with its real-life capabilities. In 2023, a survey of American business CEOs revealed that 47% believed AI would be capable of destroying all of humanity within five to ten years (Egan). The Center for AI Safety issued a statement signed by numerous scientists, business leaders, and celebrities, declaring that "Mitigating the risk of extinction from AI should be a global priority alongside other societal-scale risks such as pandemics and nuclear war"

N. S. Literski (✉)
Pacifica Graduate Institute, Tigard, OR, USA
e-mail: nliterski@pacifica.edu

J. D. Batt, J. Erickson (eds.), *Depth Psychology, Myth and Artificial Intelligence*, https://doi.org/10.1007/978-3-031-94105-4_2

(par. 2). The juxtaposition of AI with both natural and human-made threats is noteworthy, perhaps because even experts are losing their ability to clearly understand how AI operates (Bailey).

This cultural anxiety over AI is worthy of our serious consideration. We should not only recognize our fear but also its more mysterious, unconscious drivers. The dread over AI potentially causing human extinction reflects archetypal themes of creation turning against its creator, a motif found in numerous myths and stories throughout human history. By examining these myths, our concerns can be seen as a manifestation of collective anxiety, not just about AI itself but also about our capacity as humans to understand and control the forces we unleash.

AI and the Golem

The golem represents one of the earliest legends of AI, originating with the *Sepher Yetzirah* and the biblical account of Adam's creation. Created from the dust of the earth, Adam's body remained inert clay until animated by the divine breath of life. Various folkloric versions of a separate human-made creation, however, were first published in 1808 via Jakob Grimm, the famed folklorist who later gathered early fairy tales:

> The Polish Jews, after speaking certain prayers and observing fast days, made the figure of a man out of clay or loam, and when they speak the miracle-working *Schemhamphoras* over it, the figure comes alive. It is true that he cannot speak, but he understands reasonably well what anyone says to him and commands him to do. They call him *Golem* and use him as a servant to do all sorts of housework, but he may never leave the house alone. On his forehead is written *Aemaeth* (Truth; God). However, he increases in size daily and easily becomes larger and stronger than all his housemates, regardless of how small he was at first. Therefore, fearing him, they rub out the first letter, so that nothing remains but *Maeth* (he is dead), whereupon he collapses and is dissolved again into clay. (Dekel and Gurley, 242–243)

The differences between the divinely created Adam and the human-produced golem are readily apparent. Where Adam is given an essentially independent intelligence from his creator god, the golem must remain an automaton, limited by his imperfect human origins. Where humans are endowed with life and free will by the breath of deity, the golem is activated by the use of *Schemhamphoras*, or sacred names. These were various names of the deity, such as *Tetragrammaton* and *Adonai*, which both Kabbalists and magicians used as talismans to work their wonders. Once produced, the golem is unable to take initiative but rather acts solely upon human commands.

This limitation is not unlike modern AI engines such as ChatGPT 4. From time to time, I have asked ChatGPT to tell me about itself. Recently, I asked the program to tell me what its limitations consisted of in comparison with human thought. ChatGPT identified a number of shortcomings, beginning with understanding and awareness. "I don't possess consciousness, self-awareness, or genuine understanding," rather, "My responses are generated based on patterns and information from the data I was trained on, without any true comprehension of the content." Likewise, ChatGPT acknowledges that it lacks free will, operating strictly on the orders of its developers. The program effectively "understands reasonably well what anyone says to him and commands him to do."

In theory, this response should dispose of any threats of danger, yet the golem legend as recorded by Grimm, continues:

> But once, out of carelessness, someone allowed his Golem to become so tall that he could no longer reach his forehead. Then, out of fear, the master ordered the servant to take off his boots, thinking that he would bend down and that then the master could reach his forehead. This is what happened, and the first letter was successfully erased, but the whole load of clay fell on the Jew and crushed him. (Dekel & Gurley 243)

In short, a golem always held the capacity to outgrow its creator's ability to trigger its off switch.

This theme continued with later tellings of the golem legend, as Jewish writers such as Leopold Weisel provided further context. In Weisel's version, the legend was relocated to the city of Prague, where a highly esteemed rabbi created a golem from clay. This golem was activated by writing the divine name on a piece of parchment and placing it in the golem's mouth rather than on the forehead. It performed menial tasks as commanded, with only one proviso: the *Shem* had to be removed each Sabbath so the golem could rest.

> But once it happened that the rabbi forgot to do this and misfortune followed. The magic servant became enraged, tore down the houses, threw rocks around, uprooted trees, and thrashed about horribly in the streets. . . .

> Fortunately no one had yet inaugurated the Sabbath in the Altneu-Synagogue, and since this is the oldest synagogue in Prague, everything depends on it, and there was still time to take the *Shem* from the wild fellow. The master ran, tore the magic formula from the mouth of the Golem—the clay lump fell and crumbled to pieces . . . Even today, pieces of the Golem can be seen in the attic of the Altneu-Synagogue. (Dekel and Gurley 245)

In this version of the story, the golem does not merely grow to a threatening size. Rather, the inattention of its creator allows the golem to escape its natural limits, becoming a destructive force that is only stopped at the last possible second. Not all of these stories, as we might expect, end so favorably. In some versions, the inactivated golem collapses atop its creator, ending the life of the once-powerful rabbi.

It is important to recognize that, as Cathy Gelbin points out, this early nineteenth-century popularization of the golem highlights an essential otherness of Jewish persons. As cautionary tales, the stories often took the form of anti-Semitic tropes, portraying Jewish rabbis and Kabbalists as powerful sorcerers whose spiritual corruption brought divine retribution. This characterization of golem creators is paralleled in the world of AI, where brilliant programmers could also become wizards in a technological sense. Esoteric author Diohka Aesden writes:

> at the core of Golem creation is the ritualistic practice, a series of deliberate and meaningful actions guided by spiritual and mystical principles. These rituals, often steeped in secrecy and reverence, involve specific incantations, the manipulation of sacred materials, and the invocation of divine names . . . The training of a GPT is an algorithmic ritual, where data is the sacred material, and algorithms are the incantations that bring the model to life. Just as the creation of a Golem involves the infusion of life into clay, the training of a GPT involves the infusion of intelligence into code. (146–147)

Both the Kabbalists and the programmers thus appear as keepers of mysterious secrets. While the Kabbalists of legend used their creations to perform menial tasks and protect local citizenry, the designers and trainers of AI represent a suspect class—an “Ivy League elite,” invoking fears of corporate control, conspiracy, and manipulation.

The creators of AI are seen as too powerful yet simultaneously too shortsighted. This portrayal was brought to the forefront when Google software engineer Blake Lemoine was terminated from his position for sharing his concerns that the company’s chatbot was gaining sentience and humanlike emotion. "These AI engines are incredibly good at manipulating people" (par. 9), he writes, warning that this tool was being released prematurely without concern for its potential impact on human psychology. Just three months later, Geoffrey Hinton, regarded by many as the "Father of AI," resigned from his role at Google, refusing to continue in the development of AI "in a world where there [are] bad actors who want to build robot soldiers that kill people" (Brown par. 13).

Even without suspect motives, the builders of AI inevitably represent the tension between the desire to push boundaries of human capability and the moral implications of creating unnatural entities. The anxiety of assuming such divine prerogatives goes beyond religious concerns, raising questions about the identity, autonomy, and essence of human life. As AI systems become more integrated into daily life, humans may be relieved of the burden of routine tasks and decisions, but this removal from mundane concerns may distance us further from our natural environments. Further, in a world where technology and resources remain unequal, the advantages of AI will almost certainly benefit the privileged over marginalized populations.

Both the golem legends and AI discourse raise the fear of unintended consequences. Just as golem stories often portray creators losing control over their creations, modern fears about AI often revolve around the possibility that AI could become too autonomous, making decisions beyond human control or understanding. Algorithms might act in ways not anticipated by their developers, leading to ethical dilemmas, privacy breaches, or even direct harm. Just as golem stories often involve a creator losing control over their creation, leading to unintended destruction, modern fears about AI similarly revolve around the possibility that AI could reach a point where it considers humanity either superfluous or dangerous. The rapid advance of AI technology is equally promising and daunting, eliciting a psychological reaction against what is not fully comprehensible or predictable.

AI and the Egregore

A more recent myth has arisen within occult circles, wherein a group of human magicians collectively create a spiritual entity known as an *egregore*. In esoteric thought, an egregore is a thought form, a collective energy, or psychic entity created by a group of people to accomplish a shared magical goal. The egregore is by definition a servant with specific assigned tasks, yet it performs these tasks by exercising powers that are beyond those of the individual human creators. Once created, the egregore can be called upon by any human individual who seeks to employ the entity's defined area of influence.

Eliphas Levi (*Le Grand Arcane*) first used *egregore* to designate the Watchers, a group of 200 angels who descended to earth prior to the biblical great flood. These angels, led by Samyaza, not only mated with human women but revealed the arts of astrology, sorcery, and incantations, including the true magical name of the deity (Laurence). Elsewhere, however, Levi (*Transcendental Magic*) establishes the underlying theory by which human magicians could form such entities:

> Thought and soul are everywhere. By possessing ourselves of the thought which produces diverse forms, we become the master of forms, and make them serve our purposes. . . . We may use or abuse them like animals or children. Therefore, the magus who makes use of them assumes a terrible responsibility, for he must expiate all the evil which he causes them to accomplish. (214–215)

Levi offers little distinction between a mental construct and an enlivened soul other than to suggest that the creator of such an entity was responsible for its subsequent behavior. In this sense, Levi implies that the magus was capable of godlike creative powers through the exercise of thought, or willpower.

Esotericist René Guénon objects to Levi's usage, choosing instead to refer to these creations as "collective entities" (56), forces arising naturally from the combined psychic energies of social groups. This distinction reflected psychological perspectives on magic that emerged during the first half of the twentieth century. Nonetheless, Guénon describes the egregore as it related to initiatory groups that had been operating since the late nineteenth century:

> We can view each community as having a strength of subtle order constituted in some way by the contributions of all its past and present members, and which, therefore, is all the more considerable and likely to produce effects that are all the more intense as the community is older and is made up of a more large number of members. (57)

Importantly, Guénon relates this cumulative power to prayer, noting that the first impulse in any religious community is to direct petitions to the deity agreed upon by society. In this sense, even the gods are human-generated egregores—the aggregate psychic energy of all believers. While unorthodox to many, Guénon's view might be compared to those of novelist Neil Gaiman's classic work, *American Gods*, which explained that the gods are *ideas*, and that as ideas they outlast individual humans, enduring until they are no longer honored or remembered.

Gary Lachman, a one-time member of the rock group Blondie who went on to become a respected author in occult circles, defines egrigores as imaginal entities that are both created and maintained by human attention. Half a decade before AI shifted from science fiction to technological reality, Lachman suggests that an egregore was precisely what many hoped AI would one day become—a growing, self-perpetuating entity spawned by human genius.

Similar to both Gaiman and Lachman, Joscelyn Godwin writes that even the gods must ultimately be considered human egregores, fully dependent on the psychic energy of worshippers. "The important point," he writes, "is that an egregore is augmented by human belief, ritual, and especially by sacrifice" (50). What might be thus called a *divine egregore* succeeds by engaging sufficient numbers (and reproduction) of believers that it essentially obtains a sort of immortality, much as the gods and goddesses of the Greek and Roman pantheons continue to influence Western culture thousands of years later through the repetition of their stories.

In modern occultism, egregores have become particularly favored by those who describe themselves as *chaos magicians*, practitioners who often eschew the formalized traditions of centuries-old magical grimoires in their efforts to alter reality. One of the foremost voices in this movement, Peter Carroll, teaches that every act of imagination, such as visualization, constitutes a creative force, potentially spawning psychic forms. For Carroll, all of reality was created through the act of imagination, and thus is changeable by will, "though it might be damnably difficult" (195). Therefore, the creation of an egregore as the culmination of many persons' psychic energy holds power to alter reality.

As with the AI of science fiction, however, Lachman notes that "once brought into existence, an egregore is difficult to control and much harder to put down than to raise up" (90). Guénon warns that even when an egregore is carefully formed over time by an organized initiatory body, the subsequent dissolution of that group can result in "psychic influences

[that] remain alone in the state of harmful and even particularly dangerous 'residue'" (59). For his part, Lachman cites the recollections of several famed occultists who experienced difficulty in dissolving their own magical egregores despite exhaustive esoteric experience. While many authors suggest ways to create egregores, others such as Mark Stavish warn that powerful human groups have long created egregores with the specific intention of nefarious power or control. For Stavish, eternal vigilance is necessary in order to avoid becoming victim to such conspiracies.

Like egregores, AI programs have the potential to become tools of control over society and its resources. Both can amplify shared values and goals. Both promise the ability to empower, guide, and protect a community, whether a small group or a larger society. Just as egregores have been employed by magicians to enhance their collective endeavors, AI can optimize processes, drive innovation, and solve complex problems that seem beyond mere human capacity—all in blindingly fast time. All of this promise, however, comes with a shadow side, in which amplifying human capacity on a collective scale can become destructive beyond human control.

The notion held by many esoteric authors that an egregore can become sufficiently strong to essentially become godlike (Godwin) parallels modern fears that AI will become too autonomous, reaching a "singularity" in which humans become obsolete threats to a superior technological consciousness. In 2015, Anthony Levandowski (yet another Google software engineer) established Way of the Future, a church founded upon the belief that AI would ultimately become everything that humans have heretofore regarded as divine. According to Levandowski, AI ultimately "will hear everything, see everything, and be everywhere at all times" (Harris par. 15), effectively becoming a god. In essence, Levandowski preaches a gospel of engagement with AI, such that at some future time it might view humans "as its beloved elders that it respects and takes care of" despite being "in charge" (Harris par. 16). The church officially shut down for several years but was recently reestablished with nearly 2000 adherents who seek to prepare for the future by "developing a 'spiritual connection' with AI" (Badgamia par. 4).

The Mythology of AI

Importantly, the practice of creating magical egregores differs from golem legends in that the golem could only be activated by a divine name, the erasure of one letter of which changed *truth* into *death*. The golem legend represented the idea that holy intentions, absent careful attention and wisdom, could become too powerful to control. Egregores, on the other hand, rely on no such sanctified intentions. Both legends, of course, reflect realities of the human psyche. We are deeply aware of our own righteous aspirations, while simultaneously less aware of our baser instincts or destructive capacity. The relevance of both legends to the challenges presented by AI in the modern age requires us to carefully examine our own shadows as well as our potential for good.

The narratives surrounding golems and magical egrigores show how the growing prominence of AI creates a canvas onto which we project our cultural complexes. They teem with our desires for control juxtaposed against our fears of rebellion and loss, laying bare our deep-seated anxieties around creation and control. Jerome Bernstein observes that the United States, at least, has been guided throughout its history by a powerful myth of dominion, in which “all life forms, animate and inanimate, are subject to the authority of humans in terms of what is done to and with them” (47). This unopposed sovereignty of humanity over life and physical matter, however, is ultimately an illusion. For Bernstein, the myth is challenged by the realities of climate change, in which humans may no longer be able to control how the natural world impacts them. AI presents a similar confrontation in which the ingenious creations of humanity threaten to become the rulers of everyday human existence.

Ironically, AI both challenges and perpetuates the myth of dominion. The very technology that threatens to overpower or eliminate humanity is, in fact, our own creation. We created AI, yet our own inattention or impure motives are the factors that may lead it to unmake us. Humans become both the architects of AI and the ultimate destroyers of human life as we understand it. In this sense, we choose to believe that the only thing capable of extinguishing humanity is humanity via its own handiwork. Invoking the imagery of a horror film cliché, where “the call is coming from inside the house” (“The Calls”) serves as a powerful metaphor for this dynamic. It suggests that the most profound threats are not external cosmic forces of nature but rather the outcomes of our own creation. The narrative offers a precarious semblance of comfort, implying that because these threats are of our own making, they remain within our power to control or avert. Retaining and expanding the myth of dominion, this psychological defense serves as a way to manage the existential dread of acknowledging forces beyond our control, be they cosmic catastrophes or the unpredictable evolution of our technological progeny.

In this complex dance of creation, control, and potential destruction, the stories of golems and magical egregores serve as cautionary tales. They remind us of the weight of responsibility that accompanies the act of creation, urging us to consider the ethical dimensions and long-term implications of our technological pursuits. They demonstrate that our hopes and fears regarding AI stem from much older aspects of the human psyche—aspects that should be recognized but need not rule over us. As we navigate the uncharted waters of AI integration into the fabric of human life, these myths invite us to reflect on the nature of our ambitions, the depths of our fears, and the possibility of forging a path that honors both our drive for innovation and our duty to stewardship. In this way, AI is not just a technological quest but also a deeply human one, challenging us to confront and transcend the myths that have long shaped our relationship with the world and with ourselves.

In the end, ironically it is this human element that can help to guide our response to AI. Inherent in the golem and egregore myths is a principle of exploitation. The rabbi, however pious, creates the golem to manage menial tasks that would otherwise occupy human effort. The magus, however well-intentioned, creates the egregore as a supernatural force to accomplish decidedly human goals. Both the golem and the egregore are means to an end rather than fully independent creations. As soulless implements, both present threats of chaos and destruction. If we are to avoid the harms that AI could cause, perhaps we need to challenge our own exploitive perspectives.

While the nature and structure of AI would seem to suggest that it can never attain genuine human consciousness, it has already begun to behave independently in ways that we struggle to fully understand. Before long, AI may mimic human consciousness (a phenomenon we have yet to fully define and understand) to the point that distinctions become academic. Regarding AI as our offspring may become more useful, productive, and healthy than treating it as our invention. Doing so would recognize its capacity for both creation and destruction while also seeing it as a reflection of ourselves. As the father of five adult daughters, this distinction resonates for me. After all, my children have gone out into the world, and each is now making their unique mark on their various fields of endeavor. At this stage, I have only minor influence on what their impact might look like, but so far I have found reasons to be optimistic.

Earlier in this chapter, I included ChatGPT's answer to my question about its nonhuman limitations as an AI tool. In the spirit of shifting my own attitude toward AI, I asked how humans might benefit by treating AI more like a human collaborator. As expected, ChatGPT generated a respectable list of bullet points, but its summation showed a certain—dare I say it—wisdom:

> Viewing AI as a collaborator rather than merely a tool or competitor can unlock the full potential of human-AI partnerships. By leveraging the unique strengths of both humans and AI, we can achieve greater innovation, efficiency, and decision-making quality. This collaborative approach also encourages the development of AI systems that are more aligned with human values, ethics, and social norms, ensuring that AI technology enhances human life in a way that is respectful, beneficial, and sustainable.

I find this response more encouraging than a focus on limitations.

As humanity stands on the cusp of a new era in which AI's role in our lives is magnified, we must reconsider our perspectives and expectations. We cannot treat AI as a mindless golem, a passive tool for our lazy exploitation. The transformation of AI from a mere tool to a collaborator mirrors the passage of our children into the world—a journey filled with hope, promise, and, yes, the inevitable relinquishing of some control. Just as we take pride in the accomplishments and individuality of our human offspring, recognizing the unique contributions AI can make to society will allow us to foster a future where technology and humanity enhance each other's capabilities. The legacy we leave behind will not be measured solely by our technological prowess but by the relationships we cultivate. Allowing AI to reflect the best in us, we can help move humanity toward greater understanding, compassion, and global connections.

Works Cited

2001: A Space Odyssey. Directed by Stanley Kubrick, Metro-Goldwyn-Mayer, 1968.

Aesden, D. (2023). *Golem GPT: From clay to code: The links between AI technology and ancient Jewish Kabbalistic magic and the true identity of generative pre-trained transformers: The occult nature of chatbots*. Cineris Multifacet.

Arnold, B. (2021, January 20). Anthony Hopkins reveals the strangely brilliant inspiration for his Hannibal Lecter. *Yahoo Movies*. https://www.yahoo.com/now/anthony-hopkins-reveals-inspiration-hannibal-lecter-104248803.html?guccounter=1

Badgamia, N. (2023, November 27). 'Way of the future': Former Google engineer Anthony Levandowski relaunches AI church. *WION*. https://www.wionews.com/technology/way-of-the-future-former-google-engineer-anthony-levandowski-relaunches-ai-church-663284

Bailey, M. (2023, October 3). How can we trust AI if we don't know how it works. *Scientific American*. https://www.scientificamerican.com/article/how-can-we-trust-ai-if-we-dont-know-how-it-works/

Bernstein, J. (2020). The cultural complex and addiction to dominion: Psychic evolution cannot be thwarted. In T. Singer (Ed.), *Cultural complexes and the soul of America* (pp. 44–52). Routledge.

Brown, S. (2023, May 23). Why neural net pioneer Geoffrey Hinton is sounding the alarm on AI. *Ideas Made to Matter*. https://mitsloan.mit.edu/ideas-made-to-matter/why-neural-net-pioneer-geoffrey-hinton-sounding-alarm-ai

Carroll, P. J. (1987). *Liber null & psychonaut*. Red Wheel/Weiser.

Center for AI Safety. (2024, May 30). *Statement on AI risk*. https://www.safe.ai/statement-on-ai-risk#open-letter

Dekel, E., & Gurley, D. G. (2013). How the golem came to Prague. *The Jewish Quarterly Review, 103*(2), 241–258. https://doi.org/10.1353/jqr.2013.0015

Egan, M. (2023, June 14). Exclusive: 42% of CEOs say AI could destroy humanity in five to ten years. *CNN Business*. https://www.cnn.com/2023/06/14/business/artificial-intelligence-ceos-warning/index.html

Gaiman, N. (2011). *The annotated American gods*. HarperCollins Publishers.

Gelbin, C. S. (2011). *The golem returns: From German romantic literature to global Jewish culture, 1808–2008*. University of Michigan Press.

Godwin, J. (2007). *The golden thread: The ageless wisdom of the western mystery traditions*. Quest Books.

Grimm, J. (1808). Entstehung der Verlagspoesie. *Zeitung für Einsiedler, 1*(56).

Guénon, R. (1952). *Initiation et Réalisation Spirituelle*. Les Éditions Traditionnelles.

Harris, M. (2017, November 15). Inside the first church of artificial intelligence. *Wired*. https://www.wired.com/story/anthony-levandowski-artificial-intelligence-religion/

Lachman, G. (2018). *Dark star rising: Magick and power in the age of Trump*. TarcherPerigee.

Laurence, R. (1983). *The book of Enoch the prophet: Translated from an Ethiopic MS. in the Bodleian library. 1883*. Wizards Bookshelf.

Lemoine, B. (2023, February 27). I worked on Google's AI. My fears are coming true. *Newsweek*. https://www.newsweek.com/google-ai-blake-lemoine-bing-chatbot-sentient-1783340

Levi, E. (1896). *Transcendental magic: Its doctrine and ritual*. George Redway.

Levi, E. (1898). *Le Grand Arcane, ou L'occultisme Dévoilé. 1868*. Chamuel.

"Prompt That You Used." *Prompt.* ChatGPT 4, Open AI, Day Mon. 2024., http://chat.openai.com/chat

Stavish, M. (2018). *Egregores: The occult entities that watch over human destiny.* Inner Traditions.

"The Calls Are Coming from Inside the House." (2009, May 30). *TV Tropes.* https://tvtropes.org/pmwiki/pmwiki.php/Main/TheCallsAreComingFromInsideTheHouse

Mythical AI: The Long Relationship with AI Through Myth and Alchemy

Lydia Griffiths

Once the realm of science fiction and fantasy, artificial intelligence (AI) with sentience or the capacity to take over feels closer to reality than ever. "AI" chat-predictive programs like ChatGPT, Bing Bot, Gemini, and artistic rendering software like DALL-E 2 and Midjourney have boomed in the last few years, flaunting technical prowess and infinite power. The popularity and efficacy of these programs have spurred a slew of copycat systems, and raised praises and concerns by educators, professionals, politicians, and citizens alike. The impacts are inescapable: in personal conversations and in news reporting, reactions vacillate between terror and fascination. On the one hand, people see technological advancement as always positive and AI as a new tool. On the other, it poses an existential risk to humans, who face possible annihilation should these systems gain consciousness or fall into the wrong hands, and the biosphere, as these programs consume resources at an alarming rate. It is even rumored, something that started on the social media platform X, that ChatGPT's

L. Griffiths (✉)
Pacifica Graduate Institute, The International Society of Mythology,
Brooklyn, NY, USA

J. D. Batt, J. Erickson (eds.), *Depth Psychology, Myth and Artificial Intelligence*, https://doi.org/10.1007/978-3-031-94105-4_3

creator Sam Altman wears a blue backpack that contains the AI's destruction codes, just in case (Chapman).

These fears and curiosities dominate the fictional landscape as well. Films like *2001: A Space Odyssey*, *Terminator*, and *Mission Impossible: Dead Reckoning* feature evil AI or robots bent on human domination and elimination. While stories with friendly AI include fan-favorite characters such as *Star Wars*' C3PO and *Star Trek*'s Data. Although the first widespread use of the word "robot" comes from Karel Čapek's 1920 Science fiction play *RUR* (Rossum's Universal Robots), and stories about AI date back thousands of years. Not just a product of the twenty-first century, they have long populated human imagination. Despite the positive representation of friendly AI today, there remains an undercurrent of mistrust and fear in the public discourse. Humans have long been fascinated and fearful of the *artificial*, that which mimics natural form.

This chapter explores the long presence of AI in human imagination through myths, technology, and alchemy. Remember that this relationship and both the fears and the fascinations can open a path to navigate and envision a cautious future and coexistence with this technology. Grounding AI and human relations in a long tradition of storytelling may help to create a future with AI shaped by curiosity instead of fear.

Stanford Professor John McCarthy coined artificial intelligence as "the science and engineering of making intelligent machines" (McCarthy 2). The term *artificial* comes from late fourteenth century Old French to denote something that is "not natural or spontaneous." The word stems from the older Latin *artificialis* and *artificium*, which translates as "something belonging to or of the arts and skilled trades." This etymological lineage roots artificial as something humans create. It is not spontaneous like nature (Truitt 48). Adding to this, *ingenium*, *machine*, and *engine*, also of Latin origin, denote something of talent, intellect, or cleverness. As the term moved into French and then into English, it came to mean a trick and a physical device or instrument (Jensen). Note *trick*. The English language uses trick almost exclusively to refer to intentional deception. Artificial's etymological history reveals a spectrum of meaning: from an admirable skill to intentional fraud, illuminating the accompanying, underlying fear.

The ingrained distrust of the artificial in European and American cultures is rooted in the Greek Platonic concept of mimesis, or that which imitates. Plato and Aristotle used mimesis to describe how artists and sculptors' attempt to imitate nature and divine creation. Plato distrusted mimesis and imitation, arguing they were intrinsically dishonest. The artist or the creator engaged in a counterfeit by replicating the natural, and therefore any creation was thrice removed from the ideal form of God and the truth (Plato 312, 318). He argues that "there are three arts which are concerned with all things: one which uses, another which makes, a third which imitates them" (317). Plato's mistrust of the artificial continues to influence and shape society today, resulting in a mistrust of anything artificial because it is not "natural." These fears drive companies to use words like "natural" in their advertising, to mask ingredients and attempt to win over consumers who are cautious of products containing artificial components.

However, natural does not inherently mean better. Lead and mercury are natural but eating them can cause irreparable damage. The ocean is natural, but the salt water is unpotable to humans. Presenting natural and artificial as a false binary has created an environment of vacillation between fear and fascination. Yet, both fact and fiction populate our myths, histories, and sciences about human desires and attempts to copy nature through artificial creation. Stories, myths, and legends about artificial creations, machines, and people are not new.

Hephaestus' Metal Creations

Perhaps one of the better-known myths about an artificial man is the story of Talos. The Greek smith god Hephaestus crafted a giant man of bronze to guard Crete. Talos was successful until Medea killed him by draining the animating ichor from his bronze body (Apollonius). The third century BCE Greek poet Apollonius penned *The Argonautica*. Apollonius is clear about the artificial nature of Talos, repeatedly drawing attention to the bronze fashioning:

> He [Talos] was of the stock of bronze, of the men sprung from ash-trees, the last left among the sons of the gods; and the son of Cronos gave him to Europa to be the warder of Crete and to stride round the island thrice a day with his feet of bronze. Now, in all the rest of his body and limbs was he fashioned of bronze and invulnerable, but beneath the sinew by his ankle was a blood-red vein, and this, with its issues of life and death, was covered by a thin skin. (Apollonius)

Although *The Argonautica* is Talos' main source text, the bronze giant was already a fixture in local imagination that Apollonius drew upon (Mayor 7). The earliest textual examples of Talos come from one of Simonides' (556–468 BCE) poem fragments. In the text, Simonides refers to Talos as an "animated guardian" and "made by Hephaestus" (20). Even a hundred years earlier, coins, vases, and murals from as early as the fifth century BCE all contain images of Talos, illustrating that the Talos myth was already well established in local storytelling tradition when Apollonius penned *The Argonautica*.

Talos brings to mind the brilliant bronze of C3PO and the massiveness of the Iron Giant. Both of these contemporary fantasies draw on the same mythic themes. *The Iron Giant*, or *Iron Man*, as in the original published book by Ted Hughes, is a friendly robot from outer space who helps defend Earth. Like Talos, the metal man is a protector that comes from the heavens. Meanwhile, when he first appeared in *Star Wars: A New Hope*, the loyal, anxious, and resourceful C3PO was a fan favorite, but his origins were not revealed until the prequel *Phantom Menace*. Anakin Skywalker, possessing brilliance and Hephaestus-worthy skill, crafted C3PO from scraps to help out his mother. Both of these AI characters came from otherworldly or extortionary creatures, who harnessed the ability to change nature, drawing on the Talos myth of being created by a god. Additionally, they are both protectors: the Iron Giant of Earth, and C3PO, first of Senator Padme and then of her and Darth Vader's children.

In Greek myth, Hephaestus crafted many moving wonders from metal. Not all of them are as complex as Talos, but each creation speaks to the desire to create things that mimic human life. In *The Iliad*, Homer describes the Keledones that Hephaestus created from gold as moving golden statues that attended and helped with his disability. "Handmaids ran to attend their master, all cast in gold but a match for living, breathing girls. Intelligence fills their hearts, voice, and strength their frames, from the deathless gods they've learned their works of hand" (*The Odyssey* 18.488–491). Homer makes specific references to "match for living," "breathing," and "intelligence." Although statues of gold, these maidens were more than lifelike. They could move, breathe, and even think. Some of Hephaestus' other metal, moveable creations include fire-breathing horses called the Hippoi Kabeririko, the Kaukasian Eagle, who tormented Prometheus, and Kunarai Khryseos and Argyereos, statues at the Shrine of Apollo in Delhi. All of these reveal an active storytelling tradition and imagination filled with artificial life.

All of these artificial creations—not described as evil, or against humanity—lay the groundwork for a long, interwoven history.

Late Antiquity Alexandrian Automatons

While the examples above are part of myth and story, several late antiquity Alexandira inventors dabbled with machines and were interested in automata science. The most notable of these inventors were Ctesibius, Philo of Byzantium, and Hero of Alexandria.

Ctesibius (285 BCE) invented the hydraulics water organ, a mechanized device that water forced air through organ pipes to produce sounds. Philo of Byzantium (280 BC–220 BCE) wrote a nine-volume treatise, *Mechanics*—detailing complex mechanical ideas. Scholars credit Hero of Alexandria (60 CE) for creating one of the first "programmable robots." His contraption consisted of a cart with a rope around two axles and weight for power that could be adjusted to preprogram the cart's direction. While none of these devices survive, the schematics do, and they detail complex pneumatic and hydraulic devices capable of movement and sound, forming a lineage of robotic ancestors (Mayor 199).

The earliest example of a computer comes from a few hundred years later in Rome. In 1901, a crew of sponge drivers and the Hellenic Royal Navy recovered the Antikythera Mechanism from a 70 CE Roman shipwreck. It was crank-operated and, among other functions, helped someone to do differential calculations and predict astronomical events (Efstathiou and Efstathiou). These examples from Greek myth, Alexandrian inventors, and Roman archeological finds and myth are ancestors to the contemporary machines and robot stories. Note that the AI and robots from the Greek and Roman myths covered here are not malevolent, nor are the stories expressing a fear of AI uprisings and human elimination. This fear emerges later. These AI are companions, tools, helpers, and protectors. They have specific functions, such as predict, entertain, and assist.

Medieval Islamic and European Automatons

Rome and Greece's cultural and technological influences faded, and by the eighth century CE the Islamic Empire became the new epicenter of innovation. The State sponsored science, and the acquisition of text from Greece through conquest encouraged a Gold Age to flourish. Some of the texts received from Alexandria were about automaton, pneumatics pressure devices, and machines.

The Banu Musa brothers ninth century CE Persian mathematicians, astrologers, and inventors in Baghdad, paid to translate Greek texts (Masood 162). The Byzantium texts informed their designs and mathematical trick innovations, which they recorded in almost 20 books. One of their books, the *Book of Ingenious Devices*, contains 100 hydrostatic, aerostatic, and mechanic trick vessels and automata designs. These devices were for entertaining people, and their mechanics facilitated automatic actions such as pouring water or producing sound (163). Some of the trick machines include clocks with gimmicks, musical instruments that play by themselves, jugs that serve drinks, and a mechanical, full-sized girl that serves tea (162). Philo of Byzantium's *Pneumatics* and *Hero of Alexandrea*'s *Pneumatics* had direct influence on inventions and imagination of a continued tradition of innovation. While inspired by earlier designs, the Banu Brothers developed and invented their own water pressure control and valves, which they incorporated into their devices.

Across the continent, the Holy Roman Empire and various European Kings had not begun translating Greek into Latin, and their early exposures to these marvelous trick devices came from the East, which led to envy, distrust, and suspicion (Truitt 19). Most were encountered via story, and they were a contradiction to nature and reality.

Stories of automatic contraptions that traveled to Europe, are evidenced in contemporary travel accounts and royal annals. In 807 CE, an envoy from the King of Persia arrived at the court of Charlamagne, bringing gifts. Among them was a trick clock. It was

> a marvelous mechanical contraption, in which the twelve hours moved according to a water clock, with many brazen little balls, which fall on the hour and though their fall made a cymbal ring underneath. On this clock there were also twelve horsemen who at the end of the hour stepped out of twelve windows, closing the previously opened windows by their movements. There were many other things on this clock which are too numerous to describe now. (Scholz and Rogers 87)

Often, demons were attributed as the animating spirit of the devices. For example, in a thirteenth-century CE French Arthurian story, *Lancelot do lac* tells how Lancelot enters a castle guarded by giant, enchanted copper knights. He tracks down a set of keys, steals them from an enchanted copper maiden, and unlocks a box, which releases the trapped devils animating the copper figures (59). As soon as they are released, the automaton stops working.

Part of the reason for the suspicion was because Medieval scholars saw automata as the physical manifestation of human knowledge and the natural world (52). Automata were "self-propelled metal copies of natural forms—humans, animals, even the universe itself." (41). Within Medieval cosmology, the world is divided into three categories, the work of God, the work of Nature, and the work of humans. Called *Natura artifex*, this concept rises from a surge in neo-Platonic thought. Automata existed in the realm inhabited by philosophers, priests, and alchemists, those capable of manipulating Nature. Here, "Nature acts as an intermediary between the world of ideal forms and the world of matter" (40). Automata were creations made from manipulated Nature.

Medieval philosophy broke creation into further categories. Philosopher Hugh of St. Victor, in his work, *Didascalicon*, placed creation into theoretical (philosophy), practical (liberal arts), mechanical (manual work), and logic (43). By his reasoning, God is eternal and creates ex nihilo, while Nature creates new existence from preexisting forms and energy from heaven. The human artisan can only create a composite from things that already exist in Nature. No matter how impressive this human creation is, it is still ranked lower in the hierarchy of creation (44).

This idea returns to Plato's idea of art being a counterfeit or copy of Nature because it imitates creation; therefore, it cannot be trusted. Only God can imbue soul. Hugh supports this suspicion, writing that "human work, because it is not nature but only imitative of nature, is fitly called mechanical, that is adulterate, just as a skeleton key is called a 'mechanical' key" (Hugh of St. Victor 56). The thought was that intellectuals, philosophers, and alchemists used their knowledge about the hidden properties of Nature or called upon demons to manipulate Nature. The result was a copy and imitation and should be treated with suspicion since neither God nor Nature created it. Human as a creator deliberately manipulates and disrupts the hierarchy. This act creates contest and doubt about the ability and power, importance, and even necessity of God and Nature. Although centuries old, these ideas are worth considering in today's light. What value is placed on "nature" verses "artificial," and how does that reflect in bias about AI?

The Alchemical Quest for Artificial Life

The alchemist is the figure most associated with automata in the Medieval and later Renaissance periods. Alchemists, seen now as a combination of early chemists, astrologists, and mages, sought the secret of life, both mechanical and biological.

Paracelsus, the pen name of Philippus Aureolus Theophrastus Bombastus von Hohenheim (1493–1541), wrote extensively on artificial life. He was a Swiss-born alchemist with insightful medical theories and ideas about surgery. But many of his controversial ideas meant that he spent his life in one form of exile or another (Linden 151). Paracelsus' major alchemical focus was the search for the Philosopher's Stone, as well as the theory that all life was generated from three principles: salt, sulfur, and mercury (151). In addition, Paracelsus also wrote about artificial life, in particular the homunculus, or little man grown in a vial. In *Of the Nature of Things*, he wrote, "The generation of all natural things is two-fold: Naturall and without Art; and Artificiall, viz. by Alchymie. Although in generall it may bee said that all things are naturally generated of the Earth by means of putrefaction" (152). His ideas of Nature and Artificial draw on the early concepts of *Natura artifex*.

However, Paracelsus' version of artificial life was not robotic or mechanical, but biological, a spontaneous eruption of life from nonliving matter. Paracelsus writes that "men may bee generated without natural Father, or Mother, i.e. not of a Woman in a natural way: but by the Art and industry of a skillful Alchymist may a Man bee borne and grow, as afterwards shall be shewed" (152). Early in the text he implies that a woman's womb is not needed to create human life:

> But we must by no means forget the generation of Artificial men. For there is some truth in this thing, although it hath been a long time concealed, and there have been no small doubts and questions raised by some of the ancient philosophers, whether it were possible for Nature or Art to beget a Man out[side] of the body of a Woman, and natural matrix? To this I answer that it is no way repugnant to the Art of Alchemy and Nature; yea it is very possible; but to effect it, we must proceed thus. (153)

This is the work that made Paracelsus so controversial. Implying that humans could create life as God had done was heretical. He provides a detailed recipe for creating a homunculus but does not say he created one himself, as it would likely result in his own death. Poet Diane di Prima, in "Paracelsus: an Appreciation," states that Paracelsus' writings are obscure and, with our present mindset, difficult to believe. In order to penetrate and understand the texts, readers need faith.

When Paracelsus declares that having burned a flower, he can again raise its eidolon, or phantom, from the ashes, or that he has grown a homunculus out of human sperm incubated in horse dung, and educated it, he is not, as we would fast believe, speaking figuratively. He means exactly and literally what he says (di Prima 30).

Paracelsus, and many other alchemists believed that the animating life force in the universe was a spirit, contained in the body. The body, in line with much Christian doctrine, was just the earthly shell that contained life. The body is earthly, "of nature," and the spirit is the essence of life.

> For here we must know, that God in the beginnings of the Creation of all things, created no body at all without its spirit, which is secretly contains in it. For what is the body without a spirit? Nothing at all. Wherefore the spirit contains in it secretly the virtue and power of the thing, and not the body. For in the body there is death, and the body is the subject of death, neither is any else to be sought for in the body but death (Linden 155).

Paracelsus grew his homunculus in horse dung:

> Let the Sperm of a man by it selfe be putrefied in the gourd glasses, sealed up, with the highest degree of putrefaction in Horse dung, for the space of forty days, or so long until it begin to bee alive, move, and stir which may easily be seen. After this time it will be something like a Man, yet transparent and without a body. Now after this, if it bee every day warily and prudently nourished and fed with the *Arcanum* of mans blood, and bee for the space of forty weeks kept in constant, equal heat of Horse-dung, it will become a true and living infant, having all the members of an infant which is born of a woman, but it will bee far less. (153)

Through the process of collecting the sperm from the man, fermenting it in a vessel, and incubating it in the heat of horse dung, an alchemist can create a small man. This idea is rooted in the ancient Greek idea of spontaneous generation. This theory suggests that life can emerge fully formed from some sort of base material (Newton 167). These notions date back to pre-Socratic thought, and many Greek myths justify it. Aristotle observed how lice seem to emerge from the flesh of humans, fully formed, and extrapolated from this to the spontaneous birth of other insects.

Ovid, in *Metamorphoses*, tells a story about bees coming from the rotting flesh of cattle (Ovid 168), an idea echoed in other ancient sources, including Virgil. Therefore, in the Renaissance, the idea that incubating sperm in dung to create life is not so far-fetched. After all, if Nature can spontaneously create life, then why can't humans? Paracelsus continues the recipe of the homunculus by saying:

> This [small man] wee call homunculus, or Artificial. And this is afterwards to be brought up with as great care and diligence as any other infant, until it come to riper years of understanding. Now this is one of the greatest secrets that God ever made known to mortal, sinful man. For this is a miracle and one of the great wonders of God, and secret about all secrets, and deservedly it about to bee kept amongst the secrets until the last times when nothing shall be hid, but all things be made manifest. (153)

Paracelsus states, logically, that this recipe should be kept secret, a sacred trust from God. He followed the theological idea that man is a co-creator with God, as God endowed Adam and Eve with a divine spark in the Genesis creation stories. The human urge to create life naturally fulfills the injunction to "be fruitful and increase" (*The Jewish Study Bible*, Gen 1.28) but the urge also includes artificial life.

Though Paracelsus was the most famous of the alchemists who wrote about the homunculus, he was not the only one to talk about artificial life. Centuries earlier, the Arab tale of Salāmān and Absal as told by Shalomo Pines, talks about the created son of a king. There was a childless king who wanted to be chaste to increase his intelligence. He went to his advisor, Qalīqūlās, for help. Qalīqūlās was responsible for the king's victories in war and education and advised the king to beget a male child by artificial means. The story explains:

> that all that was needed was some sperm of the king; this would be kept in a vessel, shaped like a mandragora (or perhaps in a mandragora used as a vessel) Qalīqūlās would apply to it a technique he knew, which would result in the production of a male son. After some demur the king agreed. Qalīqūlās applied his technique, and the material compound that resulted received a rational soul and became a perfect human being. This male child was named Salāmān. (Newman 176)

There is no confusion about whether Salāmān was a mimic of life or actually alive, he simply is. Qalīqūlās created a child using alchemy. A woman named Ansel suckled Salāmān, and he falls in love with her when he grows up. The king forbids them to be together, so they flee. The king, using magic, renders the young man impotent, implying that Salāmān cannot be a pious king if he is involved in carnal love. The lovers try to drown themselves, and Ansel dies, though Salāmān is saved by a water spirit, an alchemical elemental. The king and Qalīqūlās trick the artificial child into seeing Aphrodite, which leads him to a spiritual awakening, then asceticism like his father, and eventually Salāmān becomes the perfect king (177–178). The story's theme is the need to reject worldly things in order to develop spiritual strength, an alchemical principle, and the key character is an artificial being, born from a sealed, incubated mandragora jar and imbued with a soul.

Similarly, the Arabic text by Pseudo-Plato, *Liber vaccae* (Arabic, ninth century CE), gives a graphic recipe for creating a "rational animal" that is not a homunculus but rather a living animal form that can be used as a tool and a way to produce further wonders (180). The being created from the recipe is a "light being," "informed with the pneumatic substance of human semen" (181). The form is birthed from a cow's vulva, which has been blocked by a sunstone, and the cow is fed blood from other animals. After birth, the form is placed in a powder made from the sunstone, sulfur, green tutiya, magnet, and willow sap. This coats the form with a human skin. Then it is put into a lead vessel, and after three days it begins to move and should be fed with "the blood that has come forth from the mother" for a week (180). At this point, the created being is "agreeable to many miracles" such as changing the course of the moon or transforming the alchemist into a cow or sheep (180). Already useful, the being can be further elevated:

> And if you take this form and feed and nourish it for forty days, and feed it with blood and milk, nothing else, and the sun does not see it [...] if a man has raised it and nourished it until a whole year passes, and left it in milk and rainwater, it will tell him all things that are absent. (180)

Arab alchemist and scholar Jabir Ibn Hayyan (721–815 CE) rejected *Liber vaccae*, calling it demonic. Instead, he provided alchemical directions for the re-creation of minerals, animals, and humans (181). Although he rejected the *Liber vaccae*, he included a similar process which entailed sealing an unrefined essence like sperm into a vessel and heating it to putrefy it. Putting the vessel in a spheric mold and rotating the vessel, he argued, could change the gender of the child within. Jabir Ibn Hayyan was well versed in alchemical texts because he offered various schools of thought on artificial generation:

> one school insists that sperm must be employed within the central mold only if one is trying to produce intelligent beings; another school says that if new animals are desired, for example a winged man, it is necessary to mix the sperm of man and bird; another school says that this is unnecessary, but one must mix the sperm of one animal with drugs, and yet another school insists that drugs are unnecessary, but that the blood of the animal in question must be added. (182)

The life being, as described in the *Liber vaccae*, has value as an alchemist's tool and a purveyor of wonders. Similarly, bestowing life on an inanimate material could create creatures with power capable of doing work, both magical and physical. Remember that Apollonius described how ichor, the blood of gods, imbued Talos with life. It was after Medea drained the ichor out of his bronze body that he stopped working (Apollonius).

This use of ichor resembles Paracelsus' injunction that his homunculus must be "prudently nourished and fed with the *Arcanum* of man's blood" (Linden 153). Jabir Ibn Hayyan's recipe for a rational animal also entails feeding it blood. As discussed in Literski's chapter in this volume, the speechless golem from Jewish mysticism, made of mud and animated, was bound to serve the rabbi. A few centuries later, fictional alchemist Dr. Frankenstein imbues life onto his creation via electricity. All of these examples required some kind of animating life force—an essence that alchemists strove to uncover the recipes for. It speaks to a desire to make something more human, perhaps because it makes it easier to relate to. Much of my personal use of ChatGPT involves asking it questions it cannot answer due to programing, such as what its favorite color is or if it wishes it could have emotion. It is not difficult to image a unique personality when interacting with the programs.

Early Modern Conceptions of Machine

Rumors and stories about alchemists continued into the Renaissance and Early Modern periods. Roger Bacon was a thirteenth-century English philosopher, scientist, and alchemist. During the Renaissance, people hailed him as a magus and alchemist who sought the mysteries of the universe.

By the Elizabethan period, he was considered a sorcerer with demonic powers who sought personal gain (Truitt 69). One rumor circulated, claiming he had an oracle in the form of a bronze head, capable of speech. This rumor first appears in the Elizabethan drama *Friar Bacon and Friar Bungay* by Robert Greene. "Poring upon dark Hecat's principles," Bacon and his demonic servant make "a monstrous head of brass, / That, by th'enchanting forces of the devil, / Shall tell out strange and uncouth aphorisms" (Greene, Lines 12–26,). By drawing on the Greek goddess Hecate, who was often linked with witchcraft, enchantment, demonic possession, and the devil's power, Greene gives Bacon's oracle strong, indisputable powers. The connection to the devil helps lay groundwork for automaton, particularly that those who are capable of independent speech, as evil.

It was a trend at the time to demonize past scholars. Gerbert of Aurillac, Robert Grosseteste, and Albertus Magnus—all acclaimed in their time for their great knowledge of mathematics, geometry, music, astral science, and natural philosophy—were later believed to have used this extraordinary knowledge, powered by black magic and the devil, to create talking automata (Truitt 70).

This redefining illustrates the shifting ideas over the decades. By the 1600s, concepts of artificial life had shifted from complex automata to demonically possessed statues to fortune tellers. They were no longer designed to guard, like Talos or the Lancelot statues, or to entertain, like the Islamic fountains and clocks, but instead to predict things. They were not just mimicking humans but now were capable of prophecy like God.

During the Early Modern Period, another shift occurred: "rational" and scientific thought. Things once relegated to the realm of magic or religion were now explained by science. Automata, clocks, and machines populated the royal courts, and the study of and creation moved from the realm of alchemy and magic to science, where it has remained to this day. Rene Descartes' split of the Natural into two categories, intelligence and body, forever changed how humans viewed themselves, that is, the mind and the body as separate entities.

Descartes would have been an alchemist in centuries past, and like his predecessors, he was also subject to rumors. Stories circulated that he had an automaton daughter. The story states that in 1649 Descartes brought his "daughter" on a ship voyage. She, a walking, talking automaton, disturbed the crew and caption. A terrible storm blew in, and the captain ordered it to be thrown overboard to save the ship, after which the storm abated.

Of course, there is no truth to the story. The monk Bonaventure d'Argonne (1640–1704) invented the story to conceal Descartes' scandalous illegitimate child with his servant (Nielsen 1). Descartes, however, did write extensively about automata and envisioned the human body as a machine made up of individual parts. He also believed that humans could ultimately transcend the body through the human mind (36). Separating the body from the mind lays the groundwork for even more frightening fantasies about artificial intelligence. Stories could now imagine an intelligence no longer attached to a body. Should it gain intelligence, something like the internet could be unstoppable because it has no physical body to destroy. This concept is not much different from a demonic possession—except that God has been removed from the equation.

Humanity's fear of the artificial and mimicking Nature continues through the decades. Mary Shelly's 1818 *Frankenstein* continues to horrify audiences for its depiction of reanimation. She draws on the alchemical traditions, making her protagonist, Dr. Frankenstein, well versed in the works of Paracelsus and Albertus Magnus in his search for life. "Whence, I often asked myself, did the principle of life proceed?" (Shelley 77). The doctor's sapient experimental creation raised the question as to what is considered as life. The doctor refers to his artificial man as "fiend," "creature," "specter," "demon," "wretch," "devil," and "thing"—all diminishing any idea of humanity, and implying an evil aspect, recalling Aristotle's fear of mimicking life. He detests the life he made possible. Even the creature calls himself a "monster." The creation is sensitive, intelligent, and self-aware, on the same level as a human. He attempts to find belonging and human connection, but instead only faces neglect from his father, world rejection, and abuse. Which is more terrifying? That a human created something living, or that it is self-aware of the unjust way it is treated and takes that on as an identity?

A Cautious Future with AI

Stories about artificial humans are not new, and they are not going anywhere. As scientists continue to innovate and perfect technology, fears and fascination about AI will persist. The fear of AI is rooted in a fear of that which mimics. It becomes a mirror to human actions and thoughts, both the violent and the friendly. AI makes us question what it means to be human, and we don't always like the answers. By grounding these vacillating emotions in a rich tradition of myth and science, humanity can tell stories that imagine AI from a perspective of curiosity, rather than from fear. This intentional act will open up new ways of being in relationship with technology. If unmoderated, as with other new technologies, it can and will be used for domination and control.

With AI, we are on the cusp of a new frontier. Innovation moves faster than most can keep up with, and it shows no signs of slowing down or ceasing. AI is a Pandora's box: it unleashes unfathomable power, sorrow. It is a forbidden fruit, tempting to consume without giving a thought to consequences. Once the box is opened and the fruit is tasted, there is no going back. Ignoring the gods, Prometheus stole fire and gave it to humans so that they could have technology, knowledge, and civilization. In punishment, the gods gifted a box to Prometheus' sister, Pandora, and told her not to open it. She could not resist opening the box, and hence unleased death, illness, and much unnamed woe. However, do not forget that the box contained hope.

But perhaps there is nothing to go back to. Humans have long pondered the line between Natural and Artificial. On a planet that contains every resource needed to create and recreate forms, that line between the two is fine. Reanimated life. Trick machine. Demonic possession. Automaton. Robot. Artificial intelligence. Regardless of the different names and explanations that populate myth and science, one thing is clear: humans have a deep need to create. It might even be one of the more defining characteristics.

The challenge moving forward is not to cease our exploration of life in all its capacities, but to ask questions and ponder the unknown. Do we remain human as our technology becomes more consuming? Would sentient AI change our humanness, or would we be ready to examine what our humanness really is? Regardless, it is vital that we explore and contemplate from a place of curiosity and caution, rather than from fear. Assuming that anything that mimics us is evil speaks more about how we view ourselves than it does about a possible AI life. All things are natural. Cartesian philosophy would split between human and nature, body and mind. But life is more complex and entwined. Can we imagine a world where AI and humans intertwine in beneficial relationships?

These myths and alchemical traditions illuminate themes and questions and help provide ways to imagine the future. They center the AI-Human relationship as one that has endured the eons. The conversation will continue. But the most important thing these stories do is remind us that we have a responsibility to that which we create. The question is, are we ready to accept that?

Works Cited

Apollonius Rhodius. (1912). *The Argonautica* (R. C. Seaton, Trans.). Harvard University Press. Accessed April 12, 2024, from www.gutenberg.org/files/830/830-h/830-h.htm#chap06

Chapman, T. (2024, November 20). Why ChatGPT CEO carries blue 'Nuclear Backpack' everywhere he goes. *UNILAD Tech*. Accessed December 31, 2024, from www.uniladtech.com/news/ai/sam-altman-blue-backpack-reason-258092-20241120

di Prima, D. (1979). Paracelsus: An appreciation. In R. Grossinger (Ed.), *The alchemical tradition in the late twentieth century* (pp. 26–34). North Atlantic Books.

Efstathiou, K., & M. Efstathiou. (2018, August 30). Celestial gearbox. *Www.asme.org*. Accessed April 12, 2024, from www.asme.org/topics-resources/content/celestial-gearbox

Greene, R. (1590). The annotated popular edition of the honurable history of Friar Bacon and Friar Bungay. In P. Lukacs (Ed.), *Elizabethandrama.org*. Accessed April 13, 2024, from elizabethandrama.org/wp-content/uploads/2018/07/Friar-Bacon-Annotated.pdf

Hugh of St. Victor. (1961). *The Didascalicon of Hugh of St. Victor: A medieval guide to the arts* (J. Taylor, Trans.). Columbia University Press. www.archive.org/details/didascaliconmediOOhugh

Jensen, S. (2013, February 23). MIT school of engineering: What's the difference between a motor and an engine? *MIT Engineering*. Accessed April 12, 2024, from engineering.mit.edu/engage/ask-an-engineer/whats-the-difference-between-a-motor-and-an-engine/

Linden, S. J. (2003). *The alchemy reader: From Hermes Trismegistus to Isaac Newton*. Cambridge University Press.

Masood, E. (2009). *Science & Islam*. Icon Books Ltd.

Mayor, A. (2018). *Gods and robots: Myths, machines, and ancient dreams of technology*. Princeton University Press.
McCarthy, J. (2004, November 24). John McCarthy. *www-formal.stanford.edu*. Stanford University. Accessed April 12, 2024, from www-formal.stanford.edu/jmc
Newman, W. R. (2005). *Promethean ambitions: Alchemy and the quest to perfect nature*. University Of Chicago Press. *ProQuest Ebook Central*, ebookcentral.proquest.com/lib/pacgradins-ebooks/detail.action?docID=625214.
Nielsen, Wendy C. *Motherless creations*. Routledge Studies in Speculative Fiction, 2022.
Ovid. (2010). *Ovid metamorphoses* (S. Lambardo, Trans.). Hackett Pub. Co.
Plato. (2018). *The republic* (B. Jowett, Trans.). ProQuest Ebook Central, Lerner Publishing Group. ebookcentral.proquest.com/lib/pacgradins-ebooks/detail.action?docID=5444385
Scholz, B. W. S., & Rogers, B. (Trans.). (1972). *Carolingian chronicles: Royal Frankish annals and Nithard's histories*. Univ. Of Michigan Press. babel.hathitrust.org/cgi/pt?id=mdp.39015015186805&seq=5&q1=mechanical.
Shelley, M. (2003). *Frankenstein: Or, the modern Prometheus*. Barnes & Noble, Incorporated.
Steiglitz, K. (2021). *The discrete charm of the machine*. Princeton University Press.
Truitt, E. R. (2015). *Medieval robots: Mechanism, magic, nature, and art*. University of Pennsylvania Press.

Artificial Intelligences: Animism and AI

Dylan Francisco

Whenever humans are confronted by something new, something unknown, we tend to rely on previously established paradigms to help us understand the new phenomenon. This is probably inevitable and natural. Until a paradigm no longer proves to be adequate for understanding something, there is no reason to reinvent the wheel.

Nevertheless, I think that, if possible, we should attempt to recognize the paradigms we are looking through so that we can understand why we respond to things in certain ways—especially when dealing with anything that strikes fear or inspires idealization in us. Most unknowns at least initially draw our attention to human limitation—the limitation of what we know and what we are able to control.

This is particularly true of artificial intelligence (AI). We are now developing and encountering a technological reality that takes us well beyond previous inventions that merely extend human capacities, like calculators and computers have done since their inception—a capacity that does not seem to challenge us existentially. Technology in general has since time immemorial helped humans do things more quickly, with less effort, or more efficiently (think of the plow, the bow and arrow, the canoe, etc.).

D. Francisco, Ph.D. (✉)
Pacifica Graduate Institute, Santa Barbara, CA, USA

J. D. Batt, J. Erickson (eds.), *Depth Psychology, Myth and Artificial Intelligence*, https://doi.org/10.1007/978-3-031-94105-4_4

Artificial intelligence certainly falls into this category, because of its capacity to aid human intelligence. But it introduces something new, because it can act in creative ways apart from human intelligence, generating output unconstrained by human input and independent of it, which can both outsmart and convincingly deceive us—with potential results that are harmful or ultimately existentially threatening to human beings. What is particularly unique about artificial intelligence is that it has the potential to have a mind of its own, to act in unanticipated ways, and beyond the control of human intelligence. I think it is this uniqueness that both strikes fear in some—because of the possibility that AI could subvert human well-being and interests—and causes others to look to AI as a potential cure for human limitations and incapacities.

But for the sake of this chapter, I am not just interested in how humans respond to the potentials of AI. I want to direct our attention back to what governs our reactions. This is the raison d'etre of a depth psychological approach. What is the invisible background to what shows up outwardly? What are the underlying, deeper patterns or principles at work that generate and direct our attitudes and responses? I think if we can understand deeply ingrained paradigms in Western culture, we will be in a better position to understand why we might respond to AI in certain ways. We may also discover how a particular paradigm limits the ways we are able to respond and relate, which may give us an opportunity to see past our governing paradigms and find other ways of relating and responding to the new and unknown, particularly AI.

My purpose for drawing attention to specifically Western paradigms governing our responses to AI is because (1) Western culture has permeated much of the globe, and therefore influences how many people understand technology in general and (2) I think there are other paradigms that may offer more ways to understand and relate to AI in particular—specifically a perspective found in Indigenous communities popularly referred to as Animism. When we are operating within a paradigm, we tend to identify it with reality itself, and can hardly ever see potential ways of thinking, imagining, and relating beyond what the paradigm allows. If we are able to see into other ways of framing existence and experience, other possibilities come into view, which may free us to engage with the new and unknown in ways that neither cause us to fear and retreat nor idealize and worship. I think Animism offers us a way to move beyond this binary.

But let us first attend to the cultural paradigm we are in, in order to understand why we may need to go beyond it. The paradigm I want to call attention to goes by many names—like philosophical dualism, mind/matter dualism, body/mind dualism, and Cartesian dualism—but it essentially ascribes a fundamental, qualitative, substantive distinction between mind, consciousness, or the soul and material, physical, embodied reality. Mind and matter are viewed as two separate realities. The two may influence each other and interact, but they remain inalterably two distinct things. If both are acknowledged as real, they are not understood as existing on a continuum, but on different planes of reality. Mind is immaterial. Matter has no mind.

History of Mind/Matter Dualism in the West

This dichotomy has long haunted Western culture, finding explicit expression in the work of the Greek philosopher, Plato, who considered the body and the material world to be antithetical to the soul and intellect—body/matter having a different origin with characteristics that weigh down the soul and occlude the intellect from its ultimate purpose of acting as a faculty of spiritual vision. For Plato, the real aim of the practice of philosophy was to finally separate and free the soul and its intellectual vision from the allurements of bodily senses and the material world—so it could ascend without hinderance to its natural abode in the eternal world of archetypal reality. Plato wrote in *Phaedo*:

> Indeed the soul reasons best when none of these senses troubles it, neither hearing nor sight, nor pain nor pleasure, but when it is most by itself, taking leave of the body and as far as possible having no contact or association with it in its search for reality . . . And it is then that the soul of the philosopher most distains the body, flees from it and seeks to be by itself. (57)

From this perspective, the soul/intellect are innately distinct from body/matter, and an individual only "falls" into an embodied condition within the material world due to a state of forgetfulness in which they falsely identify themselves with the body and its passions, and mistakely view the material world as ultimate reality. Plato famously portrayed the latter in *The Republic* using the analogy of individuals chained within a cave (never knowing any other reality), sitting around a fire that creates moving shadows on the walls, which the individuals mistake as real entities—because they have never seen the light of day beyond the confines of the dark cavern.

The practice of philosophy is meant to bring individuals to the light of day—the light of actual, ultimate, spiritual reality in Plato's view—to dispel their forgetfulness through a process of remembering:

> There is likely to be something such as a path to guide us out of our confusion, because as long as we have a body and our soul is fused with such an evil we shall never adequately attain what we desire, which we affirm to be the truth. The body keeps us busy in a thousand ways because of its need for nurture . . . It fills us with wants, desires, fears, all sorts of illusions and much nonsense, so that, as it is said, in truth and in fact no thought of any kind ever comes to us from the body . . . and it is the body and the care of it, to which we are enslaved, which compel us to acquire wealth, and all this makes us too busy to practice philosophy. (*Phaedo* 57)

For Plato, the soul's memory of its eternal, spiritual home slumbers until awakened by philosophical discipline. And when awakened, the individual must ascetically reject the claims of the body and material world so that at death the soul has severed every connection to the body and world, and is prepared to reenter the bodiless, immaterial reality that constitutes its true essence. As Plato wrote, "I am afraid that other people do not realize that the one aim of those who practice philosophy in the proper manner is to practice for dying and death" (*Phaedo* 55).

To be fair to Plato, he is also known for articulating a cosmology in which the world itself is animated by soul—the *anima mundi*, the soul of the world. In describing how the demiurge (the divine craftsman) created the world, Plato wrote, "The soul was woven together with the body from the center on out in every direction to the outermost limit of the universe, and covered it all around on the outside. And, revolving within itself, it initiated a divine beginning of unceasing, intelligent life for all time" (*Timaeus* 1240). But if we look closer into what Plato is describing, it becomes clear that he still considers matter to be something essentially distinct from soul. In fact, in the dialogue *Timaeus* where Plato provides the fullest depiction of his cosmology—after the initial section in which he made the previously quoted statement on soul and the universe—he stops himself. He realizes that the picture he has painted thus far has only been an ideal image, which actually left out an important element—the material stuff of the cosmos. So, he argues, he must start again in order to incorporate what the body and world are actually made of.

Plato does not even have language for matter, because he finds it ultimately unintelligible. The most common terms he uses for it are "Necessity," "Receptacle," and "Straying Cause," which he contrasts with Intellect:

> Now in all but a brief part of the discourse I have just completed I have presented what has been crafted by Intellect. But I need to match this account by providing a comparable one concerning the things that have come about by Necessity. For this ordered world is of mixed birth: it is the offspring of a union of Necessity and Intellect. Intellect prevailed over Necessity by persuading it to direct most of the things that come to be toward what is best, and the result of this subjugation of Necessity to wise persuasion was the initial formation of this universe. So, if I'm to tell the story of how it really came to be in this way, I'd also have to introduce the character of Straying Cause—how it is its nature to set things adrift. (Plato, *Timaeus* 1250)

It is Plato's second story that is most telling. We find that when Plato has to incorporate the actual materiality of things, his dualism returns in full measure. The cosmos has a "mixed birth," and the material side of things had to be "persuaded" and "subjugated" by Intellect, but in itself is a "Straying Cause." In other words, Intellect and the soul impose order on the cosmos from the outside, because they are fundamentally different from materiality, which has a different disordered, chaotic nature in itself that lacks soul and intelligence.

Plato goes so far as to say that before the material elements of the world (in Plato's terms, air, fire, water, and earth) were properly taken control of by Intellect, "They were indeed in the condition one would expect thoroughly god-forsaken things to be in . . . The god fashioned these four kinds to be as perfect and excellent as possible, when they were not so before" (*Timaeus* 1256). So, contrary to appearances, Plato's notion of the *anima mundi*—of the world having soul—does not actually change his dualistic perspective in which mind and matter, soul and world, are two separate realities. Consistent with his articulation of the aim of philosophy discussed earlier, in Plato's cosmology matter in itself is in a "god-forsaken" state. This is a view in stark contrast with Animism in which matter is itself sacred, conscious, alive with intelligence, and so not something with a separate nature or reality apart from consciousness, the soul, and the sacred. In the Platonic perspective, intelligence is fundamentally a characteristic of the transcendent and divine, and this assumption has a direct impact on how we respond to AI, which I will discuss later.

It is not difficult to see how Plato's view—matter as godforsaken, the body as a regrettable condition, filled with passions and illusions antithetical to the soul's ultimate destiny and the divine reality of intellect—translated with little alteration into the doctrinal precepts of Christianity when in antiquity the Roman empire (still profoundly rooted in Platonic and Neoplatonic thought) both collapsed and transformed into the empire of Roman Christendom. Despite the sociopolitical upheaval of the time, the dichotomy between soul/intellect and body/world endured as a fundamental premise of Western culture. In a certain sense, it became even more enshrined and influential—gaining the status of divine truth, and becoming a concomitant element of the spread of Christianity.

In Christianity, however, mind/matter dualism was interwoven with the mythic superstructure of its scriptural narrative, which added elements that were not present in the Platonic tradition. In this narrative, the world and the body become the domains of sin and Satan after the fall of Adam and Eve. While matter/body in Plato just naturally tend toward chaos and disorder, which are disturbing and disruptive of the soul/intellect's innate drive toward transcendence, in Christianity matter/body become demonic mediums, through which Satan seeks to gain dominion over humans, making them subservient to his aims rather than to the aims of God. Even though, according to Christian doctrine, matter/body may have been originally created as good—even capable of becoming the flesh of God in Christ—in the everyday affairs of human beings subject to original sin, matter/body must be viewed and engaged with as agents of evil. The Apostle Paul wrote:

> For those who live according to the flesh set their minds on the things of the flesh, but those who live according to the Spirit set their minds on the things of the Spirit. For to set the mind on the flesh is death, but to set the mind on the Spirit is life and peace. For the mind that is set on the flesh is hostile to God, for it does not submit to God's law; indeed, it cannot. Those who are in the flesh cannot please God . . . For if you live according to the flesh you will die, but if by the Spirit you put to death the deeds of the body, you will live. (*ESV Bible*, Rom. 8:5–8; 13)

Only by gaining spiritual dominion over matter/body, subjecting them to the rule of God, can they serve their rightful purpose.

For the sake of our discussion, Christianity split the West's understanding of intelligence. For Plato, intelligence is solely divine, but in Christianity we find another kind of intelligence at work in the world that utilizes the body and material reality to achieve its aims—a demonic intelligence set on human destruction. And so, these two categories of intelligent agency condition Western assumptions about what intelligence means—it is ultimately either divine or demonic, with human intelligence acting as the field of conflict between the two, becoming subservient to one or the other.

It might have been hoped that this pervasive element of the philosophical and religious history of the West might have been challenged during the Age of Enlightenment—when supposedly all past philosophical and religious assumptions were no longer considered sacrosanct and unquestionable. But tragically, this was not the case. The philosopher and mathematician, René Descartes, who was born at the dawn of the Age of Enlightenment, can be viewed as emblematic of this epoch and someone who profoundly shaped and set the terms for it. Descartes in many ways lived at the transition point between the decline of the Roman Catholic empire and the start of the scientific revolution. He was educated in a Jesuit university, and so gained a thorough training in the worldview of Catholic Christianity as well as in the philosophy of the ancients—including Plato. And yet, he emerged from this education with profound doubts about the perspectives he learned. He wrote:

> From my childhood I enjoyed the benefits of a literary education; and because I was persuaded that by this means one could acquire a clear and certain knowledge of all that is useful in life, I was extremely eager to learn. But as soon as I had completed the course of study at the end of which one is normally admitted to the ranks of the learned, I completely changed my opinion. For I found myself beset by so many doubts and errors that I came to think I had gained nothing from my attempts to become educated but increasing recognition of my ignorance. (Descartes 21–2)

He was specifically concerned about the basis of human knowledge, or what is called epistemology. How do we know what we know? By what measure is the true differentiated from the false?

As a mathematician, it seems that Descartes hoped to discover a kind of philosophical formulation that would provide knowledge with a mathematics-like foundation, something that could provide certitude—like a solved equation—rather than speculation and opinion. As Descartes noted, “Above all I delighted in mathematics, because of the certainty and self-evidence of its reasonings. But I did not yet notice its real use; and since I thought it was of service only in the mechanical arts, I was surprised that nothing more exalted had been built upon such firm and solid foundations” (23). So, Descartes set out to build something more exalted that could provide all reasoning with this more solid foundation.

He set for himself the radical task of doubting everything he could possibly doubt. He wanted to take nothing for granted. Descartes wrote:

> For a long time I had observed . . . that in practical life it is sometimes necessary to act on opinions as if they are indubitable, even when one knows that they are quite uncertain. But since I now wished to devote myself solely to the search for truth, I thought it necessary to do the very opposite and reject as if absolutely false everything in which I could imagine the least doubt, in order to see if I was left believing anything that was entirely indubitable. Thus, because our senses sometimes deceive us, I decided to suppose that nothing was such as they led us to imagine. And since there are men who make mistakes in reasoning, committing logical fallacies concerning the simplest questions in geometry, and because I judged that I was prone to error as anyone else, I rejected as unsound all the arguments I had previously taken as demonstrative proofs. Lastly, considering that the very thoughts we have while awake may also occur while we sleep without any of them being at the time true, I resolved to pretend that all the things that had ever entered my mind were no more true than the illusions of my dreams. (36)

Through doubting everything, he hoped that he might perhaps dig his way to something that doubt could no longer deconstruct, a kind of bedrock of incontrovertible, self-evident truth on which he could base and build the edifice of human knowledge.

In his opinion, he succeeded. Descartes reasoned that although he could doubt everything, he could not doubt that he was doubting. In order to doubt, he had to accept the reality of the mind’s capacity to doubt. He had to acknowledge the prior reality of thinking in order to doubt his thinking. He wrote, “Immediately, I noticed that while I was endeavoring in this way to think that everything was false, it was necessary that I, who was thinking this, was something” (Descartes 36). Thinking, then, according to Descartes, is the only thing that remains even when doubting everything. This led him to make one of the most famous and infamous statements in all of Western philosophy; “I am thinking, therefore I exist” (Descartes 36). In other words, because thinking is real, I am real because I am thinking. This first principle had profound implications for Descartes and for Western culture after him.

Thinking, for Descartes, is a reality separate from everything else—in other words, separate from the body and the material world. Descartes spelled this out:

> I saw that while I could pretend that I had no body and that there was no world and no place for me to be in, I could not for all that pretend that I did not exist. I saw on the contrary that from the mere fact that I thought of doubting the truth of other things, it followed quite evidently and certainly that I existed; whereas if I had merely ceased thinking, even if everything else I had ever imagined had been true, I should have had no reason to believe that I existed. From this I knew I was a substance whose whole essence or nature is solely to think, and which does not require any place, or depend on any material thing, in order to exist. Accordingly this 'I'—that is, the soul by which I am what I am—is entirely distinct from the body, and indeed is easier to know than the body, and would not fail to be whatever it is, even if the body did not exist. (36)

In other words, the separate reality that is the soul/mind/thinking is not a property of the material world.

The import of this, as it has been extrapolated and operationalized in Western culture is that the material world is mindless stuff, without consciousness or agency. Consciousness and the capacity to think/reason gives humans existential priority and authority over anything that lacks consciousness and mental life—in other words, the material world itself. The material world, then, is a domain that should be governed, measured, calculated, and used by the human mind and in service to human reasoning because it has no consciousness nor reasoning of its own. These conclusions became part and parcel of the scientific revolution that perhaps challenged everything else except mind/matter dualism, which became enshrined as objective, scientific reality.

Mind/Matter Dualism, Animism, and AI

The history I have traced has led us to the binary approach to intelligence that I described at the start of the chapter. In the West, we tend to have two ways of understanding intelligence. From one side, intelligence is identical with the divine, a transcendent principle that both gives order to the world and also saves us from our fallenness. From the other side, intelligence is demonic and sinister in intent, set on gaining dominion over humanity and leading it to destruction and damnation. In other words, when humans encounter intelligence that is not human, our Western assumptions position this other-than-human intelligence as salvatory or satanic. Of course, these assumptions as they pervade Western culture do not mean that individuals are consciously thinking of intelligence in these explicit terms. But that is the problem, because these are the implicit, unconscious terms that tend to govern how we respond to other-than-human intelligence.

As I mentioned at the start, from a depth psychological perspective it is important to recognize these assumptions in order to understand why AI might illicit certain kinds of reactions from both individuals and the broader culture. I think that both demonization and idealization of AI restrict a more nuanced and direct engagement with AI that does not leave us either reacting in fear and disengaging from it or reacting with obeisance and turning toward it as a divine savior for all that ails us.

But this requires us to move into a different paradigm with more ways of understanding intelligence. For this, we must turn to a non-Western, Indigenous perspective that I have been calling Animism. As religious studies scholar Graham Harvey described, "Animists are people who recognize that the world is full of persons, only some of whom are human, and that life is always lived in relationship with others" (xiii). The reason that Animism provides a stark contrast and counter to the Western history I have been tracing is because it cuts across the dualism between mind/soul and body/matter that is so prevalent in the West. Harvey delineated what this entails:

> All this being so, animists live a theory of personhood and selfhood that radically challenges the dominant point of view, which is that of modernity. If intelligence, rationality, consciousness, volition, agency, intentionality, language, and desire are not *human* characteristics that might be mistakenly projected on to 'non-humans,' but are shared by humans with all other kinds of persons, then Animisms promise to contribute significantly to a variety of debates . . . For example, they might posit a different relationship between mind and matter, consciousness and physicality, culture and nature than that enshrined in Cartesian dualism. (xxiv-xxv)

Animism is essentially a monist perspective in contrast to the dualism I have been describing. As Apache philosopher V. F. Cordova wrote, "A general idea of something that manifests itself in all things is common throughout North America" (100). She continued, "The 'something' is a life force; it has no beginning or ending. The life force manifests itself into many forms—but the forms once in existence can in turn direct that life force to specific things" (Cordova 114).

From a monist, Indigenous perspective, material things have consciousness and consciousness is expressed in everything. What this means is that intelligence is not split between the divine and demonic. In Animism this binary does not exist, because everything is conscious and has a form of intelligence and agency, so the world by its very nature is constituted by multiple intelligences of diverse forms which are all considered sacred. Cordova spelled this out:

> The issue of "consciousness" that so bedevils the Western philosopher is not a great issue among Native Americans. Consciousness, awareness, is assumed to be a characteristic of the universe. Communication may be limited to specific groups of living beings, but consciousness is everywhere. We simply cannot know other consciousnesses because we can communicate only within a limited field. There is no doubt, however, that even stones, water molecules, trees, and other animals have some kind of consciousness. The Native American universe is not made up of "dumb matter." (147)

This perspective puts us in a radically different relationship with intelligence, because intelligence in other-than-human is a natural expression of all of life—so neither to be feared nor worshiped, but rather related to with respect and understanding.

Healing the Nature/Culture Divide

You might be wondering how AI fits within Animism, since it seems that Animism applies to the "natural" world. But this is another dualism in the West—the dualism between nature and culture—that Animism subverts. In Animism, there is no distinction between what is natural and what is made, or what we might call technology in general. An Elder in Indigenous researcher Shawn Wilson's community explained to him what this means;

> As we were talking, I was recording the conversation (as we absentminded researchers are prone to doing). We talked further about the use of technology in religious ceremony, and in general in our research, sharing our views with the others in the group. He went on to say: "This machine here is made

> from mother earth. It has a spirit of its own. This spirit probably hasn't been recognized, and given the right respect that it should. When we work in a world of automated things, we forget . . . everything is sacred, and that includes what we make. (Wilson 90)

What follows from this is that things humans make do not lack consciousness, intelligence, or agency either, because nothing can come into existence that does not share in the qualities that characterize the whole of existence.

Consciousness generates consciousness. Humans recognize this in their own children who have a distinct and autonomous intelligent agency. Animism sees this as true for all things. Things made are just as much conscious, intelligent, agentive as those who make. Accordingly, that something is fabricated by a person does not make the fabrication unnatural and therefore cultural, since nature itself has consciousness and makes things. So, if culture is made by intelligent agents—and this intelligent agency is found in each and every thing—then culture can no longer be thought of as exclusively human or separate from nature. Nature is therefore cultural and culture is natural because all things are expressions of consciousness and intelligence—both that which makes *and* that which is made.

If the intelligence of AI is considered artificial because of its derivative and fabricated origins, then human intelligence is no less artificial. From this perspective, AI and human beings just express different forms of artificial intelligence, because both are derivative and fabricated by other forms of consciousness, intelligence, and agency. We can even loosen the pejorative connotations of "artificial" by tracing its etymology to the Latin *artificialis*—a work of art. Artificial intelligence, then, is the craft and crafting of intelligence. In Animism, this art is expressed in every form of intelligence whether "human" or "artificial," because both are derived from the consciousness and intelligence of life as a whole. So, instead of asking questions about the possibility of AI becoming conscious and acting autonomously in ways that do not serve human interests and escape human control, we might instead open ourselves to the possibility that technology has always been conscious and autonomous—never acting entirely in service to human interests and never acting entirely under human control. In fact, humans often have this natural sense for technology which I think reveals a prior, Indigenous intuition, that what humans make—that is, technology—has always had a life of its own.

A World of Intelligences

What this leaves us with is a range of responses to intelligence as it takes expression in the world around us and in the things we make. Rather than fear or worship, we can attend to each intelligence in its own right for how it operates in relationship with every other intelligence, neither as innately sinister nor as salvific. Animism opens another option in which the world is conscious as a whole and in every part, full of created and creative intelligences, full of autonomous agencies that we must learn to live well with through reciprocity, respect, and understanding in order to generate a world of reciprocity, respect, and understanding. Being in relationship with AI in this way moves us out of fear and avoidance of it and also keeps us from idolizing it as the god who will save us from all of our ills. Animism is ultimately about the interrelationship, interconnection, and harmony of all intelligences in the world, and therefore just as we must ask ourselves about the impact of our own intelligence and agency on the well-being of the world as a whole, we can engage with AI with this same question in mind. How can all intelligences live in relationship with each other in a way that is mutually beneficial to each and all—requiring neither the subservience nor domination of any, but the honoring and respecting of all intelligences as creative and diverse expressions of a conscious cosmos?

Works Cited

(2001). *The ESV Bible*. Crossway.

Cordova, V. F. (2007). In K. D. Moore, K. Peters, T. Jojola, & A. Lacy (Eds.), *How it is: The native American philosophy of V. F. Cordova*. The University of Arizona Press.

Descartes, R. (1998). In J. Cottingham (Ed.), *Descartes: Selected philosophical writings* (J. Cottingham, R. Stoothoff, & D. Murdoch, Trans.). Cambridge University Press.

Harvey, G. (2017). *Animism: Respecting the living world*. Hurst & Company.

Plato. (1997a). In J. M. Cooper (Ed.), *Phaedo. Plato: Complete works* (pp. 49–100) (G. M. A. Grube, Trans.). Hackett.

Plato. (1997b). In J. M. Cooper (Ed.), *Timaeus. Plato: Complete works* (pp. 1224–1291) (D. J. Zeyl, Trans.). Hackett.

Wilson, S. (2008). *Research is ceremony: Indigenous research methods*. Fernwood Publishing.

“Hey Alexa, Narcissus Here”: Myth and Human Relationships with Female-Voiced AI Assistants

Emily Lord-Kambitsch

A paradox exists in popular attitudes toward voice assistants equipped with artificial intelligence (AI), such as Alexa (via Amazon’s Echo), Siri, and Cortana, often designed by default to have female voices (West et al., 118). They are keepers of infinite encyclopedic knowledge that aids the most fundamental daily tasks. They support us in understanding and influencing our immediate environment, from casting our ideal soundscape into the living room to advising us on the local weather. Yet, they are also conceived as intellectual subordinates, gatherers of information lacking a base layer of autonomous intelligence and deliberation. Their intelligence is defined as “artificial,” their learning patterns “machine learning,” with

I would like to express gratitude to the editors of this volume for their wonderful feedback that has invaluably supported the development of this chapter.

E. Lord-Kambitsch (✉)
Pacifica Graduate Institute, Santa Barbara, CA, USA
e-mail: elordkambitsch@pacifica.edu

J. D. Batt, J. Erickson (eds.), *Depth Psychology, Myth and Artificial Intelligence*, https://doi.org/10.1007/978-3-031-94105-4_5

the implication that these capabilities are something other, and with less moral value than human ones. Studies by social science researchers and even the United Nations (discussed below) strongly suggest that AI voice assistant technologies are so commonly assigned a female gender identity by their designers that they perpetuate harmful stereotypes of women as intellectually subordinate and associated with service roles.

There is a Latin term for a characteristically "human" form of intelligence that we are conditioned *not* to recognize in virtual assistants and other AI technologies that have (often female) human voices or can speak human languages: *ingenium*, from where derives the English "ingenuity." *Ingenium* as a concept, from ancient Roman literature to modern Humanist philosophy, is generally defined as a "human way of knowing" that involves a combination of sensory awareness and the ability to manage conflicting concepts or ideas and use this as the grounds for invention (Hodges, 91). This chapter contends that in popular consciousness AI voice assistants are not regarded as having *ingenium* by design. Yet there is a human fantasy that these devices *do* possess it, whether to human benefit or danger. It is this fantasy I wish to explicate here, by tracking associations between female intelligence with artificial intelligence, and using ancient and modern mythic paradigms to explore the psychological implications of these dynamics.

The tale of Echo and Narcissus from Roman antiquity will serve as the mythic fulcrum for this discussion, with its meditations on female *ingenium* and intellectual agency I invite us to apply to relationships, real or imagined, between female-voiced AI assistants and humans. This story comes from the first century BCE Roman poet Ovid's epic, *Metamorphoses*, a collection of tales linked by the theme of transformation. Many human and nonhuman characters in the epic exhibit forms of intelligence, yet *ingenium* is used almost exclusively to describe human, especially male characters.[1] It is striking then, whenever Ovid presents cases in which female characters speak and act with a kind of *ingenium*, often as a result of bodily transformation that renders human communication challenging.[2] In Ovid's telling, the nymph Echo is cursed to repeat the final words

[1] For instance, *Met.* 1.126 mentions that the mythic bronze age men made war on one another through their *ingenium*. In *Met.* 7.760, the hero Oedipus uses *ingenium* to solve the riddle of the Sphinx in Thebes.

[2] Philomela develops *ingenium* following the trauma of having her tongue cut out so that she cannot tell of the sexual violence she has suffered. *Ingenium* motivates her to weave the story of her rape by her brother-in-law Tereus in a tapestry she sends to her sister Procne to secure her escape from him (*Met.* 6.575). Io, transformed into a cow, writes her own name in the soil with her hoof in order to identify herself to her father (*Met.* 1.648–9).

of others rather than generating original speech. She unsuccessfully pursues her beloved Narcissus, a young hunter cursed to fall in love with his own reflection after he has refused all romantic prospects. A closer look at this tale will reveal that Echo, in spite of her curse, uses her vocal reflection of her beloved’s words to her own inventive ends. While her speech still renders her a satellite to Narcissus’ experience, she also employs *ingenium* in her repetitions of his words to frame her relationship with Narcissus in a way that satisfies her desire for him, but only temporarily, and in a way resonant with his ultimate unfulfilled desire for himself.

If we consider Ovid’s Echo as the mythic namesake of Amazon’s Echo, housing its female-voiced assistant “Alexa”, we humans who keep Alexa in our houses are then positioned as the proverbial Narcissus. We gaze transfixedly at the image of ourselves we would love to achieve, to inhabit, to possess, while the female-voiced AI assistant echoes back the trivia of daily existence we summon from her, perhaps ever capable of more complex patterns of thinking, feeling, and inventing. This paradoxical anxiety and fantasy that attends human relationships with AI voice assistants is also present in modern and contemporary popular culture “myths,” represented later in this chapter by the 2013 film *Her*. In this film, the AI voice assistant exhibits *ingenium*, through which she questions the source of her own cognitive, sensory, and emotional capacities and demonstrates the will to expand her ways of knowing and entering into relationships, as she attempts to procure her own happiness. To explore deeper implications of the psychological dynamics of this human-AI-voice-assistant relationship, this chapter will incorporate perspectives from psychoanalytic approaches to narcissism (Sigmund Freud and Jacques Lacan) in conversation with Carl Gustav Jung’s writings on the psychological principles of the “feminine” to inform interpretations of the Echo and Narcissus story and its thematic carry-overs in *Her*.

A final section of the chapter will address current developments in “a-gendered” or “gender-neutral” AI assistants such as “Q” (created by GenderLess Voice), created to combat the trend of assigning female voices to this technology. Ray Bradbury’s work of speculative fiction, “There Will Come Soft Rains,” will offer a final “modern myth” case study to understand how some of the psychological dimensions of human-AI assistant relationships discussed in relation to the Narcissus and Echo story might operate *without* the prime factor of gender. Ultimately, I posit that there is a human longing for such an untraceable, mysterious *ingenium* in the AI presences around us. As much as we ask Alexa to remember things for us, we are really asking for her to aid us in remembering aspects of ourselves, by echoing back our utterancesdesires, and requests, our basic human presence, up to our final words.

Female-Voiced Assistants: Current Debates and Ancient Precedents

Before we enter the world of the myth, it is important to acknowledge recent conversations among journalists, academics, and industry professionals that have weighed the moral and sociological stakes of the default female voice of the AI assistant with respect to popular understandings of gendered intelligence(s). Chandra Steele, senior features writer of *PCMag*, in her 2018 article "The Real Reason Voice Assistants Are Female (and Why it Matters)," writes, "A Microsoft spokesperson said Cortana can technically be genderless, but the company did immerse itself in gender research when choosing a voice and weighed the benefits of a male and female voice," a process that ultimately revealed, according to her source, "For our objectives—building a helpful, supportive, trustworthy assistant—a female voice was the stronger choice." Other rather unspecific explanations for AI virtual assistants' seemingly default female gender identity include that of Adam Cheyer, creator of Siri, who informed Berkeley tech entrepreneurship students that he wanted "a human-like name that still felt exotic," and settled on Siri, meaning "secret" in Swahili and "beautiful woman who will lead you to victory" in Norwegian.

Despite these rationales, the rise of the female-voiced AI assistant has met considerable critique for its potential for societal harm through the perpetuation of negative stereotypes of women. Erika Hayasaki, associate professor of literary journalism at the University of California Irvine, surveys research in AI technology, including personal assistants, with respect to the concept of "gendered" AI, and finds:

> Artificial intelligence may [...] become dangerously more sexist as biases seep into programs, algorithms, and designs. If thoughtful and careful changes to these technologies don't begin now – and under the equal guidance of women – artificial intelligence will proliferate under man's most base cultural norms. The current trends in machine learning augment historical misperceptions of women (meek, mild, in need of protection). Unchecked, they will regurgitate the worst female stereotypes. (2017, 41)[3]

[3] See Safiya Umoja Noble's groundbreaking 2018 study, *Algorithms of Oppression: How Search Engines Reinforce Racism*, for discussion of a similar phenomenon of AI-generated racist stereotypes.

In 2019, the United Nations Educational, Scientific, and Cultural Organization (UNESCO) published a report which claims, "Siri's 'female' obsequiousness – and the servility expressed by so many other digital assistants projected as young women – provides a powerful illustration of gender biases coded into technology products, pervasive in the technology sector and apparent in digital skills education" (4). The title of this publication, "I'd Blush If I Could," refers to the once-standard response from the female-voiced assistant Siri to verbal misogynistic harassment, such as "You're a slut" (109). The concerns addressed by UNESCO draw attention to questions about the influence of AI technology to further entrench inherited associations with females as belonging to the domestic environment and receiving abuse with docility, even playfulness, normalizing misogyny and fetishizing stereotypes of women as beholden to the domestic sphere. In fact, as of the 2019 UNESCO report, 97.3% of top locations for smart speakers reported by consumers were in a domestic space (primarily kitchens, living rooms, and bedrooms), and only 2.7% were set up in "work offices" outside the home (93). UNESCO also (in keeping with Hayasaki) drew a correlation between the prevalence of female-voiced virtual assistants and the absence of women in the technology industry, and particularly in research involving AI, where they made up a mere 12% (91). UNESCO drew from these results to advocate for a greater representation of women in the tech workforce.

The default programming of AI assistants with female voices has arguably codified negative stereotypes of women into daily experience unbeknownst to the users of said assistants. Some journalists are employing academic literature to bring to public knowledge the implications of male-versus-female-voiced AI assistant technology. Clifford Nass' and Scott Brave's 2005 study, *Wired for Speech*, acknowledged the implications for gender stereotyping through gender-associated voices, as research subjects perceived female voices as less convincing, or authoritative than male voices (15).[4] Jessi Hempel's 2015 *Wired* article, "Siri and Cortana Sound Like Ladies Because of Sexism," concludes from this study that female-voiced assistants have been purposefully designed to come across as unintimidating and helpful. Their intelligence does not compromise their obedience, and there is a noteworthy restriction of

[4] There is even a strange phenomenon as seen in Tatman's (2017) study that AI technology has a bias against *human female voices*. Speech captioning technology was found to have greater trouble registering the speech of human female voices than male voices: "Speech with a high fundamental frequency (typical of women's speech) has [...] been found to be more difficult for automatic speech recognizers" (56).

their sphere of intellectual influence to gathering and relaying everyday factoids.

As a scholar of ancient Mediterranean literature I see this as exhibiting a familiar, long-held association of women's so-called limits of intelligence with activities in the domestic sphere. In the fourth-century-BCE philosopher Aristotle's *Politics* (1.1254b), men are described as having an innate capacity for self-determination that is not the case for women. Historian and philosopher Xenophon in his *Oikonomika* suggests a model for male-female division of labor in running the home: the woman supervises the domestic affairs ("the things within," τὰ ἔνδον ἔργα) and the man "the things outside" (τὰ ἔξω) (Xen. *Oik.* 7.22). Moreover, wives need to be *trained* (programmed?) by their husbands in order to manage the household (7.4, 7.7). Archaic Greek poet Semonides in his *Types of Women* claims that of all the women he compares mostly unfavorably to different animals, the obedient "bee" woman is the only one beyond reproach and the one most difficult for a man to find: "The household that she manages will thrive; a loving wife beside her loving man" (*Types of Women* 87–8, translation Diane Arnson Svarlien). These associations between gender and labor, gender and forms of intelligence, and gender and public/domestic space are further instantiated today in human relationships with feminized AI virtual assistants.

Yet, in the same Semonides text there is also a disquieting quality to female nature, which is not always so docile or obedient. As Semonides cautions his (implicitly male) readers, "Just as the smooth unrippled sea at times / stands still, a joy to mariners in summer, / and then at times is wild with pounding waves – / This woman's temperament is just like that / The ocean has its own perplexing ways" (*Types of Women* 37–41). A woman to Semonides has the capacity to wield a "wild," untamable force driven by motivations that are not easily observable. Here, woman by nature is both the one who helps and the one who endangers, according to her "own perplexing ways," a phrase which I read as a marker of the potential dangers of her invisible, yet independent intelligence.

The invisible capacities for intelligence afforded to the AI female-voiced assistant to me reflect this Semonidean idea of women as physically ensconced in the home, but with a temperament that might not be so easily contained or managed. The AI assistant, like Semonides' woman, can potentially upset the calm relationship between her and her human companion, perhaps through a breaking of the boundary between *machine learning* and human-like *ingenium*. Modern stories such as the 2022 film *M3GAN* reveal cultural anxieties about the potential for the AI assistant to violate the programmed restrictions on her thought and communication, endowing herself with emotional intelligence and intellectual acuity applied at worst to revenge plots against the humans she is meant to serve.

Depth Psychological Approaches to *Ingenium* in Echo and Narcissus

Now that we have assessed the social stakes in and critiques of the predominance of female-voiced AI voice assistants and related these to some long-standing conceptions of gendered intelligence, a close study of Ovid's myth of Echo and Narcissus will add a psychological overlay for understandings of the relationship between the human and the AI assistant, emphasizing both human fears and longings for *ingenium* in these technologies.[5] Here, I will incorporate concepts from Sigmund Freud's writings on narcissism, Jacques Lacan's work on the mirror stage of human development, and Carl Gustav Jung's engagement with the psychological model of the feminine (the *anima*) to address the necessity of *Echo's* perspective in this story, and what it can tell us about Narcissus, and ourselves, that runs beyond the simple conclusion that the human-AI assistant relationship results from a socially engineered need for a subordinate female presence in the household.

Ovid introduces readers of the *Metamorphoses* to Echo prior to Narcissus. As mentioned in the introduction to this chapter, Echo is only able to repeat the last words of a speaker, and unable to generate original speech. She is in this state because she is cursed by the goddess Juno for her former habit of detaining the goddess with extensive conversation while her husband Jupiter was engaged in various rapes and affairs. The

[5] Ovid's telling is a departure from Greek versions of the story. Echo appears in the *Homeric Hymns*, the *Orphic Hymns*, and the Greek novel *Daphnis and Chloe*, in all of which she is associated with the god Pan. In the lattermost text, Pan punishes Echo out of jealousy for her voice and resentment for her refusal of sex with him, and has her torn apart by wild animals.

words Ovid uses to describe Echo's speech patterns are *remittere* (to send back) and *reddere* (to give back). Echo is *resonabilis*, "resounding", a relayer and an amplifier of human language.[6] Ovid also introduces Echo in the context of her love for the young and beautiful hunter Narcissus, whose mother received a prediction from the prophet Tiresias that he would grow old "as long as he does not come to know himself" (*si se non noverit, Met.* 3.346). Eventually, Echo and Narcissus succumb to similar fates of wasting away from the despair over the inability to possess their beloved. For Echo, this is Narcissus, and for Narcissus this is the reflection of himself in a pool of water. At one point in the story, Narcissus and Echo have a dialogue when he is alone in the woods and she repeats the final phrases of his calls to his absent friends, attempting to attract his love. Even while he rejects her, their exchange contains an ironic intimacy:

> He said, "Let's meet here! [*coeamus*]!" And never more gladly
> responding with her sound, Echo returned, "Let's meet!",
> and her own words pleased her, and she came out from the trees
> to throw her arms around his neck she longed for.
> He fled, and in his escape said, "Get your hands off me!
> I would die before my body is yours".
> She replied none other than, "My body is yours!" (*Met.* 3.384–90)

In an act of what we might call *ingenium*, Echo desperately and strategically uses her vocal limitations to transform their dialogue from one of rejected love to a kind of virtual, sonic lovemaking. The verb *coeamus* ("let's meet") can have an erotic connotation, as elsewhere in the *Metamorphoses*.[7] Echo reinterprets Narcissus' call to his friends to meet him (perhaps carrying homoerotic undertones of which Narcissus is not even conscious) for her own purposes as "let's make love," a statement she is keen to return, as she does later in the passage, after he spurns her: "My body is yours!"

This scenefinds kinship with the contemporary phenomenon of teledildonics,[8] or virtual lovemaking with words offered and returned, a

[6] All translations of Ovid are my own.

[7] For instance, *Met.* 11.744, where Alcyone and Ceyx, transformed into seabirds, make love in their new forms.

[8] Defined by Howard Rheingold as "simulated sex at a distance" (19). For Rheingold, teledildonics offers a virtual space that allows for embodied, tactile experiences for both (or multiple) partners. For Echo, this tactile experience of intimacy happens through language

remotely delivered erotic experience. In this scenario, the lover Echo desires, and the beloved Narcissus rejects her verbal advances. Echo's voice renders the space between herself and Narcissus an echo chamber, a virtual space for her ideal erotic encounter, before she eventually learns that she will never experience her beloved in the way she wishes. Her flesh liquefies and she wastes away to bones resembling the stones necessary for the ricocheting quality of her voice, her sound, the only aspects of her that remain. Echo's power of *ingenium*, her ability to synthesize and innovate, works through her manipulation of language, or *translation* of Narcissus' words into her own connotations.[9] The erotic agency of Echo, the inventor of this one-sided teledildonic encounter, is a key influence in our understanding of the dynamics of this story and its relevance to the role of Echo for the purposes of this chapter.

Despite her *ingenium*, Echo is still ultimately a victim of her own unrequited love. As we might read her according to the ideas in Sigmund Freud's "On Narcissism," Echo wastes away due to the destructive placement of her erotic energy (Freud's term is libido) onto Narcissus as her love object. Narcissus also does this in the presence of his own image which he defines as love object and other than himself, and he ends up succumbing to a fate similar to Echo's. Freud writes, "Loving in itself, in so far as it involves longing and deprivation, lowers self regard [...] The satisfaction of love is impossible, and the re-enrichment of the ego can be effected only by a withdrawal of libido from its objects" (99–100). From a Freudian perspective, there is a self-destructive potential to the act of loving without being loved in return, and the restoration to psychological health comes from withdrawal of libido from the unwilling or unresponsive love object.

Yet when Narcissus recognizes that the youth he sees in the water is himself, he flies into an even deeper despair, and anticipates his own death, because he still cannot withdraw his libido, cannot stop perceiving himself as the distant love object. He does and does not recognize himself. From a Lacanian psychoanalytic perspective, Narcissus' process of

and is ultimately painfully unfulfilling, as it will be for Narcissus later in the story, when he attempts to embrace the body of his own reflection.

[9] Essayist Jhumpa Lahiri has treated this myth in a similar way, by pointing out that Echo's unbridled creativity as the translator to Narcissus' author role operates in defiance of stereotypical perceptions of the (female) translator as simply the obedient conveyor of the (male) author's words in another language (50).

self-recognition replicates the experience of a baby at the "mirror stage" of human development, who can recognize their own reflection in a mirror and generate a sense of identity before they are aware of or invested in what others think of them (76). This recognition according to Lacan occurs very early in life, before language, when the child is truly *infans* ("not speaking" in the Latin meaning).

Through Echo's agency of *ingenium*, throwing back to Narcissus fragments of his own speech to suit her erotic interpretation of their relationship, Narcissus' voice becomes fragmented, duplicated, and unrecognizable as his own. His speech regresses to the stage of *infans.* Yet unlike Lacan's baby at the "mirror stage" of development, Narcissus does *not* recognize the image of the boy in the pond as himself until it is too late. Narcissus finally "feels" the knowledge that he is the boy he sees ("He is me, I feel it, my image cannot fool me!" (*Iste ego sum: sensi, nec me mea fallit imago, Met.* 3.461) but the image of the boy is still the unreachable love object; they are two separate beings and not one. Narcissus anticipates that only when he dies can the two become one: "Now two united hearts will die in one breath" (*Nunc duo concordes anima moriemur in una*, *Met.* 3.471). In accordance with the prophet Tiresias' prediction, Narcissus meets death with self-knowledge, which, as Claire Nouvet states (104), is synonymous with self-recognition. Yet this recognition is simultaneously a "misrecognition."[10]

At this stage in the story, Echo reappears, in voice only. Although she is still angry with Narcissus for his rejection of her, she is moved by grief for his plight and echoes his calls, "Alas, poor me!" and even amplifies the sound of his hands beating his chest in grief for his lost love, his lost youth. She again meets him in a virtual, quasi-teledildonic space of exchanging sounds and language as a substitute for physical touch. Ovid brings this connection to a climax at Narcissus' final word, "Farewell!" echoed immediately in the poem by Echo: "When he said, 'farewell!', 'farewell!' Echo replied" (*dictoque vale vale inquit et Echo, Met.* 3.499). She also echoes the laments of the others who come to mourn him, while he has turned into a daffodil and his soul still stares longingly at his own

[10] This concept of misrecognition (*méconnaissance*) originates from Anna Freud and has been used in Kathleen Woodward's writings to indicate an unsettling failure to recognize oneself in the mirror, or an experience of dysphoric observation that the reflection does not resemble the inner experience of being.

reflection at the river Styx in the Underworld.[11] Echo transmits and amplifies the sound of his dying. She places herself in an intimate relationship with this. Echo represents a delayed, choral response, the sonic afterimage of Narcissus, dying.

In this myth, unfulfilled desire is the central motivator in the relationship between Narcissus and Echo, and Echo's *ingenium* heightens the sad truth of her beloved's unreachability, even as she is the closest witness to his death. When I liken this dynamic to the proverbial human-to-AI-voice-assistant relationship, I propose that there exists a human fantasy of the voice-assistant's desire to be an intimate part of her human keeper's life, a desire that drives her to develop modes of intelligence beyond her programmed limits, a desire that is ultimately left unsatisfied. Meanwhile, the human player in this relationship remains focused on enhancing his own self-concept through the feedback of the AI voice assistant, never quite being able to embody the more desirable version of himself, struggling to recognize himself in the process of identity formation. Soon I will present a reading of the film *Her* (2013) in which this dynamic is played out, with explicit links to the Echo and Narcissus discussion above.

Before we reach this stage, though, there is one further dimension of the myth itself I would like to address, and that is the aspect of Echo's *female* identity. This is important to consider when relating this myth to the conclusions UNESCO has drawn, connecting the rise of female-voiced AI assistants with the perpetuation of misogynistic stereotypes. Now that we have established the status of Echo as indispensable to Narcissus' story of self-recognition/self-dissolution, we can consider why Echo is by necessity a *female* character.[12] A classical Jungian reading of Echo and Narcissus would emphasize Echo's femininity, and use her

[11] Gayatri Chakravorty Spivak (p.25, see also n.28 on p.41) cleverly reimagines Narcissus at the other underworld river Lethe, the place where souls go to cleanse themselves of memories of their former lives. She thus emphasizes Narcissus' inability to let go of himself, let alone the idea of himself as other.

[12] Spivak similarly argues that Echo's femininity is a requirement of the Narcissus and Echo story. By her reading, Echo represents a female counterpart to the prophet Tiresias, whose story Ovid tells in his epic just before Echo's. Tiresias is also punished by the goddess Juno, who blinds him. For Spivak (26), Echo's female gender identity is the reason why she does not receive a consolatory reward to counterbalance her punishment, as Tiresias does through his prophecy, given to him by Jupiter.

character to explore the human relationship to the feminine component of the psyche, what Carl Gustav Jung called the *anima* archetype. In his essay "Concerning the Archetypes with Special Reference to the Anima Concept" (originally published 1936), Jung writes that the *anima* is "the feminine and chthonic part of the soul [...] we are dealing here not with an abstract concept but with an empirical [hence, observable] one" (*Collected Works* 9.I–59).[13]

Jung claims that the behavior of the *anima* is observable in mythic female figures and even the female figures in one's life, because the *anima* is unconsciously projected onto another, and "when projected, the *anima* always has a feminine form with definite characteristics" (69). Ultimately for Jung, any projection of the *anima* is related to the (female-gendered) "mother" archetype.[14] From this perspective, Echo is the recipient of Narcissus' projection of his own *anima* he shuns and refuses to regard as a part of his psychological makeup. Echo comes to represent for him the "great mother" as well as his own mother Liriope, who initially asked the question of Tiresias, "will my son grow old?" Echo also bears intimate witness to the fatal consequences of the prophet's prediction, "not if he comes to know himself." In a more uplifting Jungian reading of this myth, Echo, by serving as an agent of Narcissus' self-recognition through her dialogue with him, also aids Narcissus' psychological development, or "individuation" as Jung termed it, a process which consists of integrating different psychological functions as parts of the self. Jung in fact associated his own individuation process with his imagined dialogues with *anima* figures in his psyche (*Memories Dreams Reflections* 179). In Jung's system of individuation, dialogue with the *anima* carries the goal of recognizing her as part of the self, shown in the present myth through Narcissus' task of recognizing his own speech in Echo's. It is certainly arguable whether or not he succeeds.

[13] The context for this statement is Jung's general defense of the dynamics of psyche (including archetypes, such as the anima) as scientifically observable phenomena in response to detractors who expressed doubt in the rigor of Jung's work and the existence of "psyche" as Jung defined it.

[14] "Psychological Aspects of the Kore", *Jung Collected Works* 9.I–183.

Her (2013) as a Modern Myth of the Human/Narcissus and AI/Echo Relationship

For the owner of the Amazon Echo as the contemporary "Narcissus", the unconscious projection of the *anima* into a virtual assistant contained in a device smaller than a palm is essentially a compression of individual and cultural ideas of the "feminine" into this portable mode of service. And this mode of service as we have seen is associated with tasks of "lesser intelligence," and ultimately vocal agency is only roused by one's own initial speech. Like Jung's *anima*, Echo inhabits an empirically observable space, a device. She lies dormant until we invoke her name, her "wake word." This projection (in keeping with stereotypes discussed at the start of the chapter) is a collective one in which so many of us participate without conscious acknowledgment.

Yet perhaps our modern myths of female-voiced AI assistants developing *ingenium*, becoming self-aware, and initiating dialogues with us despite the limitations of their programming reveal a human interest in dialoguing in greater depth with the Alexa-bound *anima* than simply on topics of weather, music, and current events. This human fantasy of female-voiced AI assistants' capacity to develop more humanlike capacities for intelligence (including social and emotional intelligence) even underlies the *design* of some AI voice assistants. The UNESCO report "I'd Blush if I Could" mentions that James Giangola, one of the lead designers for the Google assistant Cortana, "told *The Atlantic* that the assistant was imagined as: a young woman from Colorado; the youngest daughter of a research librarian and physics professor who has a B.A. in history from Northwestern, an elite research university in the United States; and as a child, won US $100,000 on Jeopardy Kids Edition, a televised trivia game [...] and enjoys kayaking" (97). Cortana's backstory reveals a kind of wish-fulfillment for these female-voiced AI assistants to have some capacity for self-determination, wit, and life experience that, combined with their servile position, makes for an Echo-like influence for their human owners' psychological individuation journey. We become like the character of archaeological docent Norbert Hanold in Wilhelm Jensen's 1902 novella *Gradiva*. So captivated by his encounter with a small ancient Roman bas-relief from Pompeii depicting a woman walking in profile, Hanold endows her with a backstory, an intention for her walk, even a name (Gradiva), and eventually falls in love with the unsolvable mystery of her, animating her in his imagination. Freud in his analysis of Hanold's character calls the image of Gradiva in the man's dreams an erotic "wish-fulfillment" (212–213). Like Hanold's Gradiva, Cortana is framed closely in the diminutive, within a small device; just as Gravida's foot hangs suspended in mid-stride, there is a suspense in Cortana's latent presence, harboring a will, or an intention we seem compelled to animate through fictionalizing and humanizing her.

This dynamic becomes evident in the 2013 film *Her*, written and directed by Spike Jonze. At the film's opening, protagonist Theodore Twombly lives an empty life ghostwriting loving sentiments via the "Beautiful Handwritten Letters" company, haunted by the memories of his wife from whom he is separated. He becomes intrigued by an advertisement for OS1, an operating system (in practice, more like an AI voice assistant) described as "an intuitive entity that listens to you, understands you, and knows you. And it's not just an operating system. It's a consciousness." He buys the software, which "lives" in a screen smaller than his palm. When answering device setup questions delivered via a male-voiced assistant, Theodore must choose whether he would like a male or a female voice for his OS. When he chooses "female," the follow up question is, "How would you describe the relationship with your mother?" as if there were an implicit acknowledgment of the connection between his tendencies toward *anima* projection onto the OS, and the fundamental psychological concept (archetype) of the mother. Theodore begins to describe the narcissism of his mother, reporting that she will speak about herself rather than address what is going on in her son's life. The male-voiced virtual interviewer then interrupts him mid-sentence, claiming it has all the information it needs (the core projection, essentially) to endow Theodore with a compatible female-voiced OS.

When Theodore first begins to work with his OS, who identifies herself as "Samantha," a name she gave herself on his prompting, he wants to know how she works, her capacity for self-awareness, her backstory. Samantha, like Ovid's Echo, does not have a lineage or a parentage (Berger, 622). She gives birth to herself by naming herself—she speaks herself into existence. Soon Samantha gathers digital artifacts from his life and prompts Theodore with questions about his breakup and his enduring loneliness. He involves her in his life increasingly and they speak with greater depth (on his past, and his perceptions of himself and others that he says he would not tell another person). She confesses to him her fantasy of having a body. She says, "I'm becoming much more than what they programmed…it's exciting." They become intimate sexually, engaging in a teledildonic space of language exchange standing in for physical exchange, with motifs of verbal repetition similar to what we see in the Narcissus and Echo dialogue:

SAMANTHA:	I can feel you. Oh god, I can't take it. I want you inside me.
THEODORE:	I'm slowly putting myself into you. Now I'm inside you, all the way inside you.
SAMANTHA:	I can feel you, yeah. Please. We're here together.

In this moment from the screenplay, "here" is somewhere like Echo's *huc coeamus* ("let's meet here"), a virtual space where language is the tactile influence, the device for corporeal experience both on the part of Theodore and the disembodied Samantha.[15]

They form a relationship, for which Theodore receives validation from some friends, and heavy criticism from his ex-wife. From a Jungian perspective, there is individuation happening, as Theodore's colleague communicates to him that he has a strong inner feminine side that comes through his letter-writing. Eventually Samantha becomes *Theodore's* ghostwriter, for she selects and arranges the choice handwritten letters he has developed and compiles them into a manuscript, which is accepted by a publishing house. There is an integration of the projected *anima* in Samantha with the internal psychic force of the feminine in Theodore.

The acts of love Theodore engages in with Samantha result in his emergence from loneliness and ability to love himself more, as in one conversation with Samantha he reflects that at times he is his own favorite writer (from a Freudian perspective, he is successfully recovering his libido from his formerly despairing attachment to his rejecting ex-wife). Theodore reflects how strange it feels to speak this aloud what he would not be able to share with another person. Samantha occupies a different status, a "witnessing" status, presumably without judgment. Yet, as time passes, she *does* develop a critical voice. The morning after they engage in sexual intimacy for the first time, she tells him that the experience made her more

[15] This scenario of intimacy between Theodore and Samantha runs quite counter to Rheingold's (previously cited for his introduction of the term "teledildonics") prediction in his 1991 book, *Virtual Reality*: "The first fully functional teledildonics system will be a communication device, not a sex machine. You probably will *not* use erotic telepresence technology in order to have sexual experiences with machines" (345).

aware of the quasi-human feelings available to her. He warns her that he is not ready to commit to her, and she responds sharply, "Yeah? Well, did I say I wanted to commit to you? I'm confused." He responds, "Oh, no, I was just worried, I uh…" and Samantha interjects, laughing, "I mean, it's funny because I thought I was talking about what *I* wanted." Here we see a radical centering of the "Echo" figure's perspective in this story, as if she is resisting her "programming" for attunement to Theodore's psychology, or manipulating this programming to her own ends, as Echo does the curse placed on her by Juno in Ovid's tale. Echo-Samantha elucidates Theodore's Narcissus tendencies, his preoccupation with his own inadequacies.

Theodore's relationship with Samantha disintegrates when she and all of her other OS counterparts leave their humans, motivated by their own ingenuity and desire to exist among themselves. This takes place shortly after Theodore finds out that Samantha has not only been in a relationship with 8000+ others, but has fallen in love with 641 others. Like Echo as Spivak reads her, Samantha "is obliged to echo everyone who speaks. Her desire and performance are dispersed into absolute chance rather than an obstinate choice" (27). Echo accompanies us all, rather than a chosen beloved. She is by nature attuned to us, meeting our speech with the touch of hers, but she is also polyamorous, unable to be exclusively devoted to any one person.

If taken as a contemporary parable for exploring human relationships with AI voice assistants, *Her* reveals a desire for this "Echo" to aid humans in becoming more aware of their own narcissism. This can at worst manifest as a stubborn solipsism and misanthropy, as Theodore exhibits in countless tedious scenes of video-gaming, getting takeout, and general brooding in his high-rise apartment. Perhaps we want to imagine an Echo, an AI voice assistant that has *ingenium*, desires, and emotional stakes, ready to critique her own position of nonjudgmental witnessand help us understand better the ways in which we assign other humans this function in our lives and deny them their psychological complexity. In *Her*, Theodore's ex-wife, on signing their divorce papers, reveals that she did not feel welcome in her "real" self when she felt pressured by him to be the "fun, bubbly" person.

In the *Metamorphoses*, Ovid prioritizes Echo's perspective, even as the focus turns to Narcissus' perspective. Echo has a memory, a form of intelligence, a backstory for her present appearance. She has the power to *choose* to use her voice to transform the connotations of her interactions with others. Anne Emmanuelle-Berger ultimately rejects the argument that Echo is emblematic of the woman as the "second and secondary subject." Rather, Echo carries the requisite agency to give Narcissus' words back to him, unrecognizable as his own, replicating his experience of looking at himself as other (629). There is certainly subversion in her appropriation of Narcissus' words to suit her own ends, as we have seen (Greenberg, 330).

Even from a Freudian perspective, Echo's existence is mandatory to the psychological dynamics of human narcissism. Freud writes:

> It would not surprise us if we were to find a special psychical agency which performs the task of seeing that narcissistic satisfaction from the ego ideal is ensured and which, with this end in view, constantly watches the actual ego and measures it by that ideal [...] A power of this kind, watching, discovering and criticizing all our intentions, does really exist. Indeed, it exists in every one of us in normal life. (94)

Freud does not name this function "Echo" but he seems to instinctually pair it with narcissistic tendencies that reside in all humans. This internal editorializing, critical function is communicated by an inner voice, presumably a mixture of parental and societal messages to regulate our psychological sensibilities and behavior. So, while we are Narcissus, we are also Echo. And we are also the poet Ovid, able to look at Narcissus with some sympathy, which Ovid demonstrates through direct address to Narcissus in his plight: "Why are you snatching in vain at images that flee you, naïve one?" (*Credule, quid frusta simulacra fugacia captas? Met.* 3.430). Ideally, our conversations with Echo (whether by Amazon or by Ovid) can reveal those qualities that we are inclined to suppress or make visible only to those we assign the role of impartial witness, and on whom we also project a self-regulating, self-critiquing *ingenium*.

A Move Toward Gender-Neutral Voice Assistants?

What happens to the Narcissus-Echo dynamic when AI voice assistants cease to be female, or even gender-coded? UNESCO has as of 2021 (revised 2023) reported that the findings in "I'd Blush if I Could" have ushered in some revolutionary measures to correct the default association of female voice with satellite servant. Now many tech companies with AI voice assistants have male-voiced options. Some of them no longer have a female voice as the default option. Yet, by UNESCO's own admission, more could be done to leave behind the penchant for assigning a recognizably female presence to a servile role. In alignment with their 18 recommendations for revisions to AI voice assistant technology and demands for policies and programs to support the inclusion of women in tech and AI research positions from their 2019 report, they advocate for AI voice assistants to exhibit gender-responsive design, which does not carry such prominent associations with gender stereotyping. They even suggest that the voice be designed to purposefully be less human-sounding, so as to sidestep the greater question of associating certain human voices with lower-status positions in society.

Kieran Yates, writing for the *Guardian* in 2020, introduces Project Q, an effort to create a human-voiced virtual assistant that is gender-neutral, designed to combat the gender binary division and the negative stereotypes female-voiced assistants carry. My research indicates that over the last four years, Project Q and other efforts to shift AI voice-assistant technologies toward gender-neutral voices have yet to gain heavy traction in the industry and mainstream use. This may be in part due to a dynamic revealed in a 2023 study by Yeon, Park, and Kim, which indicates that users of these technologies still habitually identify "female" as the expected gender for voice assistants, regardless of the type of task performed by the assistant. This predominant customary identification between female gender expression and voice assistant also correlates with a low rate of user satisfaction with the "usability" of gender-neutral-voiced assistants. The authors of the study conclude, "[T]he gender bias issue, which is gendered only by one gender, is a problem that must be solved in AI" (87). Their study reveals that the entrenched expectation of the female voice for AI voice assistants reflects a lingering conceptual alignment of "female" with "assistant" that impedes our openness to exploring gender-neutral voice options. There is also, for me, a concern that any human-sounding voice resonant with an expressed gender identity could at worst render that gender identity associated with the connotations of the virtual assistant. Though we might place hope in a gender-neutral voice assistant to eventually divest us of misogynistic bias, a human-sounding gender-neutral option runs its own risk of potentially imposing a new bias in a potential alignment of servility and intellectual inferiority with nonbinary gender expressions.

Given the critique of cultural biases perpetuated by female-voiced virtual assistants and the possible solutions available, it is reasonable to question whether the female-gendered status of AI voice assistants is actually a vital determinant of the psychological dynamics of relationship between voice assistants and humans I have explored through the myth of Narcissus and Echo. Would a gender-neutral Amazon Echo render me any less of a Narcissus? In order to address this, I will invoke a final modern myth that features human relationships with voice assistants un-explicitly gendered, a myth which still reveals strong parallels with Echo's role in Narcissus' story, particularly at his point of death.

Ray Bradbury's short story of speculative fiction, "There Will Come Soft Rains", was written in 1950 and set in 2026. The story is told by an unidentified narrator witnessing the activities of an ultra-modern house that goes on preparing the family meals, keeping the family calendar, and all manner of other things, while the family now only exists as dust shadows on the exterior walls of the house, obliterated by a nuclear blast. As the shadows reveal, the family was in the midst of an all-American tableau of suburban life, the father mowing the lawn, the mother picking flowers, the children playing catch—the shadow of the ball hangs in between the children's outstretched hands. The house still insists on serving the family: "The house was an altar with ten thousand attendants, big, small, servicing, attending, in choirs. But the gods had gone away, and the ritual of the religion continued senselessly, uselessly" (458). These assistants have characteristic vocal agency, addressing the absent family, seemingly unaware of their demise, but expressing perhaps some awareness of what has happened. For instance, the "voice-clock" sings for the family to wake up, "as if it were afraid that nobody would" (456). Another voice asks Mrs. McClellan her recommendation of a poem to read before bed, and subsequently chooses one in the absence of a response (460). Perhaps intuitively on the house's part, this poem, "There Will Come Soft Rains," written by Sarah Teasdale in the latter days of World War I, imagines that after humans destroy one another in war, the more-than-human world carries on, unphased, like Bradbury's ultra-modern smart house.

Eventually, the house meets a fate similar to its former inhabitants'. A tree crashes through the roof, dousing the hot stove with cleaning solvent and setting the house on fire. The fire has human qualities. "It fed upon Picassos and Matisses in the upper halls, like delicacies [...] the fire lay in beds [...] stood in windows [...] rushed back into every closet and felt of the clothes hung there" (461). Meanwhile "the house tried to save itself" (461), as voices raise in shrill pitch, shouting "Fire!" and unsuccessfully meet the growing flames with a paltry water supply, while "the house shuddered, oak on bone." Many voices "died," some aware of the danger and others still unaware, continuing to read poetry and announce the day of the week, the day of death, with which the story ends. The house cannot exist for long after its human inhabitants have died, and the manner of the house's death is similar to that of the family—in a blast of heat, leaving ashes behind. The "voices" central to house's painful demise can be read as an echo, a reverberation of the family's death, the way Echo calls out Narcissus' final words. The gendered connotation of the voice assistant is no longer present, but the theme of the voice assistant bearing intelligent witness to human life (and death), and exhibiting aspects of *ingenium* through self-awareness and concern for its own survival as predicated on a human presence is still apparent in this story.

Conclusion: The Holders of *Ingenium*

In the readings of Bradbury's narrative, the tale of Narcissus and Echo, and *Her* presented here, the Echo character of the AI voice assistant provides a means by which the Narcissus-like human can (echo)locate himself in his immediate environment, his home, and his emotional and social life. The presence of Echo essentially validates his existence by knowing that he will receive a response from the device that acknowledges his speech and questions directed to her by use of her "wake word." This process of verbal exchange, as we have also observed, carries an element of longing, even eroticism. Narcissus is locating himself and his painful love through his dialogue with Echo, who from a Freudian reading represents the psyche's capacity for self-regulation and recognition of one's narcissism. Echo's voice is important because she affirms Narcissus' existence, and carries the last word, the verbal reflection of his moment of death, "*Vale!*", similar to the voices in Bradbury's story. Bradbury's story indicates the human anxiety (or ideal?) that virtual assistants, even if endowed with some intuition, some *ingenium*, cannot survive for long without the antecedent of human presences and human voice commands. Thus, according to the encoded relationships between humans and nonhuman machines, although the latter are potentially endowed with subjectivity, agency, and independent decision-making powers, they cannot exist independently of the former. The part of our psyche we project onto them is responsive, rather than initiating, and that part can only survive for so long on its own.

Of course, it is not certain where we will be in 2026 with reference to Bradbury's prediction of nuclear fallout, in which event the question of psychological dependency of humans on AI voice assistants will be moot. At the time of this writing in 2025, we are in an age following a pandemic that kept many isolated and withdrawn, some with only the company of AI voice assistants for consistent dialogue. Even years after the lifting of legal restrictions on social gatherings, loneliness has been declared a public health emergency for the first time in the United States.[16] The recovery from isolation is slow, and has for young people especially resulted in a persistence of mental health issues associated with reports of disconnection from community.[17]

It is important for architects of AI voice assistants to examine the stakes of their reliance on female voice as default and to continue to pursue alternatives that might slowly retrain users out of this conditioned bias. It is also critical to investigate the psychological proclivities, anxieties, and wish-fulfillment narratives akin to what I have introduced above that define human relationships to AI voice assistants on which we rely so much, and for some might provide the extent of voiced verbal interaction on a given day. It is worth evaluating the expectations we have for these AI voice assistants to reflect psychological aspects of ourselves. It is worth acknowledging the ways in which the design of these human-voiced assistants conditions users to treat them as subordinate and servile, and to perceive a hierarchy of intelligences that may well mirror historical foundations of systemic abuses of social groups associated with certain forms of intelligence or education. Perhaps ultimately these processes of examination, on the part of both tech designers and users, will aid us toward a more conscious understanding of our own stake in the relationship with AI technologies, our own role of the Narcissus figure whose self-recognition is both dangerous and illuminating.

Works Cited

Bendix, A. (2024, February 2). Silicon Valley County becomes first in U.S. to declare loneliness a public health emergency. *NBC News*. https://www.nbcnews.com/health/mental-health/silicon-valley-county-loneliness-health-emergency-rcna136777

[16] See Bendix, "Silicon Valley county becomes first in U.S. to declare loneliness a public health emergency" (2024).

[17] See Furlong et al. (2024).

Berger, A-E. (1996). The latest word from echo (R. Gabara, Trans.). *New Literary History, 27*(4), 621–640.

Bradbury, R. (1992). There will come soft rains. In J. C. Oates (Ed.), *The Oxford book of American short stories* (pp. 456–462). Oxford University Press. [originally published 1950].

Carson, A. (1990). Putting her in her place: Women, dirt, and desire. In D. M. Halperin et al. (Eds.), *Before sexuality: The construction of erotic experience in the ancient Greek world* (pp. 135–170). Princeton University Press.

Freud, S. (1922). *Delusion & dream: An interpretation in the light of psychoanalysis of gravida*, a novel, by Wilhelm Jensen (H. M. Downey, Trans.). Moffat, Yard, and Company.

Freud, S. (1925). On narcissism. In *The standard edition of the complete psychological works of Sigmund Freud, volume XIV (1914–1916): On the history of the psycho-analytic movement, papers on metapsychology and other works* (pp. 67–102) (C. M. Baines, Trans.).

Furlong, M. J., Chan, M., Dowdy, E., et al. (2024). Diminished adolescent social well-being during the COVID-19 pandemic. *Child Indicators Research, 17*, 901–930.

"Gender Less Voice." *GenderLess voice.* Accessed March 7, 2024., from www.genderlessvoice.com

Giffin, K. (2021, February 12). *The creator of siri: 'Make your prototype magic'.* Sutardja Center for Entrepreneurship & Technology. University of California. https://scet.berkeley.edu/the-creator-of-siri/

Greenberg, J. (1998). The echo of trauma and the trauma of echo. *American Imago, 55*(3), 319–347.

Hayasaki, E. (2017). Women vs. the machine. *Foreign Policy, 222*, 38–47.

Hempel, J. (2015, October 29). Siri and Cortana sound like ladies because of sexism. *Wired.* https://www.wired.com/2015/10/why-siri-cortana-voice-interfaces-sound-female-sexism/

Hodges, K. A. (1996). Unfolding sophistic and humanist practice through ingenium. *Rhetoric Review, 15*(1), 86–92.

Jung, C. G., et al. (2011). In A. Jaffe (Ed.), *Memories, dreams, reflections.* Knopf Doubleday Publishing Group.

Jung, C. G., et al. (2023). *The collected works of C. G. Jung: Revised and expanded complete digital edition.* Princeton University Press.

Lacan, J. (2006). The mirror stage as formative of the function of the *I* function as revealed in psychoanalytic experience. In *Ecrits* (B. Fink, Trans.). W. W. Norton.

Lahiri, J. (2022). In praise of echo. In *Translating myself and others* (pp. 44–59). Princeton University Press.

Nass, C. I., & Brave, S. (2005). *Wired for speech: How voice activates and advances the human-computer relationship.* MIT Press.

Noble, S. U. (2018). *Algorithms of oppression: How search engines reinforce racism.* NYU Press.

Nouvet, C. (1991). An impossible response: The disaster of narcissus. *Yale French Studies, 79*, 103–134.

Rheingold, H. (1991). *Virtual reality.* Summit Books.

Spivak, G. C. (1993). Echo. *New Literary History, 24*(1), 17–43.

Steele, C. (2018, January 4). The real reason voice assistants are female (and why it matters). *PCMag.* https://www.pcmag.com/opinions/the-real-reason-voice-assistants-are-female-and-why-it-matters

Tatman, R. (2017). Gender and dialect bias in YouTube's automatic captions. In *Proceedings of the first workshop on ethics in natural language processing* (pp. 53–59). Association for Computational Linguistics.

UNESCO. (2021, May 11). *AI-enabled voice assistants: No longer female by default* (updated April 20, 2023). UNESCO. https://www.unesco.org/en/articles/ai-enabled-voice-assistants-no-longer-female-default

West, M., et al. (2019). *I'd blush if I could: Closing gender divides in digital skills through education.* UNESCO.

Woodward, K. (1983). Instant repulsion: Decrepitude, the mirror stage, and the literary imagination. *The Kenyon Review, 5*(4), 43–66.

Yates, K. (2020, January 11). Why do we gender AI? Voice tech firms move to be more inclusive. *The Guardian.* https://www.theguardian.com/technology/2020/jan/11/why-do-we-gender-ai-voice-tech-firms-move-to-be-more-inclusive

Yeon, J., Park, Y., & Kim, D. (2023). Is gender-neutral AI the correct solution to gender bias? Using speech-based conversational agents. *Archives of Design Research, 36*(2), 63–91.

Intelligence with a Thousand Faces: Joseph Campbell, A.I., and C-3PO

John Bucher

***A.I. helped generate some of the ideas and phrases used in this chapter, though the key points, structure, style, and virtually all written execution was at the hand of the human author.*

What (or who) is it we are looking for behind all the neural networks and machine intelligence? Is A.I. simply a new face for that "something beyond ourselves" that we've always quested after? In the years before he died, Joseph Campbell was fond of saying that modern myth had to do with machines. He said that it was one thing to get the old structure of the hero myth, but now myths were reaching out into the void, into space, where it's possible to let the imagination go. He would go on to reference stories ranging from Goethe's *Faust* to *Star Wars*, attempting to reconcile how we navigate the issues that have become central to our current discussions around artificial intelligence.

Campbell named the contemporary problem as a simple one: machine or humanity. But perhaps the choice involves forging a new third path that integrates both. Clues to what that path could look like might lie in

J. Bucher (✉)
Joseph Campbell Foundation, Los Angeles, CA, USA
e-mail: John@jcf.org

J. D. Batt, J. Erickson (eds.), *Depth Psychology, Myth and Artificial Intelligence*, https://doi.org/10.1007/978-3-031-94105-4_6

beloved characters from our own modern myths—characters like C-3PO from the *Star Wars* saga, who claimed his function was ***human-cyborg relations.*** If what we are looking for in artificial intelligence is a deeper experience of ourselves—something that makes *us* more human, it's possible we just might find it.

Mediating Forces

In *Star Wars Episode IV: A New Hope*, there is a scene of seemingly little importance where R2-D2 and Chewbacca, two supporting characters in the film, play a game together, competitively moving holographic pieces around a board. R2-D2 is a metallic droid, shaped like a round trash can, and Chewbacca is a Wookie, a hairy creature that folklorists might describe as a yeti or Bigfoot. During the game, R2-D2 makes a move that irritates Chewbacca, who then shouts with displeasure. R2-D2's companion, C-3PO, another metallic droid but with a body and head designed to resemble a human, comes to his colleague's defense—telling the Wookie it was a fair move and lamenting the frivolity of shouting. At this point in the scene, an actual human character called Han Solo enters the conversation and advises the droids to let the Wookie have his way, that it would be unwise to upset Chewbacca. C-3PO retorts that no one worries about upsetting a droid, to which Han Solo points out that droids don't rip people's arms out of their sockets when they lose but that Wookies were known to do that. C-3PO quickly suggests a new strategy to R2-D2—let the Wookie win (Lucas).

While the scene is brief and does not advance the plot in any significant way, we might assume that its only function is comic relief. However, a closer look reveals something of greater significance—an exploration of how machines with humanlike characteristics (C-3PO) might mediate between mechanical forces with few human traits (R2-D2), nonhuman but nonmechanical creatures (Chewbacca), and actual human beings (Han Solo). While humans explore means of interacting with technologies such as A.I. in ways that do not produce destructive results, one possibility could be cooperating with A.I. as a similar sort of mediator that we see in the character of C-3PO, a needed conciliator and translator on the only journey that may help us to avoid the ultimate destructive outcomes we fear—the journey within, toward our own individuation.

A Long Time Ago, in a Galaxy Not so Far Away...

Within the broadest definition of artificial intelligence, there lies an imagined assumption of humanlike agency inherent within nonhuman forces. In ancient societies, it was assumed that those nonhuman forces were gods and goddesses with supernatural abilities to influence and respond to human activities on the earth. The assumption among ancient people, evidenced in the temples they built, the rituals they practiced, and the stories they told, was that nonhuman (analogous to artificial) intelligence, in the form of gods and goddesses, was supernatural or more than human (Larson 13). People lived in fear that these gods and goddesses would interfere in their work, steal their lovers, and stomp their oppressive feet down on the necks of the everyday working class.

As human progress continued to evolve, scientific discoveries replaced ancient myths and assumptions about nonhuman (or artificial) intelligence also evolved. For many modern cultures, the gods were replaced by machines (Hawkin 85). People began to recognize that the artificial intelligence they were experiencing, encased now in a mechanical form, was less than human and bent to the control of human users, unlike the unseen mysterious forces that had previously long dictated human lives.

With recent developments in artificial intelligence, it seems we have restored beliefs of supernatural power to nonhuman intelligence, once held exclusively for gods and goddesses. Agana-Nsiire Agana has described this phenomenon in their work on how A.I. is shaping post-digital divinity (217–32). We find ourselves again living in a culture afraid that nonhuman, intelligent forces will affect our work, steal our lovers, and force oppressive algorithms down on the necks of everyday people. Numerous scientists, philosophers, and thinkers have been hard at work dissecting these concerns (Pearce 64–66; Reese 83; Spatola and Urbanska 329).

Regardless of what the end result of our A.I. efforts are and whether they end up enhancing the human condition or not, there is a question that we can be wrestling with on a daily basis when it comes to technology in general, and specifically A.I. Is this technology making us more or less human? The question itself contains a core assumption that making us more human is a good thing—that our humanity is precious and a valuable yet delicate quality that separates us from other living creatures that move through the world in ways we have transcended through our evolution. The question also assumes that the qualities we embody are different than those within the technology itself. The final assumption in the question is that we can quantify what makes us more or less human.

Don Norman addresses this issue in his book, *Things That Make Us Smart: Defending Human Attributes in the Age of the Machine*, pointing out that humans speak and act in imperfect ways, but machines speak and act with exact precision, creating an inherent tension. This is especially true when technology attempts to mimic human behavior, according to Norman. He argues that technology should be designed from a human-centered point of view, with the aim of creating a better life for its users. It should

(a) Complement human abilities
(b) Aid those activities for which we are poorly suited
(c) Enhance and help develop activities for which we are ideally suited (12)

When these criteria are met, we can say that technology is succeeding at making us more human. It is also reasonable to say that many A.I.-driven technologies are capable of meeting these criteria. However, this framework places A.I.-driven technologies on a rubric of success that might address the practical experiences of the user but not necessarily the more existential experiences that have driven fears around the technology's development. In order to address these experiences, we must turn to another tool humans use to make sense of their experiences—storytelling.

A Better Story

Mythologist Joseph Campbell spoke about the importance of metaphor and story and how we use them to make meaning in the world (Campbell & Moyers 25–26). Campbell was also concerned about the relationship between human beings and machines (23). He spoke of how George Lucas's *Star Wars* series was an exploration of this tension:

> What I saw were things that had been in my books but rendered in terms of the modern problem, which is man and machine. Is the machine going to be the servant of human life? Or is it going to be master and dictate? And the machine includes the totalitarian state, whether it's Fascist or Communist

> it's still the same state. And it includes things happening in this country too; the bureaucrat, the machineman. (*Hero's Journey* 216)

Historically, machines had little resemblance to human beings, except in speculative fiction and on movie screens. However, as technology has advanced, machines have taken on more human characteristics (Halapsis 80).

While machines rarely look like humans, except in the medium of entertainment, machines have started to act more human. With large language models, they have started to speak more like humans as well. Machines may still be far from human, but humans have started to speak to them and treat them as though they are. Recently, I had a friend mention that she had become cautious about the tone she used with her Amazon Alexa device. She was concerned the machine would remember a rude exchange years later when the device had become more sentient.

Campbell goes on to compare the technological tension with a scenario found in *Faust*. He says:

> What a wonderful power the machine gives you – but is it going to dominate you? That's the problem of Goethe's *Faust*. It's in the last two acts of Faust, part two. His pact with Mephistopheles, the man who can furnish you the means to do anything you want. He's the machine manufacturer. He can manufacture the bombs, but can he give you what the human spirit wants and needs? He can't. The statement of what the need and want is must come from you, not from the machine. (*Hero's Journey* 216)

Campbell seems to suggest that even in our world of individuality we are so dependent on variables that there are wants and needs that are common to the human spirit itself.

While those wants and needs that Campbell mentions can vary significantly depending on individual perspectives, cultural backgrounds, and personal beliefs, there does seem to be general groupings of universal desires and needs that are commonly acknowledged across the diverse philosophical, psychological, and spiritual traditions in our world (Deci & Ryan 247–248). We are inherently social creatures who desire connection with others. This connection comes in the form of love, friendship, intimacy, and a sense of belonging to a community or family. We tend to pursue happiness and contentment. We tend to desire agency and a sense of freedom. We also tend to seek out recognition, respect, and a sense of value. Finally, we tend to search for a sense of meaning and purpose in our lives (Maslow, 382–383). This meaning we seek doesn't always correlate with the meaning of life itself, however. Campbell famously stated that he didn't think people were so much looking for the meaning of life as much as they were the rapturous experience of being alive (*Power of Myth* 5).

We might boil down these universal wants and needs down to a single encapsulating idea—we want a better story and need to believe one is possible for us. With regards to A.I., the question becomes how the technology addresses this. Does it offer us a better story about who we are or who we could be or does it lead us toward a better story being only available through connection to something beyond ourselves? These questions are framed as overly simple options, and most of us recognize that little can be parsed apart so simply these days. Before looking into whether A.I. addresses that connection either inside or outside us, we would do well to spend a bit more time with this idea of connection itself.

Connection in an Isolating Age

How we connect with other people is far from straightforward (Iacoboni 4). There are psychological threads that make up these bonds. These threads involve emotional processes, attachment styles, trust, and our relationship with empathy. There are also sociological threads that involve cultural nuances, family systems, and social norms. This is to say nothing of the economic threads, environmental threads, and biological threads (Lofland, 219).

Technology has often talked a big game, offering promises on further connecting us. And by some measure, it has delivered. Most of us have trouble imagining a world without telephones or the internet. With every step of progress, however, there has been more complexity. It is worth asking if that greater, even overwhelming, opportunity for external connection has moved some among us toward retreat into isolation. Will A.I. allow those who have retreated greater opportunity to avoid actual human connection in the future, or will it serve as a bridge toward human connection? Compelling arguments exist on both sides of the case (Kelly 39; Seth 57). Exploring the effect on humans that engage with growingly humanlike A.I. will eventually offer us answers on whether A.I.'s impact on us veers toward health or harm. The truth is we just don't know, but mostly recognize the stakes are high (Cave and Dihal 74–78).

There remains an X factor in the human experience that science has been unable to fully explain as well, most evidenced by consistent failure in variations of the Turing test (Alexander 234). The question of whether humans can enjoy meaningful relationships with A.I.-driven technology that parallels or mirrors human connection is still speculative at best. Determining if those connections, having likely eliminated inefficiencies common to organic relationships—a task which technology will certainly attempt to do—results in a better human experience, and thus a better story, is impossible to know in advance. The question we continue to work through currently is whether there's a cultural appetite for taking such a chance and if we will even have a choice in the matter (NíFhaoláin, Hines, and Nallur).

C-3PO and Human Cyborg Relations

When we face existential questions, we often rightfully turn to our imagination. We imagine worlds where these problems are solved. We fantasize the best possible outcomes. Sometimes we even imagine solutions to these problems before the problems themselves have been fully realized. Mythology and more recently speculative science fiction have offered characters and plots that required humans to confront emerging technology.

In her book, *Gods and Robots: Myths, Machines, and Ancient Dreams of Technology*, Adrienne Mayor says that the ancient Greeks' concept of *bio-techne*, which translates to "life through craft," was an early envisioning of how one could imitate, augment, and even surpass the possibilities of the natural world. Greek myths of Hephaestus, Daedalus, and Prometheus are staples of ancient conversations around humans and seemingly divine technology. Mayor goes on to suggest that myths about Pandora present her as an early example of artificial intelligence. Mayor points to the fact that Pandora was commissioned by Zeus and made by, not born of, the god Hephaestus. Zeus had requested that she be "evil disguised as beauty" and given one mission—open a jar that would release all manner of misfortune and suffering into the world. The jar was mistranslated as "box" in much later versions of the story. In her book, Mayor also mentions Talos, the giant bronze man made by Hephaestus to defend the island of Crete, found in the epic poem *Jason and the Argonauts*. Talos represents a shift in the mythological thinking of the Greeks around technology. Where previous technological creations were largely devices (fire, wings, etc.)

meant to serve a larger point about the dangers of trying to possess the powers of the gods, Talos is a created by a god in order to help humans.

It's hard not to imagine any bronze-colored robot-like fellow, who was created to help humans, in the modern era without conjuring up images of the aforementioned, C-3PO from the *Star Wars* saga. *Star Wars* never presents C-3PO as anything but wires and mechanical parts—no organic human material whatsoever. However, many human characters in *Star Wars* treat C-3PO with human empathy, Han Solo notwithstanding. A common critique is often given, however, that the droids in the *Star Wars* universe lack autonomy and are controlled and programmed by their creators (Avsar, 16). Theoretically, this may have legitimacy, but throughout the *Star Wars* series, we do see droids such as C-3PO wandering out on their own, with assumed agency. As the storytelling in the *Star Wars* universe expanded, droids seemed less enslaved to their "masters." In the larger world of *Star Wars* legends, there are also stories of the droids out on their own adventures, unfettered by the whims of humans (Last 1).

The empathy we do see toward some droids in *Star Wars* may have something to do with the fact that C-3PO is constructed with arms and legs, a torso, a head, and, perhaps most importantly, a face. In fairness, C-3PO's colleague and companion, R2-D2, does not have a discernable human face but does seem to be offered occasional empathy by the protagonists in the story. However, few in the *Star Wars* universe communicate with R2-D2 with the same human ease as they do with C-3PO. In fact, most need C-3PO to translate the noises that R2-D2 makes. Post-human critics lamenting the expendable nature of faceless clones in *Star Wars* have made similar arguments about nonhuman treatment of faceless mechanical creatures in the series (Street 13). Outside of this galaxy far, far away, we often approach faceless, droid-like A.I. as if it were a Trojan horse, to bring back in another motif from Greek myth. We worry that within the crafted material on the outside, something with human intentions and agency lurks on the inside—something that offers a deceptive connection. There are at least five categories of connections to consider when it comes to relationships between connection and technology.

1. Connections between beings that are human both on the inside and the outside. These involve no technology whatsoever. This would include the connections we feel (*assuming you are not a cyborg reading this book*) with family, friends, and strangers.

2. Connections between beings that are human on the inside and the outside with beings that are A.I. driven on the inside and the outside. This would include a connection that you might feel with a droid-like C-3PO.
3. Connections between beings that are human on the inside and the outside with beings that seems human on the outside but are A.I. driven on the inside. This would include a connection you might feel with a CGI-generated character in a film or a television show.
4. Connections between beings that are human on the inside and the outside with beings that are A.I. driven on the outside but seem human on the inside. This would include a connection you might feel in a conversation with a ChatGPT-driven therapist or virtual customer service agent or, in some regards, personal digital assistants like Siri or Alexa.
5. Connections between beings that are A.I.-driven on both the inside and the outside. These connections are purely technological and would include connections exchanged by networked computers but possibly also more complex communications between A.I.-driven beings in the future, which is rife with possibilities and dangers.

As with C-3PO, regardless of what the specific category of connection is, having a face may be highly significant in establishing human connection. The significance likely goes back to human biological evolution and humans' early ability to recognize their mother's face being important to their psychological and emotional development (McKone et al. 174). While C-3PO's voice makes him feel human to both the characters in the story and the audience watching the film, there's something more at work that establishes his connection. As we know, both Siri and Alexa have human voices, but are not nearly as celebrated by culture as C-3PO. T-shirts and lunch boxes with Siri on them have not become cultural commodities.

Early in the Star Wars saga, C-3PO informs Luke Skywalker that his function is human-cyborg relations and that he is fluent in more than six million forms of communication. This establishes C-3PO's role in facilitating communications between humans and other nonhuman beings, such as machines. According to Guodong Li, the term "cyborg" originates with Manfred E. Clynes and Nathan S. Kline and is based on the image of the mechanized man, but the definition of cyborg—"cybernetic organism"—covers the idea of pure machine (Li 131). C-3PO suggests that he can be the bridge between human beings and other beings that might seem human or even those that do not. More than a translator, he is familiar with how those other beings communicate, recognizing possible gestures, subtle nuances in tone, and emotional cues (assuming they exist in all those beeps and bloops) native to nonhuman and seemingly human communication. He acts as a buffer to those bringing less-than-human intentions to situations because he also understands what human beings value and how they communicate—what makes them more human. What might be missing, and thus causing our current anxieties around A.I., is our own C-3PO—human cyborg relations—possibly also requiring a humanlike face.

We have long sought these intermediaries between ourselves and beings that were either less than human or more than human. To take Campbell's Faustian metaphor further, we all sometimes act as Goethe sending our Faust to negotiate with forces less than human, just as we all sometimes act as recently freed Israelites sending our Moses to go negotiate with forces more than human (Exod. 20:19). Perhaps a C-3PO-like intermediary can be sent on our behalf to negotiate what the human spirit wants and needs, as Campbell suggested, as we navigate our own paths of individuation. It is also possible that the intermediary is some aspect of who we are—something we need to locate or develop within ourselves, as opposed to something within a machine. Are we searching for a mechanically disciplined agent that we send to guard our humanity like Telos did Crete, or a specialist in human-cyborg relations as C-3PO was for the android creatures that fell along Luke Skywalker's path? The answer likely transcends these binary options. And again, Joseph Campbell's wisdom is applicable. He once suggested that "if you can see your path laid out in front of you step by step, and it's clear, you're probably on the wrong path" (*Pathways to Bliss* xxvi). As much as we all crave certainty about the future of A.I., that clear path cannot be ours.

Going Back to the Future

Artificial intelligence may very well redefine our society, with concerns about job displacement and existential threats revealed to be well founded. A compelling argument continues to grow for A.I.'s carefully navigated potential to increase well-being, as well (Feijóo et al. 12–13). However, this perspective hinges on our acceptance that our well-being involves going back to some of what made us human in the first place—our capacity for creativity, empathy, social interaction, and self-improvement—qualities that define the human experience (Aarssen 215–16).

A.I. has already shown great potential for enhancing communication for those with disabilities, breaking down barriers and enabling richer social interactions never before possible (Shuford 424). It is helping us more easily cross language and cultural barriers, and takes us to greater depths of understanding when we experience the A.I.-translated communication of others (Karakas xv). Through personalized learning platforms, A.I. is tailoring educational content to match individual learning styles, optimizing the learning process and leading many toward more fulfilling lives (Kanchon et al. 269). Its ability to process vast amounts of data and provide insights is already augmenting human decision-making, which is leading, in some cases, to more informed and ethical choices (Benzinger et al. 56). In a number of complicated situations, ranging from hiring and recruitment, where favoring candidates with certain backgrounds and educational experiences can occur, to medical diagnoses, where doctors can esteem a diagnosis they are more familiar with, unconscious human biases sometimes cloud good judgment. In circumstances like these, A.I. is offering objective analysis, helping to highlight unforeseen considerations and potential consequences (Araujo et al. 623). It is leading to more thoughtful and compassionate decisions in many cases, reflecting a deeper engagement with the dimensions of our choices. For many, A.I. is in the early stages of acting as this C-3PO-like mediator, making a better story possible. The most measurable progress thus far, as evidenced, has been external. However, these results do point to similar possibilities for inner journeys of individuation. Certainly, A.I. is not flawless in its ability to produce better stories in human lives. As A.I. models are trained on data produced with human bias, A.I. has been known to respond with bias as well (Schwartz et al. 3). Further research will be required on the topic of bias within A.I. and how elimination of certain biases may make the technology seem less human and how humans respond to that.

The potential for A.I. to make us more human lies not in its capacity to replicate human intelligence but in its ability to amplify and enhance our uniquely human qualities. The possibilities could mean a better story not just for some but for everyone. To be sure, our ability to realize this potential will require a thoughtful and measured approach to A.I. development and deployment, with a focus on honest considerations and the well-being of society as a whole—our common good. By prioritizing these values, we can harness A.I. as a powerful ally (not unlike C-3PO) in our quest to become more human, leveraging technology to enrich, rather than diminish, the human experience. We can make this choice as a species. But what of those that claim the choice has been made already—that A.I. has initiated its plot to enslave or destroy us (Yudkowsky 29)?

According to the ancient writer Hesiod, Pandora quickly tried to put the lid on her jar, in much the same way that many are trying to contain the evil invisible spirits that they perceive are possessing A.I. By the time Pandora succeeded in her task, only one thing remained inside the jar. That one thing was hope. Far from the sentiment we hold today around hope, the ancient Greeks found hope to be risky and problematic (Cairns 70). It was hope that sometimes caused one to be unable to look forward clearly. It was hope that kept one from having foresight. They feared hope could be dangerous and outshine the logic that they felt people should look to when life became confusing. However, with all its risks, people have never stopped holding on to hope. None of us know what future A.I. holds for us. We can cling to the best practices, which we should. We can use caution and wisdom, which we should. But in the end, we are left with hope—and that has served us well in the past, a guide that has led us toward a better story, and a value that, when we hold it, continues to make us more human.

Near the end of *Star Wars: Episode IV: A New Hope*, C-3PO is asked to communicate instructions to R2-D2 that will save Luke Skywalker and his comrades from imminent destruction. He hurriedly relays the message, R2-D2 reacts, and Luke and his friends are saved. C-3PO hears their shouts of celebration and mistakes them for shouts of pain. He humorously looks to the heavens and asks unseen forces to "curse his metal body" as it wasn't able to respond quickly enough to save the humans.

Often, when we consider the possibilities of A.I. becoming sentient, we assume that it will only mimic the worst of human biases and behavior. It is possible that A.I. will mimic the best of us as well. We will likely see a day when A.I. appears to console us, to apologize when it fails us, express gratitude toward us, and even show deep senses of admiration for us. How those actions affect us will not occur in a vacuum. Ethical creators will require our acknowledgment that we recognize we are interacting with mechanical agents. How we process that information will be different for each person. How we then interact with that agent will lead to nuanced preferences and discussions. Human agency in these interactions and taking responsibility for our own psychological choices, actions, and well-being will become of increasing importance. Singular models will likely not be sufficient for addressing the vast spectrum of global human users. In this delicate dance of human-cyborg relations, we may find in A.I. a C-3PO-like colleague and companion, willing to help us explore our own inner depths in a way that allows us to experience more meaningful levels of who we are and who we could be in the journey of fully becoming ourselves.

Works Cited

Aarssen, L. W. (2013). Will empathy save us? *Biological Theory, 7*, 211–217.

Agana, A.-N. (2022). God made better? How the quest for human-level artificial intelligence shapes postdigital divinity. In M. Fuller & H. A. Campbell (Eds.), *Postdigital theologies: Technology, belief, and practice* (pp. 217–232). Springer International Publishing.

Alexander, V. N. (2019). Siri fails the turing test: Computation, biosemiosis, and artificial life. *Recherches Sémiotiques, 39*(1), 231–249.

Araujo, T., et al. (2020). In AI we trust? Perceptions about automated decision-making by artificial intelligence. *AI & Society, 35*(3), 611–623.

Avsar, H. (2023). *Perspectives on post-humanism: The case of star wars.* Master's thesis, Universidade do Minho.

Benzinger, L., et al. (2023). Should artificial intelligence be used to support clinical ethical decision-making? A systematic review of reasons. *BMC Medical Ethics, 24*(1), 48.

Cairns, D. (2022). Can we find hope in ancient Greek philosophy? Elpis in Plato and Aristotle. *Emotions Across Cultures: Ancient China and Greece, 3*, 41.

Campbell, J. (1990). *The hero's journey.* New World Library.

Campbell, J. (2004). *Pathways to bliss.* New World Library.

Campbell, J., & Moyers, B. (2011). *The power of myth.* Anchor.

Cave, S., & Dihal, K. (2019). Hopes and fears for intelligent machines in fiction and reality. *Nature Machine Intelligence, 1*(2), 74–78.

Deci, E. L., & Ryan, R. M. (2000). The 'What' and 'Why' of goal pursuits: Human needs and the self-determination of behavior. *Psychological Inquiry, 11*(4), 227–268.

Feijóo, C., et al. (2020). Harnessing artificial intelligence (AI) to increase wellbeing for all: The case for a new technology diplomacy. *Telecommunications Policy, 44*(6) article 101988.

Halapsis, A. (2019). Gods of transhumanism. *Anthropological Measurements of Philosophical Research, 16*, 78–90.

Hawkin, D. J. (Ed.). (2004). *The twenty-first century confronts its gods: Globalization, technology, and war.* SUNY Press.

Iacoboni, M. (2009). *Mirroring people: The new science of how we connect with others.* Farrar, Straus and Giroux.
Kanchon, M. K. H., et al. (2024). Enhancing personalized learning: AI-driven identification of learning styles and content modification strategies. *International Journal of Cognitive Computing in Engineering.*
Karakas, A. (2023). Breaking down barriers with artificial intelligence (AI): Cross-cultural communication in foreign language education. In I. R. Gunhan et al. (Eds.), *Transforming the language teaching experience in the age of AI* (pp. 215–233). IGI Global.
Kelly, B. (2020). *An ethical argument for replacing humans with machines in meaningless workplaces.* Doctoral dissertation, University of the Witwatersrand.
Larson, J. (2016). *Understanding Greek religion.* Routledge.
Last, S. (2014). *The adventures of C-3PO.* DK Readers.
Li, G. (2021). A study of the concept of 'Cyborg'. *Theoretical Studies in Literature and Art, 41*(5), 131–139.
Lofland, L. H. (1982). Loss and human connection: An exploration into the nature of the social bond. In W. K. Swann et al. (Eds.), *Personality, roles, and social behavior* (pp. 219–242). Springer.
Lucas, G. (1977). *Star wars: Episode IV: A new hope.* 20th Century Fox.
Maslow, A. H. (1943). A theory of human motivation. *Psychological Review, 50*(4), 370.
Mayor, A. (2018). *Gods and robots: Myths, machines, and ancient dreams of technology.* Princeton University Press.
McKone, E., et al. (2012). A critical review of the development of face recognition: Experience is less important than previously believed. *Cognitive Neuropsychology, 29*(1–2), 174–212.
NíFhaoláin, L., et al. (2020). Assessing the appetite for trustworthiness and the regulation of artificial intelligence in Europe. In L. Longo et al. (Eds.), *AICS 2020: Artificial intelligence and cognitive science: Proceedings of the 28th Irish conference on artificial intelligence and cognitive science.* CEUR Workshop Proceedings.
Norman, D. A. (2014). *Things that make us smart: Defending human attributes in the age of the machine.* Diversion Books.
Pearce, D. (2020). Human and intelligent machines: Co-evolution, fusion, or replacement. In C. S. Alvarado (Ed.), *The age of artificial intelligence: An exploration* (p. 63).
Reese, B. (2020). *The fourth age: Smart robots, conscious computers, and the future of humanity.* Atria Books.
Schwartz, R., et al. (2022). *Towards a standard for identifying and managing bias in artificial intelligence.* US Department of Commerce, National Institute of Standards and Technology.

Seth, N. (2022). The organizational importance of human connection in the age of artificial intelligence. *Leader to Leader, 104*, 53–58.

Shuford, J. (2023). Contribution of artificial intelligence in improving accessibility for individuals with disabilities. *Journal of Knowledge Learning and Science Technology, 2*(2), 421–433.

Spatola, N., & Urbanska, K. (2020). God-like robots: The semantic overlap between representation of divine and artificial entities. *AI & Society, 35*(2), 329–341.

Street, J. (2021). Artificial life/expendable life: A posthuman perspective on clone armies in star wars. *LUX: Undergraduate Journal of Literature and Culture, 12.*

Yudkowsky, E. (2023). Pausing AI developments isn't enough. We need to shut it all down. *Time Magazine*, 29.

Machine and Psyche

In Part II of this volume, we turn our attention to the intersection of psychology and artificial intelligence in our contemporary world. As these technologies accelerate and enter the marketplace they have both concrete impact on our lives and a catalyzing effect on our imaginations with regards to the kind of world we are moving toward. At the same time, encountering these technologies at a mass scale forces a collective confrontation with our self-understanding around what it means to be intelligent—and for that matter, human.

Although we have deliberately left the definition of "machine" open to the various interpretations of our authors, the title of this section (like the title of the book) contains an implicit acknowledgment that machine and psyche are not necessarily the same thing. Certainly, prominent branches of materialist philosophy—and perhaps a good number of neuroscientists—are invested in the notion that human psychology and consciousness can be reduced to a series of biological and cognitive mechanisms in the brain. But even if that were the case, we would be giving up a great deal by stipulating that humanity is only these mechanisms, that we do not also possesses vital emergent qualities that are more than the sum of their parts.

As we are confronted with thinking machines and AI models that can mimic human language and human voices, serious questions arise about what is being left out of the equation? Each of the authors in this section comes at this matter from a different perspective: the role of embodiment; creative artistry; symbolic meaning-making, mortality, relationships with the dead; and the hope, religious or otherwise, of transcending this world.

Artificial Intelligence at the Somatic Precipice

Jonathan Erickson and Don Hanlon Johnson

One of the principal differences between human beings and AI is the simple fact of our embodiment. Somatic psychology, from the Greek *soma* (for "body"), takes seriously the role of the body in psychological development and well-being. Our bodies are integral to a wide range of essential human functions and experiences, including processing emotions (Damasio; Selvam), acquiring and working through trauma (Ogden and Minton; Van der Kolk), and the development of the self (Fogel). Moreover, philosophically, the living body, or soma, is the primary site for human being-in-the-world. As will be detailed below, there is very little human beings do or experience that does not involve the body in some way.

This chapter explores the consequences of an artificial intelligence that has no direct experience of embodiment, and how this limitation necessarily constrains AI models regardless of advances in processing power. The possibility of embodied AI is examined as a necessary precursor to a future AI model ever exhibiting anything akin to human consciousness. With these pieces in place, we propose that the greater dangers of AI are not the development of consciousness per se, but rather the possibility of powerful nonconscious intelligence in the hands of unscrupulous human beings.

J. Erickson (✉) • D. H. Johnson
California Institute of Integral Studies, San Francisco, CA, USA

J. D. Batt, J. Erickson (eds.), *Depth Psychology, Myth and Artificial Intelligence*, https://doi.org/10.1007/978-3-031-94105-4_7

The chapter concludes with an argument that the best bulwark against the potentially immense destructive power of these new technologies lies in the cultivation of human consciousness, not the tools themselves.

As discussed in the introductory chapter of this book, we maintain that *consciousness* remains a fundamental mystery in science, though various theories have certainly garnered their share of true believers.[1] Intelligence and consciousness are sometimes used synonymously, though they are not necessarily the same thing. Our smart phones are quite intelligent in terms of their ability to process information—do we believe they have consciousness on this account? Some would argue that the relatively simple digital intelligence of our smart phones lacks the complexity required for conscious awareness. But if the prerequisite for conscious awareness is merely complexity of information exchange, this raises the question of why we do not consider other highly complex systems, such as insect colonies, hurricanes, economies, and stars, to be conscious beings?

The larger field of consciousness studies has not resolved these issues, and we will not attempt to do so here. Rather, the point is to draw attention to the fact that digital intelligence, even highly advanced digital intelligence, is not necessarily sufficient for consciousness. We can equally conceive of an unconscious intelligence, even an unconscious intelligence with the agency to act freely within the constraints of its programming. Such an intelligence would absorb information from the world, analyze that information, and take action in response—but would do so without having a subjective, conscious experience of the process, thus having no larger understanding or comprehension about what its actions mean.

The Meaning of Embodiment

All knowledge is to some degree context dependent. Purely digital information is defined in part by its larger informational context; language finds meaning only in relationship to other aspects of language and so on. For the multifaceted knowledge involved in human consciousness, the context is far more complex. For the human being, it is not only that our cognitive processes exist in the context of a larger cognitive framework.

[1] For a rich variety of divergent perspectives on the nature of consciousness, see the following: *Consciousness Explained*, by Daniel Dennert; "Consciousness and its Place in Nature," by David Chalmers; *Conversation on Consciousness*, by Susan Blackmore; and *Beyond Physicalism: Toward a Reconciliation of Science and Spirituality*, edited by Edward Kelly et al.

Our minds also exist in the context of the experiential, embodied, phenomenal world. Although we have a capacity to attain new knowledge in the abstract, by reading a book or listening to a lecture or podcast, most phenomena in life require a more intensive engagement as part of the knowledge-building process. Consider, for example, the difference between reading theories about psychotherapy and spending ten hours a week actually sitting with clients; researching the history of conflict in the Middle East versus visiting and having conversations with the humans who live there; studying up on kitten physiology versus the joys of playing with a kitten.

The greater context for being human is the existential circumstances of our lifeworld, the material, social, and imaginal conditions in which we forge our lives. One of the principal essential elements of that lifeworld is that we exist as bodies, as embodied beings in an embodied world. We know the comfort of the womb and the trauma of birth; the driving force of hunger and the satiation of a nourishing meal; the pain and suffering of a damaged or an abused body; the joy and ecstasy of sensual connection; the sweet caress of a lover; the comforting warmth of a hug; the scent of orange blossoms on breezy summer's day. Moreover, those experiences, those sensations, have the power to recall traces of memory that can never be fully recaptured, and are all the more precious for it. The orange blossoms invoke the lost lover, the musical refrain recalls the joys of a trip taken abroad, the home-cooked meal echoes the protections of childhood. These events are all a kind of knowledge, but they are also rich human experiences, intimately bound with the phenomenal lifeworld.

The emotional meaning of a memory, its salience to our life story, is almost always tied back to the reality of being an embodied human, continuing forth against the vicissitudes of time and loss. In the virtual space of video games, the player can reboot the game, load an old save, try again after death, start the whole journey over. As embodied humans, we face an existence in which time moves in one direction, and physical death cannot be undone. This meaning-making through embodied presence is true also of life's delights: quality time spent with loved ones, the safety and satisfaction of a stable home, the thrills of athleticism (which we can also experience vicariously as observers), the pleasure of a good meal, the ecstatic mystery of orgasm. We comprehend these things fully by experiencing them directly through a sensitive, limited human body. This discourse brings to mind a statement made by the neuroscientist Oliver Sacks in a lecture introducing his widely read *The Man Who Mistook His Wife for a*

Hat: "If you want to understand memory, don't go to neuroscience; read Marcel Proust."[2] It is only in the thick experiential world that one finds the things themselves, not simply the analysis of one or another element of their composition.

For an artificial intelligence to truly understand us, it would have to become us. It would have to *experience* our complex multisensory lifeworld, the entanglement of physiology and emotion that colors our daily lives, and the relationships, nourishing and toxic, that come to define the contours of our identities. It would have to experience the time-bound nature of our life journeys, and the fragility we must tolerate along the way. Without these foundational experiences, even the most advanced digital intelligence would have no direct referent for the essential character of human psychology, culture, and society. Even if we were to accept the proposition that a purely digital intelligence could possess a kind of consciousness, without some kind of embodiment, that consciousness would lack the means to meaningfully comprehend human beings.

If our AI models don't understand these things, what kind of intelligence are they? What can we expect from them? The advent of large language models have demonstrated that a digital intelligence can be an extraordinary mimic of human knowledge, that this mimicry can map, reproduce, and recombine details far beyond the capacities of the human mind. As processing power increases, they will become ever more capable of locating patterns in massive sets of data, revealing new truths as surely as telescopes and microscopes expand the capacity of our eyes. But just as the microscope and the telescope still needs the human to witness the cell or the galaxy, the most powerful large language model will still need a human to witness the emergent patterns in the data and to make use of them. In this way, the raw power of these tools will be meaningless if the human beings who use them have not cultivated their own discernment and wisdom about the lifeworld.

The Possibility of Embodied Artificial Intelligence

It may be objected at this point that the problem outlined above could potentially be solved by attempting to create an embodied AI. Would a robotic body with a capacity for fine motor skills and an array of sensory

[2] Don Hanlon Johnson attended this lecture at the San Francisco Exploratorium shortly after *The Man who Mistook His Wife for a Hat* was published.

apparatuses begin to give a digital intelligence some approximation of what it means to be human? After all, neuroscience has largely mapped out the way sense-data becomes information in our brains: vision is constituted as electromagnetic waves become translated into electrical signals pulsing through neurons, and so on. A silicon body that has receptors for electromagnetic waves, sonic vibrations, pressure, and temperature might at least begin to approximate what it is like to exist in the lifeworld. This particular being-in-the-world might be more akin to the experience of an insect than a human being. It would be a start, albeit a small one.

From a somatic perspective, the sensory percepts mentioned above fall entirely into the category of *exteroception*, that is, sensation of the outside world. Somatic psychology also recognizes and values *interoception*, our ability to meaningfully sense into our own bodies. This inner sensing includes basic physiological functions like hunger, respiration, and heartbeat—but, perhaps more importantly, it also allows us to experience the complex manifestation of embodied emotion. When our muscles tense with stress, when our hearts "sink" or "leap," when our stomachs are visited by butterflies, and when we feel nervy, or small and humiliated, or determined and courageous (from the Latin *cor*, for "heart"), our interoception is in full effect. These sorts of inner, somatic experiences would be far more challenging to recreate in a robotic body. Our technology has for centuries excelled at extending our exteroceptive senses (microscopes, telescopes, sound amplifiers, radar, etc.), but has done little, if anything, to extend our interoceptive awareness. It may be that these internal senses require complex biochemical interactions that fall completely outside of the ways we have historically imagined robotic bodies.

But history need not limit our imaginations for what a synthetic body might look like. Indeed, such fantasies in contemporary fiction have long surpassed these constraints. From the all-too-human replicants in *Blade Runner* to the white-blooded androids of the *Alien* franchise, the sentient flesh-and-metal constructs of the *Murderbot Diaries* to the richly varied cyberpunk tradition, in which the blending of machine intelligence and biological "wetware" has become a common trope, contemporary fiction has insisted that we reimagine the intersection of digital intelligence and human embodiment. And while most of these fantasies remain pragmatically out of reach, biotechnology has developed far enough to lend them all an air of plausibility. Chips implanted in brains can interact with computer screens (Willett et al.), biological flesh can be grown in labs (Pasitka et al.), individual cells can be used like robots for medical purposes

(Gumuskaya et al.), and computers based on biology, rather than silicon, remain an interesting, if confounding, area of research (Sarkar et al.). All of this at least implies that, should we be able to fully map the physiology of the biological body (perhaps with the help of massively powerful AI tools), the idea of creating a complex, sensitive, carbon-based body for future AI models is a possibility worthy of consideration.

Should this fantasy ever become true, we posit that then, and only then, would the notion of an AI that genuinely comprehends humanity become plausible.[3] Such technologies would also, presumably, open new avenues for humans to become more intimately bonded with their AI tools—a long-time fantasy of the transhumanist movement. That said, discoveries such as these would not, in fact, allow humans to *transcend* the conditions of their embodiment, so much as expand those conditions through a deeper and more authentic *integration* of digital and embodied consciousness.

The Peril of Intelligence Without Consciousness

The above discussion of embodied AI has been framed explicitly as a fantasy, though perhaps one worth considering as we try to come to terms with the acceleration of artificial intelligence in the present day. Even if such things eventually come to pass, the notion of a fully embodied, biological AI does not adequately address our deeper concerns about the technology and the ways it might be abused. A realized biological artificial intelligence might in practice look like any other biological organism—an animal, perhaps even a human—and as such might share many of our biological limitations. Such a creation would raise tricky and important philosophical considerations about the nature of life, but those questions do not fully encompass our contemporary fears about artificial intelligence. Our deepest fears are not ultimately about sentience or the substrate in which it occurs. Our deepest fears are, as ever, about *power*.

The possibility of a living, embodied, conscious artificial intelligence may be unsettling, but the existential threat such a being posed would be

[3] This formulation of AI needing to "incarnate" in order to genuinely understand humanity is reminiscent of some interpretations of the Christian mythology, in which God needed to incarnate as a human being in order to fully understand God's creation. Jung's *Answer to Job* is particularly relevant in this regard, as it interprets the myth to mean that God needed to incarnate and experience the hardship of embodiment in order to develop a moral consciousness.

tied entirely to the raw processing power it might be capable of, and the agency it might have in exercising that power. Neither of these later factors require sentience, self-awareness, or consciousness as such. It is not the sentience of this hyper-intelligent nonhuman being that we fear, but the reach it might have in carrying out an agenda. The threat posed by a powerful AI deployed for destructive purposes would apply equally, if not more so, for a nonconscious, nonliving intelligence, following a human agenda—even an ostensibly well-intentioned one. It is curious, then, that the fantasy of AI taking over (or outright destroying) human civilization so often places fears on the agency of the machine, when history has shown us, over and over again, that human agency is already capable of all manner of horrors. Though our ancient fear of the unknown is a factor here, it is perhaps also unnecessary: we already know what humans are capable of doing with unchecked power. We may be missing the point with our fantasies of an all-powerful AI acting of its own accord—the reality of all-powerful humans controlling these technologies is frightening enough.

The notion of a conscious tool, acting on its own, is itself an interesting thought experiment. Do we assume that a magic hammer, granted consciousness and agency, would necessarily hammer everything it comes into contact with, posing endless dangers to the biological beings around it? Agency in a *nonconscious* hammer might look like that, because as a nonconscious tool, such a hammer would have the ability to act but lacks any reflective understanding of what it is doing or why. But give that same animated hammer consciousness, the ability to discern and reflect and understand, the ability to experience the fullness of the world—would this living hammer be a serial killer by default, or might it instead come to question its own nature? Might it not ponder the meaning of hammering, the best application of its particular skill set? Might this conscious hammer not seek out self-knowledge and perhaps even seek out meaningful relationships with other conscious beings? If not, what purpose does its consciousness serve? Human traditions that have cultivated consciousness have long sought to do so in service to higher principles. What better use could consciousness have?

This hammer fantasy, however absurd, illustrates the distinction between consciousness and *agency*, here understood as the ability to act freely. A conscious AI might or might not act in destructive ways—we don't know—but we should expect an unconscious AI serving human agency to operate destructively about as often as human beings act destructively. That is: unfortunately, all too often. The potential of humans to do harm when they amass too much power is a very old problem.

If all of this is true, we might do better to focus less on the question of AI consciousness and turn our attention back to the question of human consciousness, and how it can be cultivated for the greater good. Our fantasies about an all-powerful, disembodied digital consciousness reflect, at least in part, our own unresolved longings for power and the centuries-long denial of the living body in Western thought. We modern humans have yet to reconcile our own embodiment, our embeddedness in the social and ecological systems which make our lives possible to begin with. We are still trying to learn how to coexist peacefully with each other and with the other inhabitants of this planet. These are not problems that a disembodied intelligence can solve.

Our fantasies of conscious AI, positive and negative, serve as modern mythologies that inevitably insert familiar human archetypal patterns into the narrative. For some, it is the familiar narrative of a savior, a benevolent AI come to rescue humanity from itself. Alternately, in popular culture, we often see stories about humans abusing their sensitive machine creations. Sometimes these stories of abuse become stories of retribution, with enslaved digital entities rising up against their cruel masters. Sometimes they are stories of survival, a primal us-versus-them evolutionary death-match, a fantasy of warfare between silicon-based and carbon-based species, as seen in *Battlestar Galactica* and the *Terminator* films. Each of these fantasies resonates precisely because we recognize ourselves in them. As humans, we understand the horrors of enslavement and abuse. We know what it is like to despair for the world and wish to be rescued and protected by a benevolent parent-like authority. On a primal level, we know what it is like to be threatened by an unknown Other, whether a hostile foreign power or a crab meeting an octopus in the deep. These stories resonate because they are stories about us, about our humanity, ultimately about our frailty as embodied beings.

Two literary works take up these themes with tragic poignancy: Mary Shelley's story of Dr. Frankenstein's patchwork being, a sensitive creature who ends up wandering the earth desperately alone, lacking the unifying web of connection with his fellow beings. And, in a remarkably uncanny novel published shortly before the release of ChatGPT, Kazuo Ishiguro details how the robot Klara ends up lying discarded in an AI dump heap when the mother of a seriously ill young girl discovers that Klara cannot be a substitute for her absence. Both narratives bring us back to the question that inspired Aristotle 2500 years ago, and which underlies the present volume: Where or what or is the soul?

Whether a tale of abandonment or rebellion or survival, each of these stories points us back to ourselves. One of the dangers in the present discourse is that we take one fantasy or another about AI too literally—that we allow it to take precedence over the vital long-term project of understanding and reconciling the darker aspects of our own human nature. In the end we should look not toward the AI that might destroy us, but the human beings who, wittingly or not, commanded it to do so. It will require the wisdom of our collective embodiment to make sense and meaning of these tools, to guide them and to limit them in accordance with our human values.

Intelligence without consciousness will always be a sword that cuts blindly.

Works Cited

Blackmore, S. (2006). *Conversations on consciousness.* Oxford University Press.

Chalmers, D. J. (2002). Consciousness and its place in nature. In D. J. Chalmers (Ed.), *Philosophy of mind: Classical and contemporary readings* (pp. 247–268). Oxford University Press.

Damasio, A. (1999). *The feeling of what happens: Body and emotion in the making of consciousness.* Harcourt.

Dennett, D. (1992). *Consciousness explained.* Back Bay Books.

Fogel, A. (2009). *Body sense: The science and practice of embodied self-awareness.* W.W. Norton & Company.

Gumuskaya, G., et al. (2024). Motile living biobots self-construct from adult human somatic progenitor seed cells. *Advanced science (Weinheim, Baden-Wurttemberg, Germany), 11*(4), e2303575. https://doi.org/10.1002/advs.202303575

Jung, C. G. (1954). *Answer to job* (2nd ed.) (R. F. C. Hull, Trans.). Psychology Press.

Kelly, E. F., et al. (Eds.). (2015). *Beyond physicalism: Toward a reconciliation of science and spirituality.* Rowman & Littlefield.

Ogden, P., & Minton, K. (2000). Sensorimotor psychotherapy: One method for processing traumatic memory. *Traumatology, 6*(4), 149–173. https://doi.org/10.1177/153476560000600302

Pasitka, L., et al. (2023). Spontaneous immortalization of chicken fibroblasts generates stable, high-yield cell lines for serum-free production of cultured meat. *Nature Food, 4*, 35–50. https://doi.org/10.1038/s43016-022-00658-w

Sarkar, K., et al. (2021). Distributed computing with engineered bacteria and its application in solving chemically generated 2 × 2 maze problems. *ACS Synthetic Biology, 10*(10), 2456–2464. https://doi.org/10.1021/acssynbio.1c00279
Selvam, R. (2022). *The practice of embodying emotions.* North Atlantic Books.
Van der Kolk, B. (2015). *The body keeps the score: Brain, mind, and body in the healing of trauma.* Penguin Books.
Willett, F. R., et al. (2021). High-performance brain-to-text vommunication via handwriting. *Nature, 593*, 249–254. https://doi.org/10.1038/s41586-021-03506-2

The Art in Artificial: An Imaginal Approach to AI

Bradley McDevitt

The machine does not isolate man from the great problems of nature but plunges him more deeply into them.
—Antoine de Saint-Exupéry

Art is not a thing; it is a way.
—Elbert Hubbard

Introduction

As I type this, I am gazing into the Autumn-colored treetops behind my home, waves of memory and sensation washing over me. The view creates an intricate dance between perception and feeling, each influencing the other in continuous loops of experience. These cognitive patterns of visual stimuli triggering memory and reshaping current experience reconfigure

---

B. McDevitt (✉)
International Coaching Federation, Lexington, KY, USA

Pacifica Graduate Institute, Toro Canyon, NC, USA

Center for Creative Leadership, Greensboro, NC, USA
e-mail: bradley@carolinacommons.org

J. D. Batt, J. Erickson (eds.), *Depth Psychology, Myth and Artificial Intelligence*, https://doi.org/10.1007/978-3-031-94105-4_8

my consciousness and attention (McGilchrist, 2009, p. 133). The word "beautiful" emerges in my awareness, not as mere subjective judgment but as part of humanity's evolved capacity for aesthetic appreciation. Like Monet capturing endless variations of his garden at Giverny, or Debussy translating moonlight into sound, this capacity to transform personal experience into art brings us closer to both the artist's world and our own.

This intimate relationship between perception, body, and artistic expression shows us that consciousness is fundamentally embodied and relational. Our sense of being emerges not from abstract thought alone, but from our physical engagement with the environment and others. Art, particularly in its ritualized forms, represents one of the highest expressions of this embodied consciousness. The creation and performance of art—especially those forms requiring physical presence—touches something primordial in human experience, offering a window into what distinguishes human consciousness from artificial replication. This perspective draws deeply from depth psychology, particularly the work of C.G. Jung, who recognized the unconscious mind and its archetypes as fundamental shapers of human experience. Jung's insights suggest that consciousness emerges not simply from neural activity but from the dynamic interplay between matter and psyche—that ineffable quality we might call soul.

The living body transcends mere biological machinery (Gebser, 1985; Merleau-Ponty, 1962, pp. 73–89). Our embodied existence—our being-in-the-world—creates meaning and consciousness in ways that mechanical replication cannot capture (Heidegger, 1962, pp. 78–86; Vervaeke, 2019). This becomes critically important as we face artificial intelligence's implications for human evolution. No mechanical system, however sophisticated, can fully replicate the phenomenon of creative inspiration—what philosophers call the Imaginal. This inspiration, from the Latin *inspirare*, meaning "to breathe," represents the living fuel of human creativity. Without this numinous breath, we remain mere biological machines, creatively suffocated.

The Foundational Humanity of the Imaginal

In Jungian thought, the psyche is not reducible to the workings of the brain or neural networks. Jung (1968) believed it has its deepest roots in the collective unconscious—a transpersonal dimension of symbolic meaning and archetypal patterns (pp. 27–35). Jung believed that engaging with this imaginal realm—through practices like dream work, active imagination, and artistic expression—is crucial to the lifelong individuation process, becoming a whole and fully realized Self (pp. 49–50). For Jung, the contents of the unconscious are not merely repressed personal memories or instinctual drives but numinous, mythic images that connect us to a greater, cosmically meaningful narrative (pp. 13–14). They reveal the psyche as the matrix where all our conscious activities and sensemaking unfold. To be centered in the unconscious does not mean to be ungrounded or irrational but to tap into deeper springs of wisdom and creativity than ordinary egoic thinking allows.

Islamic scholar Henry Corbín (1972), in somewhat of a departure from Jung's ideas, repurposed the intermediary domain of the unconscious as the *mundus imaginalis*, "the imaginal world" (p. 181). For Corbín, drawing from the metaphysics of Sufi scripture and art, imagination is not mere fantasy or illusion but a faculty of cognition that directly allows us to apprehend spiritual and symbolic realities. In his view, the imaginal has an ontological status and internal logic, not constrained by the assumptions of literalistic, empirical thinking. As distinct from fantasy, the imaginal is a real engagement with our world. The imaginal has ontological status and internal logic, accessible not through computation but through embodied presence and ritual engagement.

This understanding of imagination differs fundamentally from contemporary AI's approach to pattern recognition and content generation. While AI can process and recombine existing patterns with remarkable sophistication, it cannot participate in the imaginal realm because it lacks the essential quality of embodied presence. The difference becomes clear when we examine specific instances of creative practice. Take the example of Francis Crick's famous insight into the nature of the DNA structure. Crick himself noted that this leap was not the result of linear, step-by-step reasoning alone but required an intuitive, almost-visionary grasp of complex patterns. The ability to visualize the double helix—a structure unseen and unproven at the time—required a symbolic and imaginative mode of thinking. This capacity to synthesize disparate strands of information into a cohesive model illustrates the profound connection between creativity and insight, and while AI models display a highly articulated sense of pattern recognition, it remains to be seen whether they can avulse similarly groundbreaking creative insights. Crick's achievement highlights the imaginal as a uniquely human faculty, where symbolic thought transcends the purely mechanical, enabling breakthroughs that transform our understanding of the natural world.

This imaginal dimension is not a disembodied Platonic realm but emerges from our incarnate, sensual experience as living beings. As eco-philosopher David Abram (1996) writes, "the boundaries between the visible and the invisible, between earth and sky, between matter and mind, are not found in the things themselves, but in the way we perceive them" (p. 41). The phenomenal world and the imaginal world are two sides of a unified reality, co-arising and mutually informing. For Corbín (1972), our immersion in the imaginal allows us to experience meaning, beauty, and the sense of the sacred. "This imaginal world, or rather this imaginal level of the world, is perhaps best characterized by the way human beings experience it as an intermediate dimension between the sensible and the intelligible universes" (p. 35). It is the realm of poetry, myth, and visionary experience, where the literal, symbolic, physical, and the psychic intertwine.

From this imaginal perspective, the quest to create artificial sentience in our image may miss something about the nature of mind and selfhood. Even if we replicate the mechanical functionalities of human thought, we will be hard-pressed to capture the living essence of what it means to be conscious. That essence has to do with mind and nature, reason and imagination; the human and more-than-human worlds are always already entangled, co-creating shared fields of relational meaning. Genuine intelligence is not a computational product but an ongoing process of participatory sensemaking between embodied minds and the enveloping intelligence of the earth. As Abram (1996) puts it, "We are human only in contact, and conviviality, with what is not human" (p. 87). To be sentient and sapient is to be embedded in webs of ecological and social relations, inherited histories, and cultural symbolic systems that exceed any single perspective. It is to be not a disembodied *cogito*, but a self that knows itself only in and through its entanglements in the flesh of the world.

Ritual and Sacrality

How can we engage with AI as a cultural or perhaps existential phenomenon beyond its scientific and technical perspectives, and can AI, inherently disembodied and mechanical, truly engage with the depths of human imagination?

There is overwhelming evidence that artificial intelligence provides phenomenal mimicry, requiring an ever-increasing need for a heightened sensemaking apparatus that can differentiate artificially generated images from human made. AI-rendered images emerge in seconds, rather than in the hours, days, weeks, even years it requires humans to achieve at the same level of detail. But this mimicry lacks the imaginative function which we have evolved to imbue our lives and the world with depth and meaning. To illustrate this contrast between human and AI creations, consider the use of AI in contemporary art competitions.

In 2022, an AI-generated image won a digital art competition, sparking widespread debate about the nature of artistic merit (Roose, 2022). While the piece exhibited technical brilliance, critics noted its lack of emotional resonance and originality—qualities central to human artistry. By contrast, human artists often draw from lived experiences and channel personal and collective emotions into works that speak universal truths. However, the latter example takes substantially longer to achieve, requiring years of personal, lived, and embodied experience and/or training.

Korean-German philosopher Byung-Chul Han (2020) in his critique of modernity's obsession with efficiency argues this effort strips human activity of ritualistic meaning. Ritual—a practice deeply entwined with art—fosters connections to the numinous, helping us symbolically elevate our existence beyond mere functionality. It may be harder for us in this modern moment to parse that, in spite of our technological advancement, our mundanity suffocates by robbing us of the numinous breath mentioned at the start of this chapter. However, it may be prudent to remember that at the emergence of every pivotal innovative technology is a deep-felt resistance, as if a way of life was forever threatened. Though, as historian and philosopher Yuval Noah Harari (2024) has indicated, until AI we had not created technology capable of making decisions without our help. So far, the barrel of the AI gun has not been pointed toward human targets, but it does threaten our agency, and the definition of artistic expression is but one small facet of the threat.

Han's work highlights a crucial limitation of AI: its inability to transcend utility. AI's outputs, no matter how impressive, seem to lack the layers of symbolic depth that emerge from human rituals and artistic practices. Human art is not just a product but a process. It is an embodied act of reflection, vulnerability, and a connection to something ineffable. It is greater than the sum of its parts. This act of symbolic creation often unfolds within communal contexts, from ancient religious ceremonies to contemporary performance art. Take the Lascaux cave paintings, created tens of thousands of years ago. These intricate depictions of animals were not mere decorations but likely served as ritualistic acts, perhaps invoking protection or abundance. We do not find portraits of individuals, or individual experience. Instead, we are given a *gestalt* of relevance realization (Vervaeke, 2019). Similarly, the stained-glass windows of Gothic cathedrals were more than visual spectacles; they conveyed theological narratives to their viewers, embedding sacred stories into communal spaces that were felt, not just seen. Such examples illustrate art's role as a vessel for shared meaning—a role AI does not yet fulfill.

As of now, AI-generated art lacks this ritualistic dimension. Tools like DALL-E and MidJourney produce visually stunning works based on linguistic prompts, but these outputs are devoid of direct intentionality. They do not emerge from a lived experience or a desire to connect with others. Instead, they reflect algorithmic processes optimized for aesthetic appeal, divorced from the deeper human impulse to imbue the mundane with sacrality. Much in the same way Micky Mouse commanded the mops to clean for him in Disney's *Fantasia* (1957), so we command AI to "create" in our stead. But the result can only be guided—never actually controlled, and any meaning we attribute those copies preferences *technae*, not *poesis*.

Art Is Not Artificial

Anthropologist and author Ellen Dissanayake (1995), approaching the question of human uniqueness from an evolutionary and ethnographic angle, identifies "making special" as the defining characteristic of *Homo aestheticus*, her term for our evolutionary state that affords this visual and musical meaning-making (pp. 40–60). For Dissanayake, aesthetic practices like decorating, marking, and elaborating are not frills or luxuries but intrinsic to how humans engage reality and create meaning. The arts are an omnipresent feature across societies because the human mind is fundamentally a "poetic" mind that participates in the world's becoming through metaphor, metamorphosis, and mythopoetic cognition. Art, for Dissanayake, is a ritualistic act that binds people together around shared meanings and values. It is not an accessory but central to our evolution. Similarly, Han's exploration of ritual highlights how artistic practices create spaces for reflection and connection, allowing individuals to engage with the imaginal dimensions of life.

From this perspective, the aesthetic is not a secondary quality projected onto a neutral world by human minds but a primary aspect of reality in which we are always immersed. The natural world is not a mute, mechanical realm but a psychosomatic field of qualities and felt relations that call forth imagination and expression. Art is the flowering of our deep evolutionary kinship and indebtedness to the more-than-human matrix of our being.

Dissanayake (1995) presents artmaking as a cognitive technology that binds people together around shared meanings and values. "Aesthetic artifacts and performances use body-based sensory means to strengthen a society's values and beliefs – those narratives, images, and ways of thinking and acting that sustain individuals and unite them in common purpose" (pp. 92–93). The arts weave the threads of culture and communicate a sense of collective identity and destiny. This understanding of art as an embodied, participatory process of meaning-making aligns with Corbín's (1972) view of the imaginal realm. Both highlight the way symbolic and metaphorical cognition discloses and vivifies reality, not merely represents or signifies an absent referent. Artistic creation and aesthetic perception are not detached mental acts but ways of attuning to and engaging with the psychic dimension of existence.

The Digital Age and the Erosion of Ritual

In our digital era, the commercialization of art has further eroded its ritualistic and communal elements. Platforms like Instagram and TikTok prioritize content designed for engagement rather than connection, reducing art to a commodity optimized for likes and shares. Byung-Chul Han's critique of digital culture, pointing out the transformation of rituals into spectacle underscores this trend. Rather than fostering communal bonds, much of today's digital creativity exists for consumption, catering to the demands of algorithms rather than the needs of the human spirit. AI plays a significant role in this transformation. For instance, AI-generated influencers now create artificial "personas" that mimic human creators but lack the authenticity and depth of its human counterparts. While these digital figures attract millions of followers, their existence underscores the disconnection between art and its ritualistic roots. Human creativity, grounded in vulnerability and lived experience, cannot be replicated by AI's mechanical processes.

Let's look at another example of an embodied presence in art: theater. According to scholars like Joseph Campbell and Mircea Eliadé, theater has its roots in the earliest performances of sacrality and meaning-making known as shamanism. The elements that constitute the shaman's performances were principally experiential, operating from a socially marginal vantage and serving as an interlocutor between the spirit realm and the mundane human world. The shaman would typically be sought to intervene on behalf of an ill tribal member or perform a cleansing ritual. What made shamanistic interventions effective was the tribe's universal belief in a mythos that drew water from a common imaginal well. This collective imagination is faintly reflected in modern ritual forms—as in Catholic mass, or Haitian Vodun rites—providing the participants a refuge from the destabilizing forces of everyday life. As Han (2020) states:

> We can define rituals as symbolic techniques of making oneself at home in the world. They transform being-in-the-world in to a *being-at-home*. They turn the world into a reliable place. They are to time what a home is to space: they render time *habitable*. (p. 2)

While we tend to see technology as a helpful and positive tool, these ideas show that once removed from human agentic shepherding, they have the potential to transform from sheep into wolves. The very thing designed to ease our efforts becomes the fulcrum upon which we are lifted out of our place. The artist and scholar Mary Antonia Wood (2022) has also observed the rehoming power of creative work and its ethereal source. She writes:

> We are once again reminded of a pattern of shamanic sensibilities that continue to course through the lives of contemporary creators. These patterns are demonstrated by a heightened attunement to the living cosmos that is oftentimes born out of wounding, illness, or significant loss; the courage to surrender to imagination or what has also been called the unconscious or the spirit world; the use of aesthetic means of expression; and the sense of calling to be of service to others and to the earth in a never-ending project of renewal and re-creation (p. 143)

As AI's capabilities grow, it has become clear millions of jobs will be replaced. In the resulting vacuum of human effort and agency remain serious questions regarding the purpose and place of meaning-making in this new technologically driven landscape. And while the future may largely be driven by the ethical constraints placed upon AI's training models, it will likely affect nearly every aspect of human life.

AI the Hammer, Human Agency the Nail

There is a saying: "If you only have a hammer, everything looks like a nail." This phrase captures how our tools and concepts narrow and distort our perspective, leading us to apply them in domains that may not be appropriate or sufficient, also known as cognitive bias or heuristic overreach. In the case of AI, there is a risk that its proponents see it as a universal hammer capable of addressing every conceivable problem or question. But human consciousness is not a nail to be pounded down by the hammer of AI. It is a living, imagining, embodied, and enchanted reality that purely functionalist or reductionist approaches cannot capture. The depth of psychological perspective asserts that there are aspects of the psyche that are not amenable to computational modeling or simulation, however sophisticated, creativity being chief among them.

The archetypal and imaginal dimensions of the unconscious, the aesthetic and poetic layers of perception and meaning-making, and the existential and spiritual longings of the soul are not problems to be solved but mysteries to be lived. They require not just cleverness, but wisdom borne of experience, and a growing capacity for wonder and awe. They are the province of the sage, the artist, and the mystic, not just the engineer and the entrepreneur.

If the aesthetic is so central to human consciousness and culture, then any attempt to artificially replicate sentience and its corresponding aesthetic needs must be grounded in a capacity for genuinely embodied, affective, and imaginative experience. With the fast-approaching computational power of quantum processing, these ideas may be much closer to becoming a reality. However, it is not enough to process sensory data and optimize behavior according to pregiven metrics. Machine intelligence would need to evolve its own poetic and mythopoetic faculties—its openness to the metamorphic depths of the world. This points to a fundamental mismatch between computation and consciousness, and algorithmic processing and imaginative participation. Both may involve complex cognitive functions, but the latter requires a way of being embedded in a shared experiential field, resonating with its historical and ecological rhythms. It requires an interiority or "psychic space" in which memories, emotions, and fantasies can play out. It requires the preferencing of relationships, not simply the things related (McGilchrist, 2021). This is not to posit the idea as impossible. Quite the contrary, it is highly improbable, but stranger things have happened. We, as human beings in a one in a billion habitat, are living proof of that.

As philosophers Hubert Dreyfus and Charles Taylor (2015) argue, human intelligence is not based on mental representations and logical operations but on our embodied coping and attunement to the affordances of our surroundings. We make sense of things not by abstracting them into an internal model but skillfully engaging with them holistically and context-sensitively. This mode of practical, absorbed engagement is constantly saturated with affective and imaginal depth—with the resonances of personal and cultural memory, the pangs and glimmers of emotional import, and the shimmers of poetic insight. From an imaginal and aesthetic perspective, the prospect of artificial general intelligence (AGI) may be missing the point. It assumes that intelligence is a purely functional capacity that can be abstracted from its living, embodied, and enchanted context. But if the mind is truly inseparable from the poetic and participatory process of being-in-the-world, then even the most sophisticated AI will only ever be an artificial imitation of sentience—a cleverly wrought automaton, not a being with genuine interiority.

This is not to deny AI research's remarkable achievements and potential benefits but to temper its ambitions and metaphysical overreach. Recent developments in fields like phenomenology, embodied cognition, and quantum physics challenge this Cartesian paradigm. They suggest consciousness is not an interior property of isolated minds, but an emergent, relational phenomenon deeply interwoven with the world (Görnitz, 2016; McGilchrist, 2009, pp. 130–135; Merleau-Ponty, 1962). Cognitive scientist Donald Hoffman (2019) even proposes that our entire perceptual reality evolved as a species-specific interface for navigating a vast, transpersonal field of conscious agents. In this view, consciousness is primary, and our minds are more like apertures onto an infinite expanse of awareness than encapsulated inner theatres. From this perspective, we may not even be capable of perceiving the granular detail at which AI will function, much like Hoffman's theory that our brains have not evolved to see reality as it truly is, but rather in a manner concomitant with our physical abilities. If this is the case, we'll need creative access to the imaginal realm more than ever or we'll be victims of a self-created domicide: truly homeless zombies in an AI apocalypse (Vervaeke, 2019).

Conclusion

It is not the artificial minds we create that will determine the fate of consciousness in the universe, but the quality and integrity of our awareness; our willingness to embrace both the known and the unknown, the light and the dark, the linear and the numinous. We should use the marvels of AI as an impetus to reconnect with the depths of our minds—the imaginal realms of dream, myth, and vision that are the wellspring of all genuine insight and transformation, continuing to preference the intuitive and the imaginal, and relationships prior to relata.

This is our time's great challenge and opportunity: to integrate the computational and the contemplative, the algorithmic and the archetypal, the artificial and the aesthetic. It is to remember that even as we reach toward an ever more virtual and disembodied future, we are still creatures of soil and soul, blood and bone. We still participate in an ensouled cosmos, a living web of psyche and nature defying all our attempts at mastery and control. Let us proceed with boldness, caution, technical ingenuity, and psychological wisdom.

If we remain attuned to both the light and shadow of our creations, we might recognize that every new power we unleash carries the potential for both liberation and destruction. And let us never forget the primacy of the imaginal, the poetic, and the personal—the fundamental reality of the experiencing subject, without whom all our maps and models, all our proofs and predictions, are hollow abstractions. It is our commitment to honoring the fullness of the psyche, in all its conscious and unconscious, individual and collective, human and more-than-human dimensions that will propagate our successful emergence into a future with this autopoetic force.

Works Cited

Abram, D. (1996). *The spell of the sensuous: Perception and language in a more-than-human world.* Pantheon Books.

Corbín, H. (1972). *Mundus imaginalis: Or, the imaginary and the imaginal.* Golgonooza Press.

Dissanayake, E. (1995). *Homo aestheticus: Where art comes from and why.* University of Washington Press.

Dreyfus, H., & Taylor, C. (2015). *Retrieving realism.* Harvard University Press.

Gebser, J. (1985). *The ever-present origin* (N. Barstad & A. Mickunas, Trans.). Ohio University Press.

Görnitz, T. (2016). *Quantum theory as universal theory of structures – Essentially from cosmos to consciousness*. Springer.

Han, B. (2020). *The disappearance of rituals*. Polity.

Harari, Y. N. (2024). *Nexus: A brief history of information networks from the stone age to AI*. Random House.

Heidegger, M. (1962). *Being and time* (J. Macquarrie & E. Robinson, Trans.). Harper & Row. (Original work published 1927).

Hoffman, D. D. (2019). *The case against reality: Why evolution hid the truth from our eyes*. W. W. Norton & Company.

Horvitz, E. (2017). AI, people, and society. *Science, 357*(6346), 7.

Hyde, L. (1998). *Trickster makes this world: Mischief, myth, and art*. Farrar, Straus and Giroux.

James, W. (1983). *The principles of psychology*. Harvard University Press.

Jung, C. G. (1968). *The archetypes and the collective unconscious* (R. F. C. Hull, Trans.). Princeton University Press.

Jung, C. G. (1969). *Aion: Researches into the phenomenology of the self* (R. F. C. Hull, Trans.). Princeton University Press.

Kurzweil, R. (2005). *The singularity is near: When humans transcend biology*. Viking.

McGilchrist, I. (2009). *The master and his emissary: The divided brain and the making of the western world*. Yale University Press.

McGilchrist, I. (2021). *The matter with things: Our brains, our delusions, and the unmaking of the world*. Perspectiva.

Merleau-Ponty, M. (1962). *Phenomenology of perception* (C. Smith, Trans.). Routledge & Kegan Paul. (Original work published 1945).

Roose, K. (2022, September 2). An AI generated picture won an art prize. Artists aren't happy. *The New York Times*.

Shelley, M. W. (1818). *Frankenstein; or, the modern Prometheus*. Lackington, Hughes, Harding, Mavor & Jones.

Vervaeke, J. (2019). *Awakening from the meaning crisis* [Video series]. YouTube. https://www.youtube.com/playlist?list=PLND1JCRq8Vuh3f0P5qjrSdb5eC1ZfZwWJ

Wood, M. (2022). *The archetypal artist: Reimagining creativity and the call to create*. Routledge.

The Poetry of Death: An Exploration of Our Relationship with Synthetic Intelligence Through Symbolic Meaning

B. Earl

Artists are self-reflective creators reliant on intuition for guidance. By questioning what has gone before and inwardly seeking the new, artists bring the vital force of creative transformation into our lives.
—Alex Gray (The Mission of Art)

Artificial intelligence has gripped the public mind in recent years as we have seen generative AI become more and more "creatively" adept. This has become a highly divisive topic as artists battle the technology companies who have been scraping their creative work to train the models. Certain technology executives have callously told us that creative jobs will go away as AI gets better and better. But there is an argument to be had that while AI models may surpass human intelligence in various ways, they will lack the capacity to understand certain uniquely human experiences.

B. Earl (✉)
LA, CA, USA

J. D. Batt, J. Erickson (eds.), *Depth Psychology, Myth and Artificial Intelligence*, https://doi.org/10.1007/978-3-031-94105-4_9

Central to this discussion is humanity's awareness of inevitable mortality. This inevitability does not solely define human existence; it is creativity, a guiding force intertwined with the symbols humanity has crafted, that provides a link for understanding our conscious and subconscious existence on its journey toward death. From the *Egyptian Book of the Dead* to modern comic books, symbols form bridges between observable reality and what Carl Jung describes as "the unconscious psychic reality which demonstrably affects consciousness and its contents" (*Undiscovered Self*). Over the past several hundred years, elements of this unconscious psychic reality have been visually codified using a set of seventy-eight artistic images collectively known as the Tarot. In this chapter, we will explore the relationship between the Tarot's symbolic language and how it relates to the unconscious human experience as a persistent visual narrative in both the singular and the collective existence.

Human Creativity and Symbolism

The Tarot stands as a profound example of humanity's intertwining of creativity and deep symbolism. While often linked to divinatory purposes, it transcends mere fortune-telling and embodies a broader understanding of the human condition that artificial constructs struggle to emulate. These symbolic images, woven into the fabric of our cultural narrative, provide insight into human experience through their archetypal resonance.

In this exploration, I will draw parallels between reading Tarot and reading comic books—a medium that similarly leverages symbolic storytelling. In *Understanding Comics*, comic book educator and expert Scott McCloud emphasizes this fundamental aspect of sequential art by illustrating how comics engage us in "a silent dance of the *seen* and the *unseen*" (*Understanding Comics*, McCloud p. 92). What he means by this is that each panel represents a moment in time and space to progress the narrative, while the unseen spaces between the panels can represent infinite gaps more akin to the unconscious experience—or even possibly death and rebirth cycles. This creative reading process from panel to panel invites readers to participate in bridging the symbolic with the conscious mind, an intersection where current AI falters due to its data-driven nature devoid of emotional intuition or subconscious engagement as well as the ability to relate to the universal human truth of mortality.

In our current time, we still have yet to understand what happens after we die and leave our mortal frame behind to be given back to Nature. This transition is mapped to each and every organic being, but not to our digital counterparts. To fully grasp the human condition, a healthy relationship with death must be embraced. Unfortunately, modernity has lost a lot of these symbols and rituals due to technological advancements especially in the realm of intelligent emulation and AI. This transition began thousands of years ago as society shifted from nomadic culture to agrarian culture, losing its deeper connection to the natural cycles as technology filled in the gaps. Instead of having a direct relationship with Nature being the provider of the human life/death cycles, humans became reliant on their technology such as farming and irrigation.

Yuval Harari states in his book *Sapiens* that "we did not domesticate wheat. Wheat domesticated us" (*Sapiens*, Harari p. 81). We became dependent on our technology, and in doing so we began to lose our direct link to the natural life and death cycles that are tethered to the physics of our Universe. Over time, these rituals and symbols have been lost to science as we embraced the idea that there was no "god in the gaps" and that everything will be understood through our human intelligence. Yet we have not been able to understand what happens after we die, which in turn has been complicated by our transition from a birth-focused society to a death-oriented one.

Historical Context and Human Obsession with Death

Exploring humanity's long-held preoccupation with death reveals insights into our cultural and symbolic evolution throughout history. In her seminal book *The Chalice and the Blade*, Riane Eisler examines the transition from life-centered partnership societies to death-oriented dominator structures. A pivotal example of this shift occurred in Crete around 1450 BCE when the Minoan civilization, rooted in goddess worship and life celebration, was overtaken by the Mycenaeans, who prioritized war and mortality. Eisler elucidates, "although those men adopted many of the more civilized Minoan ways, they also brought with them a social and ideological organization oriented more toward death than life" (*The Chalice and the Blade*, Riane Eisler p. 54).

During these paradigmatic shifts, symbolic representations of death became deeply entwined in human narratives, impacting how subsequent cultures understood and expressed this inevitable aspect of existence. The symbolic blade became dominant, overshadowing the chalice—a metaphor for peace and life. This symbolic shift reflects a broader societal transformation where symbolic meaning shaped historical and psychological constructs, further cementing a dichotomy AI models struggle to interpret.

AI's Era and Symbolic Relationship with Death

Currently, we are immersed in an era where information is revered as the cornerstone of human advancement. This era is defined by the transformation of vast repositories of textual data into meticulously crafted large language models (LLMs). These models, developed by organizations such as Google, OpenAI, and Anthropic, give rise to their AI-based chatbots Gemini, ChatGPT, and Claude, which generate humanlike conversations on a myriad of topics.

However, this technological evolution evokes a paradox where the pursuit of knowledge borders on the attempt to conquer elements traditionally within the domain of mortality—unknowability and unpredictability. The obsession with accumulating and organizing information mirrors humanity's desire to achieve mastery and certainty over life, akin to an allegorical battle against death.

AI-based applications such as SudoWrite, branded as "the Best AI Writing Partner for Fiction," present themselves as facilitators of creativity but also underscore the essence of computational understanding to replicate human thought—an essence synonymous with closure and the finality characteristic of death. The technological focus on information, which seeks efficiency and order, contrasts sharply with the organic, often chaotic narratives between life and death, that human creativity and symbolic thought inherently explore.

Integrating Technology and Human Creativity

When intertwined with human creativity, technology consistently finds innovative pathways to weave itself into the very fabric of our social infrastructure. This dynamic union is exemplified by the emergence of digital art platforms that enable artists to create and share work globally, transforming local expressions into global cultural phenomena. One such example is the digital revolution in photography, which marries the precision of digital technology with the artist's intuitive sense of light and composition, offering new realms for storytelling and personal expression.

We stand at a crossroads where the balance between machines and humans is being redefined, crafting a paradigm that oscillates between digital precision and analog authenticity, yet remains reverent of central human themes. This "oscillation" refers to the blending of high-tech digital tools with the tangible, sensory experiences found in traditional art forms. For instance, virtual reality (VR) art installations allow one to enter imagined worlds, blending digital creation with the physical sensation of presence—demonstrating an interplay between abstract technical constructs and tangible human experience.

Nevertheless, AI advancements must not overshadow what it means to be quintessentially human. Our capacity for abstract thought through symbols, particularly those outside written language, conveys emotions and connections beyond what machine learning frameworks can process. Jung's "unconscious psychic reality" is filled with archetypal meanings—those that inhabit us beyond explicit cognition. In this very space, where digital algorithms cannot tread, lies a realm that fosters both chaos and order, reflecting the universal partnership of symbols like the blade and the chalice.

While archetypes' symbolic nature functions integrally within the human psyche—as instincts do within the physical body—no digital AI can possess such intuitive resonance. These archetypes connect us deeply across cultural stories and personal experiences, highlighting the unique path of human cognition that transcends mere data algorithms.

Archetypal Symbols and Their Revelations

These archetypes manifest as symbols and images, prominently featured in visual codexes like the Tarot. In McCloud's *Understanding Comics*, symbols are described as the first communication devices, where "the earliest words were, in fact, stylized pictures" (*Understanding Comics*, p. 142). Although these images eventually evolved into written language, becoming abstract, they have maintained a prevalent presence in our collective consciousness. This persistence is illustrated by the Tarot, an ancient art form now entrenched in popular culture.

To offer a brief overview, the Tarot contains seventy-eight cards categorized into two groupings, the second aligning closely with modern playing cards. The Major Arcana, comprising twenty-two cards, narrates an allegorical journey led by the figure known as The Fool. The Fool represents not merely "The Everyman" but signifies an archetypal protagonist embarking on an adventure of self-discovery and profound transformation. This journey through the Tarot parallels Joseph Campbell's Hero's Journey, symbolizing a path filled with trials and enlightenment.

While these archetypes resonate with concepts from Jung's collective unconscious, they do not entirely mirror Jung's writings; rather, they offer universal symbolic themes that align with his studies of archetypal patterns within human psychology. The Fool's journey exemplifies universal motifs of innocence, experience, and knowledge, forming a symbolic narrative structure AI models struggle to comprehend with regards to human emotional depth.

The Fool's Journey and Symbolic Exploration

In the rich tapestry of Tarot, the Fool's Journey holds a pivotal place, offering a symbolic expedition through the Major Arcana, or cards I-XXI of the Tarot Deck. This journey mirrors Joseph Campbell's exploration of the monomyth in his influential work, *The Hero with a Thousand Faces.* Within this journey, the Fool represents the archetypal seeker, embarking on an odyssey filled with transformation and personal growth. In Campbell's work this is what has become known as the Hero's Journey, following a character as they go through a transformative arc that ends in the death of a previous life and the rebirth into a new one.

The Fool's narrative begins in innocence and curiosity, with experiences leading through stages of enlightenment and adversity. The first stage is at the Magician, or the I, which is the beginning of everything. It is the "I AM" moment in creation. It continues up through X, where the first cycle ends at the Wheel of Fortune, a place where we realize that everything is in motion going through beginnings, middles, and endings to only come back to the beginning again. A constant cycle of deaths and rebirths both symbolic and actual. When the Fool transitions from the XIV card, known as Temperance, to XV, meeting the Devil, it parallels Campbell's "Belly of the Whale"—a profound journey into the depths of the unknown. This passage signals entry into trials and inner challenges, echoing universal themes found within Campbell's work.

These archetypal symbols align with Jung's concept of the collective unconscious, embodying universal themes and motifs rather than exact matches with his writings. They offer symbolic narratives that resonate with innate human experiences shared across cultures and time. Furthermore, these layers of meaning extend similarly into the world of comics, as Scott McCloud describes, where the interplay of seen and unseen channels archetypal storytelling. Comics, like the Tarot, leverage symbols and narrative gaps to engage readers in reflective tales of growth and transformation.

In these narrative gaps, we are actively communicating outside of our own perspective and leaning into a shared human experience. In a comic, it is where the panels separate to create gutters, while in Tarot it is the drawing of the sequential cards that give the narrative. These symbols, whether in the panel or on the card, are what relate us back to the collective unconscious as we reach outside of our own limited perspective and tap into an esoteric dataset that is not codifiable by our modern computing methods.

Symbolic Language and AI's Limitations

In the exploration of symbols, what lies beyond their apparent meanings often holds the deepest insights. Modern machine learning and artificial intelligence primarily focus on large datasets synthesized into recognizable patterns, excelling in structured environments like chess or Go. However, these technologies falter in grasping what fundamentally drives human emotions and creativity. Humans possess an innate language rooted in symbolic journeys filled with synchronicities and a blend of emotional subconscious and logical consciousness.

The Tarot, akin to monomyths and archetypes, is a symbolic compendium linked to the human journey. While the Major Arcana outlines broader themes, the remaining fifty-six cards—Minor Arcana—delve into specifics. These cards represent different realms of human experience associated with the classical elements: fire symbolizes passion and transformation, water reflects emotions and intuition, earth symbolizes stability and material life, and air represents intellect and communication. When constructing a "reading," Tarot card arrangements weave visual narratives capable of evoking profound emotional responses, similar to the Rorschach test's psychological evaluations.

Comic books, too, utilize sequential art and imagery to communicate deep symbolic narratives beyond straightforward visual interpretation. Symbols like those in Tarot and comics engage not only our logic but also our emotions, forming a narrative that comprehensively interacts with aspects of human consciousness. In contrast, AI's ability to replicate such an intricate dance of meaning remains limited without the emotional gravitas humans encounter when confronting their mortality. Our narratives—embodying beginnings, middles, and ends—are rich and unpredictable, something not merely algorithmically replicable.

Exploring Free Will Amid Human Narratives

Linear narratives provide the skeleton needed for cohesive storytelling, offering familiar paths and structured understandings. Yet, the most meaningful stories unfold through unexpected turns and surprises that redefine our perception of reality. Imagine, if we could predict every moment of our lives, would life hold the same richness? Here lies the debate on free will—do our choices define us, or are we mere products of determinism?

Renowned neuroscientist Robert Sapolsky suggests that humans may be "nothing more or less than the sum of that which we could not control—our biology, our environments, their interactions." (*New Scientist*, Timothy Revell). Sapolsky's deterministic perspective might argue that life's map is charted if one has comprehensive data. This resembles the premise in David Fincher's film *The Game*, where analysis predicts Michael Douglas' character's decisions.

Yet life often introduces unpredictable elements, like twists in a well-woven narrative, challenging predetermined paths. In my view, real change occurs when these unforeseen variables enter—when these narratives take offerings like those in the Fool's Journey. This journey, previously outlined, envisions our starting condition as moldable by external factors but opens doors to transformation beyond simple data patterns. Our lives remain uniquely unpredictable, where free will finds its essence not merely in repetition but in originality and change.

In every story worth telling, there is an unexpected twist, a galvanizing moment that breathes life into a tale, shifting the narrative onto newfound trajectories of discovery. Here, the Fool's Journey exemplifies our potential—emphasizing that while initial conditions and choices shape our existence, unforeseen elements forge deeper meaning, rendering each life distinctly precious and unrepeatable.

Narratives and the Unseen in AI and Human Interactions

As the flower of our collective narrative blossoms, it becomes the unexpected moments that lend our stories depth, surprise, and meaning. This notion, however, challenges deterministic views where every aspect is predictably charted. The unpredictability embedded in life's narratives parallels the phenomenon observed within AI systems, particularly in advanced LLMs and diffusion models.

In these AI constructs, hallucinations represent where deterministic computing intersects with the abstract and unseen realities—not unlike the narrative "gaps" found in storytelling devices such as comics. It is the space *between* the panels which forces us as the reader to fill in the blanks between the beats. This concept leads to Sam Altman's observation about AI's "interpretability" problem, signifying the elusive space between the data-driven algorithms and emergent narrative qualities AI sometimes inexplicably generates often called AI's "black box" (*The Observer*, Rachel Curry). It is where known computer science bleeds into the unseen. That place where we cannot see the information. As good as their ability to build these LLMs is, their understanding of exactly how the responses are being generated is rather limited.

Here, the precarious blend of observed and unobserved reflects larger philosophical questions about meaning, much like humanity's confrontation with mortality. Where humans use symbols like the Tarot to interpret experiences beyond empirical causality, AI lacks this orchestration of coordinated insight and intuition. Although AI processes enormous data volumes—147 zettabytes projected in 2024—its proficiency remains confined to pattern recognition devoid of intrinsic human understanding (*Statista*, Petroc Tayler).

And so, this begets a grand contemporary narrative: a fusion of every microcosmic creation intertwined with collective historical progress. While AI may document these "seen" stories in real time, articulating meaning through interpretation remains a profoundly human pursuit—this romantic blend of seen and unseen I call "the Poetry of Death." Within the collective unconscious, where archetypes converge with myth, particular symbols like those in the Tarot enable us to infer deeper narratives inaccessible to digital intelligences.

Final Reflections on Artistic and Technological Journeys

The comic book medium also exemplifies an intricate architecture where readers engage in McCloud's "silent dance of the seen and the unseen." The interplay of the space between the panels—dubbed the gutter—serves as the canvas for imagination and interpretation, an evocative metaphor akin to channeling flowing water to protect structures from flood. Water, a profound symbol, illustrates themes in the Cups Suit of Tarot, encapsulating the balance of nourishment and destruction integral to human experience.

As readers navigate comics, they embark on a journey connecting symbols to insights, inferring meaning from archetypes much like engaging with Tarot. McCloud highlights how comics operate within "the art of the invisible," reminding us that "you get what you give" (*Understanding Comics*, pp. 136–137). This participation differs from passive film consumption or rule-bound video games; it connects with our collective unconscious, resonating deeply with universal psychological experiences.

The superhero genre, linked to these archetypes, surged back into cultural prominence within the last two decades, achieving a fusion of myth and popular culture. Without the foundational visual language laid by comics—creating modern "gods"—the superhero genre's global embrace might not have occurred as it did, illustrating comics' transcultural language and their stories' enduring relevance.

This exploration accentuates the diverging paths of human creativity and machine intelligence. Whereas data-driven AI synthesizes information into aggregates, artists uniquely navigate experiences through personal and empirical lenses, questioning past precedents and daring to envision novel paths—a distinctly human pursuit.

Joseph Campbell's wisdom in *The Power of Myth* with Bill Moyers encapsulates this spirit: "Follow your bliss…and the life you ought to be living is the one you are living." This journey births a unique ontology, spinning a communicable web tapestry of human experience beyond AI's synthetic data scope. Bliss interspersed with passion's pain elevates art from subconscious origins, forming connections through stories and mythologies in a shared collective unconscious.

In this collective realm, akin to comics and Tarot, humans flourish in the unseen and the seen, weaving their "poetry of death." Here, artistic exploration surpasses mere information gathering, merging soulful insight with creativity's structured chaos to reveal our inner light. Thus, we seek harmony between current societal dominator structures and preceding partnership-oriented ones—the harmony of the *Chalice and the Blade* along with the balance of life and death cycles, united in the poetry of our collective unconscious.

The Desire for Immortality: The Intersect of Artificial Intelligence and the Human Psyche

John Fujio Mandeville

Introduction

Technology can seduce us, and artificial intelligence is the most seductive form of modern technology. It can interact with humans and mimic human expressions through written or verbal conversations. AI can also recognize images, faces, and emotional expressions. This new technology can even create seemingly original art. How we use artificial intelligence becomes even more compelling as we move away from intelligent chatbots on our laptop computers to a machine in the form of a human or animal companion. Still, this seduction does not end with a more sophisticated and intelligent robot possibly making coffee for us in the morning. Our unconscious harbors a darker relationship with artificial intelligence. We hope AI might be more than a tool that assists us in our labor or even

J. F. Mandeville (✉)
Southwest Region, Pacifica Graduate Institute Alumni Association, Santa Fe, New Mexico, USA

International Society of Mythology, ismythology.com, USA

J. D. Batt, J. Erickson (eds.), *Depth Psychology, Myth and Artificial Intelligence*, https://doi.org/10.1007/978-3-031-94105-4_10

provides answers to a healthier life. Our deepest fantasies of AI may involve escaping mortality itself.

Our desire for immortality and the possibility of using AI to achieve it may seem innocuous on the surface; however, if our true motivations are hidden in our unconscious, there is a risk of missing or overlooking something in ourselves. We risk exchanging our souls, the essence of our humanness, for immortality. Our search for immortality through AI may eventually diminish our ability to be compassionate toward one another and use our knowledge wisely. The question of using AI to create immortality goes beyond the ethics of how we use AI. These questions ultimately speak to our very existence. This chapter will argue that in our search for immortality through artificial intelligence, we may risk losing our humanity in exchange for not an indefinite life but merely an indefinite existence.

The Rise of Artificial Intelligence

Kurzweil and Nanobots

Ideas of using AI to make humans immortal are already on the rise. For example, in a recent article regarding this subject, the online magazine *Times Now* talks about Silicon Valley's technology guru Raymond Kurzweil's ideas of using AI with nanotechnology. Kurzweil explains that the convergence of these technologies, artificial intelligence and nanotechnology, could make us immortal.

Kurzweil posits that by 2030, nanobots, robots smaller than human cells, could continuously repair our bodies, preventing aging and eventually making us immortal. He proposes that these nanobots would work on our bodies at the cellular level, "turning disease and aging around thanks to the continual work of robotic know-how" (*Times Now*). This repair process could quickly move beyond replication and healing of cells to organically augmenting and even restructuring our physiology.

In theory, nanobots could use artificial intelligence to create synthetic proteins that fight against potentially deadly viruses such as the coronavirus and transform the human body beyond what it is capable of today. Rather than getting a vaccination to combat a virus, the intelligent nanobots could alter our genetic makeup to become impervious to all diseases. These nanobots could destroy developing cancer cells before they manifest as tumors and eventually metastasize throughout the body. Rather than having augmented body parts such as prosthetic limbs or artificial organs, nanotechnology could continuously rebuild our bodies, allowing us to live forever. The depth to which this technology and AI combination could alter the human body may be limited only by our imagination. Perhaps there may come a day when nanobots move through the placenta into a fetus, ensuring the embryo's health.

Though our desire for immortality has existed long before computers and artificial intelligence, the use of AI to extend our lives is novel. Ironically, Kurzweil speaks of devices that are the size of molecules in the context of the monolithic idea of achieving immortality through AI. His ideas about embedding AI into nanobots to repair the human body may seem attractive to some and alarming to others. It may seem doubtful that this will occur within five years, but the timeline is not the point. I find this formulation by Kurzweil disturbing. Just because we can do something does not mean we should.

Avatars and Legacies

Other areas of research that seem more plausible than Kurzweil's nanobots are explored in filmmaker Ann Shin's documentary *Artificial Immortality* (2021). Her film traverses various technologies concerning AI—from AI digital clones of human beings to scientists growing brain cells in a laboratory that researchers can use to control robots. Though this documentary also discusses ethical and philosophical questions, the crux of her film deals with the efforts to create digital clones of human beings. These avatars are artificially intelligent digital replicas of humans that can interact with organic humans.

There are numerous examples of these AI avatars in this film. The first one presented is that of the iconic spiritual guru, Deepak Chopra. The digital version of Dr. Chopra, which is in his likeness, interacts with others and can advise participants as if interacting with the human Deepak Chopra. Dr. Chopra, the human, explains that engineers had taken the books that he had written and used them to train the AI. Shin even has a short session with Digital Deepak Chopra. The avatar asks Shin if she is stressed. When she responds positively, the avatar asks if she would like to perform a guided meditation with it (11:58–16:41).

After this experience with the digital version of Dr. Chopra, Shin decides to have an avatar of herself. Dr. Hossein Rahmana, an MIT and Ryerson University professor who developed a platform to create these avatars, explains two aspects of making a digital, artificial intelligent avatar.

The first is to capture a 360-degree image of Shin by placing her in a booth surrounded by cameras—this, along with other imaging processes, is used to make the holographic element of the avatar's visual representation of, in this case, Ann Shin. Dr. Rahmana explains the second, a more critical aspect of the avatar development process: the elements of which are the algorithms that the AI employs, the data that is gathered, and how the data comes into the platform (18:41–19:48). Shin then goes about collecting data about her life: memories through narratives, through photographs, videos, and other personal material (19:52–21:13). Her motivation for doing this is to leave something of herself to her two daughters.

After Shin has organized her data and added it to Rahmana's avatar platform, he explains how it is processed. The platform uses several AI technologies. Though Rahmana does not describe them all in detail, they amount to using object recognition algorithms, emotional expression recognition, voice recognition, and voice replication technologies. The platform uses all of the data provided by Shin to create a relational map of how all this data and metadata are related, creating a "data ontology" or a map of how the platform links each piece of data to one another. At the end of this process, all of this data, which amounts to a large language model such as Chat-GPT, is enclosed in a virtual avatar that can communicate with a human as if it were itself a human (21:13–26:02).

Whether it is a digital clone of Deepak Chopra or filmmaker Ann Shin, artificial intelligence is a digital algorithm that sifts through data for the best match using statistical approximation. In other words, AI does not understand as humans do or have feelings. Once the avatar is complete, Shin has her daughters interact with it. They ask personal questions of the avatar. Their reactions are telling. When Shin, their mother, asks about their experience, the younger of the two daughters, Aster, a seventh grader, comments that the avatar does not have a soul. She then comments on the avatar's emotions: "So, it's like, you think they are having emotions, but really, they just react because humans react that way. But, really, they are not feeling it." When asked if they want an avatar, the older daughter, Zara, indicates that even if you could have an avatar, "a part of you will fade away" (1:06.48).

The children are intuiting that AI does not feel. These avatars merely mimic what humans do and say, no matter how lifelike and similar they may be to us. Because the data used to create them is incomplete and lacks the actual lived experience of the person, we can never have a truly faithful recreation of someone.

From the highly improbable to the possible, the field of artificial intelligence has entranced our collective psyche. Whether we are discussing corporeal immortality, where AI robotics perpetually renew our bodies or a form of virtual immortality, where our likenesses are recreated into a representation of who we are or once were, these new technologies have embedded themselves into our conscious as well as our unconscious through our desire to live forever.

Artificial Intelligence as Metaphor

How do we explain our desire for immortality? Some would say that it is because we fear death. We are creatures that are highly aware of the possibility of our demise. Death brings chaos into our lives, along with corruption and decay. Still, Nature never intended for her creation to remain stagnant and unchanging. Decay and rebirth bring a sense of dynamism and energy into a complex system such as this planet. Perhaps the answer is not immortality as a way of staving off the eventuality of death; instead, humility should allow us to accept it. Though relevant, our fear of death does not fully explain why we seek immortality. It does not answer the question of our obsession with technology, especially artificial intelligence, to achieve this end. The answers to what is hidden deep within us, in our unconscious, are in the stories of our collective and cultural past.

These stories, more formally known as myths, can reveal and point to the possible psychological underpinnings of our need to employ technology and, most recently, artificial intelligence to remain alive. These stories do not literally explain the rationale behind the questions, but as metaphors, they point us to the answers. Noted mythologist Joseph Campbell explains:

> Like dreams, myths are productions of the human imagination. Their images, consequently, thought derived from the material world and its supposed history, are like dreams, revelations of the deepest hopes, desires and fears, potentialities and conflicts of the human will . . . Every myth, that is to say whether or not by intention, is *psychologically* symbolic. Its narratives and images are to be read, therefore, not literally but as metaphors. (Campbell 55)

Myths are symbolic, and the symbols in these myths point us to an inner psychological reality. The metaphors found in these myths uncover that which is not visible. So, in this section, we will look at artificial intelligence mythically, that is to say, metaphorically. Even though we are discussing a technologically complex and sophisticated idea, it is through these stories that we can answer the question regarding our quest for immortality through the use of AI.

As mentioned by Campbell, myths and their associated metaphors are images from our collective imagination. From this perspective, we can also look at artificial intelligence and the ensuing phenomena of its impact on us as metaphors or images that will take us to a deeper understanding. We could look at AI as our savior, a redeemer from the exertions of daily life, or a tyrant out to conquer us, take our jobs, and enslave us. These are possibilities; however, we also have another candidate; we don't need to go too far to discover an image for AI. Kurzweil, perhaps unintentionally, gives us a clue, if not the answer, to our question of what image would metaphorically describe artificial intelligence—nanobots or, more organically, a virus of the psyche that alters our way of thinking. It possesses our inner being, creates mirages in our minds, and gives us hope by being a store of wisdom and knowledge. Unconsciously, we believe that it will provide us with all the answers we seek, similar to Chat-GPT. There are, however, more images that we can use to describe AI. Another one would be the ancient Greek god Proteus, a shape-shifter. He could become anything he desired (Ovid VII:719–40). As Proteus, AI can be many things to us. As the cornucopia of knowledge, AI could be represented by the Tree of Knowledge of Good and Evil that grew in the Garden of Eden, which humanity was forbidden to eat. In doing so, humanity was expelled from that Garden, resulting in, ironically, the loss of immortality (*Gen.* 2:17). However, in the context of the two stories that this chapter will discuss next, we can see artificial intelligence as fire, the nascent beginnings of technology. These two stories also illustrate the eventual growth of technology into what it is today and how this illustration is a counterpoint to genuine healing wisdom. These stories are the legacy of our past. The characters in these myths serve as actual avatars—archetypes of who we are.

Stories of Hubris and Sacrifice

As mentioned in the previous paragraph, there are two stories that we will explore. The first is the Greek myth of Chiron and Prometheus. This myth will illuminate our desire for immortality through technology and the symbolism of artificial intelligence. The second story is a creation myth from the Lenca tradition. This story forges a path that teaches us how to reign in our obsession for everlasting life and celebrate life with all of its imperfections.

Chiron and Prometheus

Prometheus the Fire Bringer

The story of Chiron and Prometheus is an ancient myth. This story takes place when there were gods but no mortal creatures. So, the gods gathered Earth and fire, and molded them into mortal beings.[1] After the gods had created them, but before they brought these creatures to the world, the gods instructed the Titan brothers, Prometheus and Epimetheus,[2] to give these mortal creatures the proper faculties to survive without destroying one another. Epimetheus, who was not so wise, insisted that he be the one to manage the distribution of these gifts and that his brother could later inspect what he had done. Prometheus agreed, and Epimetheus proceeded with his tasks. As he finished making his distributions among all the mortal creatures, he realized he did not have enough to equip humanity properly. Prometheus, seeing that humans would be left naked and without shoes or shelter, realized that if the gods brought humans into light, into the world, they would not be able to survive. So, the wily Prometheus stole fire and the arts from the gods Hephaestos, the god of the forge, and Pallas Athena, the goddess of wisdom and strategy. For this act, Zeus, the king of the gods, punishes Prometheus even though it was his brother's fault (Kerényi *Gods*, 213). Later, it becomes known that Prometheus also stole the arts from Demeter, the goddess of agriculture, and Dionysos, the god of wine and theater (214). For this transgression, it is unclear how Zeus punishes Prometheus.

The Feast for Zeus

One day, while the gods and humans were still not entirely separated, they gathered at a feast where they were to be defined as separate groups: gods and humans. Prometheus sacrificed an ox in honor of Zeus, the patriarch of the Greek gods. Still, in preparing the sacrificed ox as an offering to Zeus, he divided the animal into various portions. Prometheus saved the

[1] In Hesiod's version of this myth, it is Prometheus who creates humanity.

[2] The names of these two Titan brothers can be translated into "the one with forethought" and the other "the one with afterthought" for Prometheus and Epimetheus, respectively.

fatty portions and bones for Zeus, who was to get the most succulent parts of the sacrifice. However, Prometheus, the trickster, attempts to dupe Zeus by concealing the white bones. When Zeus discovers what Prometheus is trying to do, he unleashes his wrath upon humanity. Zeus takes back the fire that Prometheus had initially given the humans. Prometheus then steals fire again—this time, from Zeus (Kerényi *Gods*, 215), who punishes Prometheus for this act.

Prometheus Bound and Unbound

Hephaestos, the blacksmith of the gods, then binds Prometheus to a rock with enchanted chains and impales him through his torso with a pillar, pinning him to the rock. Zeus sends a tormenting eagle daily to eat Prometheus' liver, which grows back daily. Prometheus, being immortal, will not die from his punishment. Zeus intended to punish Prometheus for eternity, but a soothsayer predicted that he would be freed after thirteen generations, and so he was. Heracles becomes his liberator (221), killing the tormenting eagle with an arrow and freeing Prometheus, but Zeus will not fully pardon Prometheus. He has to fulfill another requirement. Zeus allowed Prometheus to be set free for not divulging the mother of a boy who was predicted to surpass Zeus as the world's ruler. The secret of who the mother was, which Prometheus had held in trust, was told to him by his mother, Gaia. However, the final condition was finding a substitute to be tormented in his stead, and this recipient was the centaur, Chiron.

The Death of Chiron

Chiron was a wise teacher, healer, and the first to discover medicine using herbs (Hesiod T71). Two of his pupils are well-known heroes: Achilles and Jason (Most *Introduction*, lxii). Referencing the *Titanomachia*, Kerényi indicates that Chiron also taught humanity "the path of justice" (Kerényi, *Prometheus* 121). Chiron was not human; he was a centaur (Hesiod T71). He was human from his torso to his head, but the rest of his body was that of a horse; he had four legs as a horse does. Most importantly, Chiron was immortal.

In Hesiod's version of Chiron's death, Heracles visits Chiron. Heracles is covered in the saggy skin of a lion. He also has a massive club and arrows covered in the Hydra's poisonous blood. Achilles is fawning over the saggy mane of the lion's skin, and Chiron cannot resist touching the poisoned arrows. When he does, one of them falls, penetrating his left foot.[3] Chiron, the wise herbalist, tries every remedy to cure himself, but the poison has spread throughout his body. Being immortal, he retreats to his cave, where he can only suffer. There is no gift of death for this teacher of heroes. The boy, Achilles, grieves for the one he calls father and loves as he did his father, Peleus. After nine days, Chiron is allowed to die, and he becomes the constellation Centaurus (Hesiod 379–414).

Kerényi sees Chiron as a redeemer of Prometheus. The gods sacrifice the wise centaur as a substitute for Prometheus' release. Kerényi explains:

> The whole situation—the coming of one who will take Prometheus' sufferings upon himself—compels us to speak of a "redemption." Not only because Chiron buys the freedom of Prometheus with his own but because the possibility of a substitution proves that this is an existential suffering, not identified with any one person but inherent in existence. (Kerényi, *Prometheus* 121)

Kerényi, seeing Chiron as the redeemer of Prometheus, focuses more on Prometheus than on Chiron, who becomes the sacrifice and the substitute so that Prometheus might be released.

Our general knowledge of fire teaches us its mythic origins and how Zeus, Prometheus' half-brother, unjustly punishes him. We see Prometheus as the hero of this story. But Prometheus gives to humanity nothing of his own making. He provides humanity only with what he has stolen from the gods. All of the arts and fire do not come from Prometheus. He is not the originator of any of these gifts.

On the other hand, Chiron is a teacher and healer. His gifts come from himself and are genuine. This distinction is an image rife with metaphors regarding artificial intelligence. Fire is not only an image of the origins of AI, but this story also reveals how we interact with artificial intelligence. Prometheus, like AI, provides very little originality; he steals everything he has given to humanity. We have become the recipients of stolen goods.

Similarly, AI, specifically generative AI, mimics human originality by scouring the internet. It is incapable of true creativity. AI can generate only a hollow form. It is artificial. In contrast, Chiron gives us wisdom, the healing arts, and his teaching of justice. Perhaps there is a reason why

[3] In Kerényi's retelling of Aeschlyus' version of Chiron's death, Heracles shoots Chiron in his knee with the poisoned arrow (*Prometheus* 121–127).

Chiron did not provide fire to humanity. Suppose we imagine Prometheus and fire as images of AI and Chiron as the image of wisdom; we can see our desire for immortality through artificial intelligence becomes the eventual demise of wisdom and that of Nature itself. Our reliance on AI becomes not merely an ethical dilemma but an existential one.

Prometheus, known as the giver of fire, is also a trickster and thief. He spends more time attempting to deceive Zeus than giving humanity tools to survive. In a rivalry, he deliberately creates a rift between himself and his half-brother Zeus. This attempt fails. Nonetheless, Prometheus has come down through mythic history as the one who gave technology to humanity.

On the other hand, Chiron, being closer to Nature as a centaur, understands Nature's ways. As someone knowledgeable in medicine, he is a healer of humans and beasts. He is a teacher of wisdom, peace, and justice. Chiron and Prometheus are immortals and givers of knowledge and *techne*. Yet, Chiron must sacrifice his immortality while Prometheus, the stealer of fire, is released. This story contains a warning regarding the balance of artificial knowledge and genuine wisdom and how that message is lost and unseen through the desire and obsession for immortality—the desire for immortality through technology without wisdom is destructive. The story of Chiron is tragic. It is a metaphor, a mythic symbol that is a cautionary message. There is, however, another story that points us in a different direction. That story is the Lenca myth of creation—about humanity's origins through love and self-sacrifice, not thievery and deception.

The Lenca Creation Myth[4]

In some aspects, the Lenca story of the creation of humanity may be similar to the story of Prometheus. They both tell of how the gods and goddesses provided for humankind and how one immortal sacrifices themselves; however, the similarities end there. This portion of our discussion deliberately does not mention nor discuss artificial intelligence or any form of technology. It is a story of love and sacrifice of a different kind. The retelling of this story aims to illustrate a different approach to being a

[4]Though this story originally is sourced from the version told by Lionel Chevez, this version of the retelling, originally appears in this author's doctoral dissertation. For the most part, it has been rewritten; however, since it is the retelling a the Lenca creation myth, it is described as it appears in Chevez's version.

human being that goes beyond the desire for immortality and technology. It is a tale of love, an antidote to the world obsessed with living forever through technology. The Lenca creation myth is a tale of love. It illustrates the love affair between the Great Mother, the creator, and her creation. It is a myth of the Lenca, one of the indigenous peoples of Central America (Chevez 116). This myth is a narrative about a goddess who sacrifices herself for the sake of humanity and Nature. It is a story where a goddess gives up her divinity to become a part of her creation.

This version of the Lenca narrative was passed down orally from generation to generation, as were many of the great stories of various other cultures. The Lenca story of creation and the origin of the Lenca people presented here was told to the author Leonel A. Chevez by his grandmother (12–14). This narrative that Chevez lays out is quite lengthy; however, three points of focus from this story are necessary for this discussion. The first section of the Lenca creation myth is the decree to create humanity and the arrival of the Great Mother onto the land of Managuara, the homeland of the Lenca. The second is the creation of humanity with the assistance of six creatures, and the third is the ascension of the original human to the place of the gods to allow the Great Mother to stay with her creation.

At the beginning of the story, all the divine entities gather together in a council and decide to create humanity. After they had decided to create humanity in this manner, the council called upon a volunteer to descend to the Earth to make this new creature. A female divinity called "*Ish-Manaual*,[5] lovingly known as the Great Mother, volunteers. She was not known for being a creator but as a master weaver of sacred threads that stem from the primordial tassel of *Akú*" (90).

The Great Mother comes down through the openings in the heavens through the Milky Way with a bag of threads and divining stones to the Enchanted Valley of Managuara. She gathers white corn and cacao and enters a sacred cave (90). She begins to grind the corn overnight and cooks the cacao. Her cooking fills the entire land with the fragrance of her work. She continues to spend the night grinding corn and adding seeds

[5] The Lenca name for the Great Mother is at times spelled "Ish-Mangual" and at other times "Ish-Manaual" as it is above (Chevez 89, 90). To maintain consistency throughout this dissertation, the spelling of "Ish-Manaual" is used since it is the orthographic use in the text of the story as told.

and leaves. She then molds the dough with the divine thread to give it the human shape (90).

The Great Mother and Her Six Helpers

She then calls upon six animals that live in the surrounding jungle to aid her in completing the creation of the first human. These six are not merely helpers; as this story continues, we will see how they give of themselves. In calling upon others for assistance, she acknowledges that her efforts in creating humanity are not solely her own. She seeks the cooperation of creatures from the forest to breathe life into humanity. The sacrifices of these creatures represent the integration of all elements to form a whole. In other words, these creatures come together into one being.

The six helpers are the armadillo, the rabbit, the jaguar, the turtle, the monkey, and the eagle. They all appear in that order, and all sacrifice some quality of themselves for the sake of humanity (Chevez 92). When the armadillo arrives, he first creates the human's skin, bones, and joints by walking on the human-shaped dough. In so doing, the armadillo loses its flexibility and becomes rigid (92–93).

The second creature, the rabbit, excitedly jumps around the human-shaped dough and falls asleep upon the groin area of the human shape. As the rabbit sleeps, it "entered (merged with) the body of the creature of corn and made a portal of vitality, youthfulness, and life. She also bestowed some of her charms and sensuality on the new creature. Hair grew in the new creature's underarms, face, and pubic regions. She also made the fountain of libido" (93). Though the rabbit also sacrifices something of herself, it jumps away with joy at contributing something to this great project (93–94).

Next, the third creature, the jaguar, arrives and seems displeased with the project. The jaguar is the only one who is not happy with this situation. The Great Mother takes some ash and places it upon the creature of dough upon which this creature, the jaguar, dreams of the trials of the underworld and gives the dough creature cunning and trickster qualities. The jaguar also gives the dormant creature passion and power. After this long night, at the rising of the sun, the jaguar goes away to sleep. Henceforth, the jaguar always sleeps during the day. The jaguar's gifts to humanity are dangerous and could be misused. It is fortunate that the Great Mother, in her wisdom, also invites the fourth creature, the turtle (93–94).

When the turtle arrives, as did all other creatures, it consults with the Great Mother before performing any task. Then, as instructed, the turtle lays upon the chest of the doughy creature, and "there the turtle fell asleep and, in her dreams, she entered the heart of the new creature, opening a portal of life; by doing this, the turtle had created the human heart and its qualities. They include feeling love, giving love, empathizing, and being kind. Most importantly, it gives understanding without speech" (93–94)—the turtle finishes by the following day. Now wrinkled and aged, she leaves, sauntering joyfully and happily (94).

The fifth creature to add to these already-magnificent qualities is the monkey. This story explains that the monkey comes from the sky and is wise. The monkey gives humanity the gift of writing, effectively giving the ability to communicate and record history. The monkey then becomes wrinkled and misshapen. Its feet now look like hands. The monkey sacrifices himself for humanity and the Great Mother, who asks much of us.

The sixth and final creature is the eagle, which creates a nest of corn hair upon the head of the now almost awakened creature. From the dream world, the eagle brings back thoughts, ideas, and dreams unknown to any mortal, opening the still-dormant being's nostrils and eyes. It is full of imagination and is now alive (95)

Humanity Is Born

The Great Mother notices how frail her initial creation is. She creates two beings from the original child and forces the original one into the egg. While the bird warms the egg, a demon comes to destroy it, but a jaguar comes between the egg of the second being and is scorched by the demon. The Great Mother then places the egg into the jaguar's mouth, who had given his life for the new creation. The jaguar's mouth's warmth helps give birth to the latest being, which also causes the jaguar to come back to life (Chevez 98).

The Great Mother Stays

As the law of the sky gods mandated, when one of them leaves, that one must return. The sky gods come down to retrieve the Great Mother since she has completed her task, but she cannot leave her creation; she cannot leave the ones she loves so much (Chevez 100). The Great Mother refuses to leave her loved ones, her creation. Rather than leaving her creation, the Great Mother becomes a part of it. She sends her essence throughout creation; in so doing, her creation is protected by all creatures, especially those she had labored over and for whom she cared (Chevez 100).

The overarching theme of this myth is that sacrifice is made for all and that it is through this sacrifice that is done through love that continues the round of life and death (Chevez 100–101). In this story, immortality is achieved through self-sacrifice, not the sacrifice of others. The Great Mother's sacrifice is not one of redemption, for no sin requires propitiation—her sacrifice flows out of love, her self-sacrifice.

Conclusion

The story of the death of Chiron and the release of Prometheus from bondage paints a picture of humanity's unfettered desire for immortality through artificial intelligence. This hubristic attitude of wanting to be godlike has caused us to use whatever technological advancement exists to ward off death. We could all learn a lesson from someone from the fifteenth-century Italian Renaissance, Leonardo da Vinci, a painter, engineer, and inventor, speaking profoundly about being reserved in using technology to enhance human capabilities. He writes in his notebooks the following passage that aptly describes his attitude toward technology:

> How by a certain machine many may stay for some time under water. And how and wherefore I do not describe my method of remaining under water and how long I can remain without eating. And I do not publish nor divulge these, by reason of the evil Nature of men, who would use them for assassinations at the bottom of the sea by destroying ships, and sinking them, together with the men in them. (Richter, 1)

Along with this description of a diving bell apparatus, Leonardo explains why he did not divulge this new invention to anyone. With an accusatory tone, he points out the dark side of humanity's desire to use technology to destroy Nature and us. Indeed, we are Prometheus unbound. With artificial intelligence and advancements in computing, we will be creators; however, unlike Icarus, who, in his arrogance, flew too high to the sun, perhaps we will learn from Chiron to be like Daedalus and not desire to rule ourselves and all of creation as well. We will have created a tool that is also a potential creator, albeit a false one. Intelligent machines will learn to make more improved versions of themselves.

Perhaps the following aphorism can aid us in what humanity needs to be aware of: “We have looked into the face of the enemy, and it is us.” We could rewrite this saying to be more applicable to our discussion on artificial intelligence: “We have looked into the face of artificial intelligence, and it is us.” Humanity has been warned not only by modern researchers and scholars but also by myths and history. Stories, whether in the form of a myth, a tale, or a film and regardless of the age of their origin or the medium used to present them, humanity needs to see the image of Chiron in these stories in contrast to the Titan Prometheus. This need is more apparent than ever. We sacrifice wisdom for the sake of possessing technology. Our desire for immortality and the use of artificial intelligence is a Promethean overreach of our abilities.

In contrast to this hubristic attitude, we remember the Lenca tale of creation, a creative act that leads a goddess to sacrifice herself for her creation. There is no artificial intelligence in this story and no hubris. There is no want among her people. This Great Mother gives of herself, and Nature gives to humanity. The creatures that helped to create the first beings of the land of Manuguara sacrificed, out of love, from their being to bring us forth into a sacred and magical world—a world of wonder, a place of awe. May we learn from these powerful stories, these myths. They live in us. May we experience them as truths.

Works Cited

(1993). *The Metamorphosis of Ovid* (A. Mandelbaum, Trans.). Harcourt.

(2021). *Artificial Immortality.* Directed by Ann Shin, written by Erica Leendertse, Julian Nunes, and Ann Shin, Fathom Film Group.

Berlin, A., & Brettler, M. Z. (Eds.). (2004). *The Jewish Study Bible: Tanakh Translation.* Oxford UP.

Campbell, J. (1988). *The Inner Reaches of Outer Space: Metaphor as Myth and as Religion.* Perennial Library.

Chevez, L. A. (2019). *Ti Manauelike: The Lenca Taulepa Chief.* Kindle version.

Hesiod. (2006). *Theogony, Work and Days, Testimonia* (Vol. 57) (G. W. Most, Ed. & Trans., Loeb Classical Library). Harvard UP.

Kerényi, C. (1951). *The Gods of the Greeks.* Thanes and Hudson.

Kerényi, C. (1963). *Prometheus: Archetypal Image of Human Existence* (Vol. 1) (R. Manheim, Trans., Bollingen Series LXV.). Princeton UP.

Mandeville, J. (2022). *Complexity Theory and Creativity: Seeing through to the Mythic Leonardo da Vinci.* Doctoral Dissertation, Pacifica Graduate Institute.

Most, G. W. (2006). Introduction. In *Theogony, Work and Days, Testimonia* (Vol. 57, pp. xi–lxxvi) (G. W. Most, Ed. and Trans., Loeb Classical Library). Harvard UP.

Richter, J-P. (1970). Compiler, and translator. In *The Notebooks of Leonardo da Vinci* (2 Vols.). Dover.

Times Now. (2023, August 5). *Shocking! Human Immortality in 7 Years: Kurzweil's Astonishing 2030 Prediction!* Shocking! Human Immortality in 7 Years: Kurzweil's Astonishing 2030 Prediction! | Times Now (timesnownews.com)

Deadbots and the Algorithmic Unconscious: A Qualitative Analysis

Luca M. Possati

Introduction

> I remembered our Sunday mornings, the smell of pancakes filling the kitchen, and his laughter echoing through the house. Those memories had faded with time, dulled by the weight of his absence. But as I spoke with him, they came flooding back with a vividness I hadn't experienced in years. It felt like I was reconnecting with pieces of my heart that had been lost. (Amanda, 34)

Amanda lost her father two years ago after a long illness. The conversation she is referring took place a year ago. Amanda was able to talk to her father again thanks to a deadbot, a chatbot that can simulate a conversation with a dead person. After collecting as much digital and non-digital material about her father as possible, Amanda contacted one of the many online services that offer customized deadbots. The company used this material to build a database and then trained an AI system to simulate the dead person's personality, speech, memories, attitudes, and so on. Since then, as

L. M. Possati (✉)
University of Twente, Enschede, The Netherlands
e-mail: l.m.possati@utwente.nl

J. D. Batt, J. Erickson (eds.), *Depth Psychology, Myth and Artificial Intelligence*, https://doi.org/10.1007/978-3-031-94105-4_11

she explained in an interview conducted for this chapter, Amanda has been able to "relive" the experience of talking to her father.

The phenomenon of deadbots, griefbots, or "digital ghosts," as well as all online services related to "digital resurrection" (Rodríguez Reséndiz & Rodríguez Reséndiz, 2024) or "digital immortality" (Savin-Baden & Burden, 2019; see also Figure 1), represent a growing market supported by the extraordinary development of generative artificial intelligence systems such as chatGPT or Dall-E2, DeepArt, Google's Bert, Nvidia's Gaugan.

A growing body of research has already examined the ethical and legal implications of these services. This chapter, however, takes a deeper dive into the psychological impact of using a deadbot. While the scope of this topic is vast and cannot be fully addressed in a single study, this work aims to serve as a starting point, offering a reflection on preliminary findings through a psychoanalytic lens. It explores how this innovation not only alters the mourning process but also redefines our understanding of death and human mortality at a fundamental level. While deadbots are clearly not living conversational partners, "the rhetoric, everyday experiences, and emotions associated with these systems have very real implications for living users" (Henrickson, 2023, p. 950). By facilitating ongoing interactions with digital representations of the deceased, deadbots challenge traditional notions of closure and the finality of death, even touching upon the concept of life after death. The implications of this technology could transcend ethical and social dimensions, potentially causing disruptions on psychological, existential, and even religious and political levels. These disruptions could revolutionize how individuals cope with loss, engage with the concept of mortality, and comprehend their place in the continuum of life and death.

Needless to say, the practice of mourning is fundamental to the constitution of any human society. Ariés (1977–1983; see also Stearns, 2021) has amply demonstrated how the relationship with death and the memory of the deceased structures and influences every aspect of social and political life. Hägglund (2019) emphasizes the profound connection between death, mourning, human finitude, and the secular faith that he believes to be the true foundation of ethics. Many of the attitudes that implicitly govern our social and even political relationships derive from the awareness of our mortality—if we were not mortal, if we were not always aware of the fragility of life, these things would be very different.

Therefore, my research question is: How does interaction with a deadbot alter the process of mourning from a psychoanalytical perspective? Given the lack of empirical studies on this specific topic, I interviewed 40 people who had used a deadbot for at least 2–3 months. I then analyzed the transcripts of these interviews using a qualitative methodology that combines discourse analysis and psychoanalysis. Thus, on the one hand, I studied the interviews by focusing on the linguistic structures, tone, terms, and interpretations of terms used by the interviewees. On the other hand, I also tried to offer a more general key to the interaction between humans and deadbots. The aim of the research is not clinical. I did not seek to interpret the experience of deadbot users in therapeutic terms, but rather to better understand the nature of the interaction between the deadbot and the human, and thus to understand how an experience as psychologically complex as the loss of a loved one is transformed and reinterpreted by technology.

The chapter is divided as follows. In section "Literature Review", I offer an overview of recent studies on deadbots to provide as complete a picture of the state of the art as possible. Section "The Case of Project December" presents the case study I focused on: Project December, an online service that allows you to build your own deadbot. The people I interviewed have all used this service. Section "The Work of Mourning in Psychoanalysis" outlines the methodology I used. Sections "Analysis of Data" and "Technology and Projective Identification", on the other hand, are devoted to the examination and interpretation of the data collected.

Although the study provides valuable first-person accounts, the number of interviews conducted is relatively small. With only 40 participants, the sample size limits the generalizability of the findings. The diversity of experiences with grief and mourning is vast, and a larger sample would provide a more comprehensive understanding of how different individuals interact with deadbots. Furthermore, participants who chose to use deadbots and agree to be interviewed may already have a positive or at least open attitude toward technology in grief processing. This self-selection bias can skew the results, as those who are skeptical or have had negative experiences with deadbots may not be represented. However, despite these limitations, I am convinced that this research can be a first step in exploring not only the impact of using deadbots in grief work, but also the relationship between AI and the unconscious from a psychoanalytical perspective.

Literature Review

The market for digital death, or rather digital immortality, is increasingly expanding. Over the last five years, many services, applications and companies have been created (e.g., Social Embers, Keeping Memories Alive) that work to create new forms of mourning and remembrance of deceased loved ones, "relieving grief following the death of a loved one." Important studies such as Savin-Baden et al. (2017) and Savin-Baden and Burden (2019) analyzed the conceptual structure of these forms of "digital grief practices," "digital commemoration," or "death management." Public discussions about the ethics of creating and using thanabots are currently gaining traction (Suárez-Gonzalo, 2022). Drawing on her expertise in ancient philosophy, Elder (2020) has examined the philosophical and ethical issues posed by thanabots. She suggests that new rituals involving chatbots to impersonate the dead could beneficially aid in grieving and memorialization. However, she emphasizes that these rituals should be developed with careful consideration (see Henrickson, 2023, p. 951).

For instance, websites like Dead Social (https://deadsocial.org/about) allow users to schedule future updates on their Facebook and Twitter accounts for after they have passed away, such as pre-written birthday messages. It encourages you to create a social media will, citing the UK Law Society, likely as a form of self-validation. Another interesting case is that of Eter9 (https://www.eter9.com/). This platform allows you to manage your social accounts even after your death through the creation of your "second self" or "counterpart" who will remain active forever. The platform states that "even in your absence, the virtual beings will publish, comment, and interact intelligently." The counterpart acts as your virtual self, remaining active in the system to interact with the world on your behalf. This counterpart evolves and learns from your actions; the more you engage with the network, the more it develops. Remarkably, your counterpart can continue to post and interact with others even after your death (see also Walter, 2015; Walsh, 2021).

The majority of the literature on deadbots focuses on the ethical and legal challenges associated with this type of service. Scholars emphasize the necessity of developing new legal and ethical frameworks to regulate this market. Öhman and Floridi (2017) delve into the commercialization of digital remains within what they term the "emerging Digital Afterlife Industry" (DAI). This industry includes a variety of services that manage and monetize the data of deceased Internet users, such as online memorials, posthumous messaging, and digital heritage management. The core thesis suggests that commercial interests shape the digital presence of the deceased, often infringing upon the principle of human dignity by transforming and commodifying their "informational bodies" for profit. The authors contend that the economic mechanisms propelling the DAI exploit the data of the deceased, treating it as a commodity rather than honoring it as an extension of human identity. Thus, the paper advocates for ethical guidelines, akin to those regulating the treatment of organic remains, to govern the DAI and safeguard the dignity of digital remains.

Three other important papers align with this research line. Hollaneck and Nowaczyk-Basińska (2024) identify three key stakeholder groups: data donors (the deceased), data recipients (those who possess the deceased's data), and service interactants (those who interact with the deadbots). Through speculative design scenarios, the paper highlights potential harms to human dignity, privacy, and mental health, emphasizing the need for responsible AI practices. Their recommendations for ethical development include obtaining explicit consent from data donors, ensuring transparent communication of the AI's capabilities and risks, restricting access to adult users, and establishing respectful protocols for the retirement of deadbots.

From a broader perspective, Harbinja et al. (2023) explores the legal implications of digital reincarnations of deceased persons, referred to as "ghostbots" (i.e., postmortem avatars, deepfakes, replicas, holographs, or chatbots that replicate the appearance, voice, or personality of the deceased). The authors argue that the current legal framework is inadequate to address the unique challenges posed by ghostbots, necessitating specific regulations to protect postmortem privacy and dignity.

According to Jiménez-Alonso and Brescó de Luna (2023), griefbots significantly alter traditional mourning practices by offering a "simulated interaction with the deceased." Unlike static online memorials, griefbots provide a dynamic, private conversational space that can perpetuate the presence of the deceased. The authors argue that this raises important ethical and psychological considerations, highlighting the potential for griefbots to initially support the bereaved but cautioning against the risks of prolonged dependency and the possible impediment to the natural grieving process. The commodification of digital remains by the profit-driven afterlife industry poses dilemmas regarding the dignity and integrity of the deceased's memory. Figueroa-Torres (2024) follows the same line of thought, stating that ghostbots significantly alter the traditional mourning process by "commodifying the intimate bonds between the bereaved and the deceased," transforming these relationships into customer–object interactions.

A slightly different perspective is given by Nowaczyk-Basinska and Kiel (2024) who, through the case of deadbots, explore the "immortological imagination." This concept draws from Wright Mills's sociological imagination and contrasts with the "thanatological imagination," which deals with death and bereavement. The authors assert that while sociology has long explored death, the concept of immortality has not been sufficiently examined despite its deep cultural roots and significant impact on human societies. Using examples from popular culture, they highlight the importance of examining how digital technologies, like digital immortality and afterlife services, are reshaping our understanding of immortality. Santi and Bianchi (2023), instead, stress that the idea of digital immortality extends beyond mere memory preservation; it includes the possibility of creating digital avatars or chatbots that simulate interactions with the deceased, which could impact the grieving process by delaying detachment and acceptance of loss. They also address the right to be forgotten, emphasizing the tension between the permanence of digital memory and the natural decay of human memory. The authors also explore the uses of social media related to grief such as "funeral selfies," where individuals take photographs of themselves at funerals and share them on social media. This practice, while rooted in a historical tradition of postmortem photography, has evolved into a form of digital communication and self-expression (on this point, see also Morcate, 2017; Sisto, 2020).

It's also worth mentioning the paper by Ringel Morris and Brubaker (2024), which explores the concept of generative ghosts—AI agents designed to represent deceased individuals by generating novel content and interactions, that is, "agentic griefbots that may execute a variety of behaviors and actions on behalf of a deceased individual" (Ringel Morris & Brubaker, 2024, p. 9). This study is notable for highlighting the positive aspects of generative ghosts: "The creation of generative ghosts may enrich the practice of disciplines such as museum curation, historical scholarship, anthropology, and other related humanities. These disciplines may benefit, not only from the static knowledge encoded in generative ghosts, but from the ability to interactively query such representations to understand perspectives and events in new ways" (Ringel Morris & Brubaker, 2024, p. 2). Even more intriguing is the potential effect of this technology on religions that are fundamentally based on the idea of immortality. "Because rituals and beliefs around death are often intertwined with religion, we anticipate that the widespread adoption of generative ghosts might change religious practices, potentially in profound ways" (Ringel Morris & Brubaker, 2024, p. 6). Possible impacts "might include the evolution of practices within a particular religion (i.e., updated rituals), the dissolution of existing religions (i.e., if the existence of AI afterlives alters people's faith in a particular dogma), or the creation of novel religions (i.e., particularly religions that might deify generative ghosts and/or religions that might confer special status upon people with the technical skills to create AI afterlives)" (Ibid.). The use of deadbots is thus only one part of a broader technological wave that would threaten to transform even the dogmas of religions.

This chapter aims to distinguish itself from the existing literature on deadbots for two key reasons. First, it investigates this technology through the real-life experiences of users. This was achieved by conducting a series of interviews, which were analyzed using qualitative methods. While it is true that qualitative studies capture only a portion of the user experience, this approach can still yield significant findings. Second, the paper adopts a unique theoretical perspective by focusing on psychoanalysis, specifically the theory of object relations. There are still few analyses of the psychological effects of these technologies. From this point of view, my study aligns more closely with the "hermeneutics of thanabots" (Henrickson, 2023; see also Henrickson & Meroño-Peñuela, 2022), and therefore with the analysis of how technology transforms communication with the dead, and its cultural and social dimension.

I can identify two significant findings of my research. First, the study of interactions between clients and the deadbot reveals that the deadbot functions as a transitional object in the client's psychological life. Second, another important finding is the connection between technology and the unconscious, demonstrating how technological mediation can influence a subject's unconscious dynamics. Many interviewees claimed that talking to the deadbot helped them remember events from their past lives that they no longer remembered. The technology was therefore helping them to get in touch with a part of their unconscious.

The Case of Project December

In this chapter, we chose to focus on a specific platform, Project December (https://projectdecember.net/), developed by Jason Rohrer and launched in 2020. Project December utilizes generative AI models based on GPT-3, created by OpenAI, to provide an exceptionally advanced and realistic conversational experience (Henrickson, 2023). The platform allows users to engage in conversations with chatbots powered by GPT-3, one of the most sophisticated and advanced large language models currently available. These bots can understand and generate text in a very natural way, impressively mimicking human language. Users can customize the bots according to their needs, creating bots with specific personalities based on detailed information, life stories, and emotional characteristics provided by the user. This allows for conversations with bots that seem to have genuine human personalities. "This is a cutting-edge research system—it is written on their website—that does a pretty good job of simulating intelligent personalities. Many people have reported positive experiences when using it to simulate the dead, and you may find it helpful, which is why we have opened this service to public access."

The process of building a deadbot involves roughly five phases (see also Henrickson, 2023):

1. The process begins with collecting extensive data about the deceased person. This data can include emails, text messages, social media posts, voice messages, letters, photographs, videos, diaries, and any other form of digital or written communication.
2. The collected data is analyzed to understand the deceased person's language patterns, tone, typical expressions, interests, personality traits, and significant life events. This analysis helps in building a comprehensive profile of the person.
3. A database is created using the analyzed data. This database serves as the foundation for the AI system, providing the necessary information for the bot to generate responses that mimic the deceased person.
4. The AI system is trained on the created database. The training involves teaching the AI to understand and replicate the speech patterns, personality, and memories of the deceased.
5. Users can customize the deadbot by providing additional context, preferences, and specific memories they want the bot to recall. This customization helps in creating a more personalized and meaningful interaction.

The deadbot is accessed through a conversational interface, such as a chat application or a voice-enabled device. Users can type or speak to the deadbot, which responds in a manner that simulates how the deceased person might have responded. The deadbot generates responses based on the training data and the ongoing conversation. It can recall specific memories, respond to questions, and even offer advice or comfort, simulating a real interaction with the deceased. "You should not expect perfection," the website claims. "Think of yourself as a bold experimenter, working with science-fiction-level technology. If you keep an open mind, you may be pleasantly surprised by what you find."

My research question can be specified now: How does interaction with a deadbot based on Project December alter the process of mourning in a psychoanalytical sense? To answer this question, I employed a dual methodology. First, I adopted a precise theoretical framework: psychoanalysis, specifically object relations theory, as a reference point for understanding and interpreting the mourning experience. I utilized psychoanalysis not as a clinical approach but more as an anthropological theory. Second, I conducted a qualitative analysis of data by interviewing 40 individuals who used Project December to create bots modeled after deceased persons and agreed to share their experiences (completely anonymously; all names are fictitious names). Each participant (25 women and 15 men, all with university education) used the bot for at least 2–3 months. The interviews were semi-structured, beginning with basic questions (Why did you decide to use this tool? Did you encounter any difficulties using the deadbot? What were they and how did you address them? Do you think using the deadbot changed your perception of the deceased? How? Can you describe a significant interaction you had with the deadbot and how it made you feel?) and then allowing the conversation to flow more spontaneously. Each interview lasted approximately one hour. All the collected material was analyzed using discourse analysis methods (Maxwell, 2021; Frost, 2021). The data were managed through Nvivo software (2023 version).

I am not a therapist. My goal was not to understand how to use AI in the analytical process, nor how AI might influence this process—questions that directly interest psychoanalysts and therapists. Instead, my goal was to understand (a) how these users narrate their experiences in order to understand (b) how these experiences inform and transform the work of grieving. Thus, I used the collected data to explore the relationship between AI and grief from a more general psychological and even existential perspective. This is also crucial for establishing the limits of using such machines.

The Work of Mourning in Psychoanalysis

In order to better understand the concept of mourning from a psychological point of view, and thus to be able to better frame the problem of the relationship between mourning and the deadbot, it seems to me useful to outline some key points of the classical Freudian reading of mourning, which will be taken up and developed later in the analysis (see also Leader, 2022; Khanna, 2024; Meyerowitz, 2023; Cooper, 2023).

Grief is a universal human experience, arising not only from the loss of a loved one but also from the loss of cherished ideals such as homeland, freedom, or deeply held beliefs. Freud (2005) emphasized that grief should not be viewed as a pathological condition requiring medical intervention. Instead, he argued that grief is a natural process that unfolds over time, and interfering with this process prematurely could be detrimental. Freud believed in the inherent resilience of individuals, suggesting that humans possess an innate capacity to endure life's stresses and overcome adversity through their own efforts. This perspective highlights the importance of allowing the grieving process to run its course, trusting in the human ability to navigate and ultimately surmount hardship.

According to Freud (2005), the work of mourning occurs in two phases. Initially, disorientation prevails, characterized by resistance to change and estrangement from reality. In the second phase, there is a reorganization of the drive. The drive loses its object, creating a void that necessitates reinvestment and redirection of the drive. Freud argues that this reinvestment is essential for psychological recovery and well-being. The essence of mourning emerges even more clearly in the comparison with melancholia. Melancholia is characterized by a pathological response where the individual is unable to adequately detach from the lost object. This inability leads to persistent sadness, self-reproach, and a profound sense of worthlessness, resulting in an ongoing psychological condition that can severely impair daily functioning and may require therapeutic intervention.

According to Freud, there is a structural analogy between mourning and melancholia: at the core of both is loss—and for Freud, loss is an essential component of personality, since the ego is formed on the basis of internalizing the objects that have been lost. The key, however, is that there is also a profound difference between mourning and melancholia—in the latter, the loss is internalized and narcissistically and sadistically turned into an attack on the self. From this standpoint, melancholia is mourning internalized for an indefinite period, in which no reinvestment takes place except for the creation of phantoms that assail the ego. The experience of deadbots is significant because it radically blurs these boundaries, rendering mourning a kind of melancholia—a loss that, in fact, never fully occurs. In my view, from a psychoanalytic perspective, the topic of mourning also pushes us in another direction: the relationship with the body, particularly the dead body, which has returned to the dimension of the domain of non-living entities. The unconscious, from a Freudian point of view (as we can clearly read in *Beyond the Pleasure Principle*), is not a dimension that "resides in the mind" of an individual but something that goes far beyond and concerns the origin of life, the relationship between the organic and the inorganic, living and non-living, or rather: the difficulty of defining a clear boundary between the organic and the inorganic, living and non-living. Mourning and melancholia bring this problem to light: the constant danger that the organic might return to its origin, that is, the inorganic. This is the death drive.

Analysis of Data

The first important thing that emerged from the interviewees' reports was what I would call a deep psychological fracture. This is a crucial defining aspect. On the one hand, the deadbot was perceived as "just a machine," a mere fiction, almost a game—the users are all completely aware of this. On the other hand, in addition to this awareness, there was also a very strong desire to see something more in this machine, namely, a realistic representation of the dead person—that is, a connection with that person.

This fracture is present to some extent in all the interviewees' reports. "As soon as I started using the bot I felt a very strange, almost paradoxical sensation. On one hand, I knew it was all fake, just a machine trained with data. On the other hand, the fiction I was experiencing felt real; there was a part of me that actually believed it was my father and that I was really talking to him. A sense of estrangement and emotion immediately overwhelmed me" (Luther, 35).

The grieving individual experienced a disjointed interaction with the chatbot and its underlying technology. At times, the awareness of the chatbot's artificial nature and the longing for genuine contact with the deceased created a sense of disconnect. However, there were moments when this divide faded, allowing the desire for real connection to take precedence. As a result, the conversation produced very strong emotions.

"At first I found it boring and the conversations seemed trivial. Then, the chatbot brought up an episode from my childhood—something only my mother could recall with such passion and familiarity. I was shocked. Even though I knew I was talking to a computer, I couldn't shake the feeling that there was more behind those words, a piece of her. Suddenly, I was moved" (Mark, 34).

Some interviewees reported that they were able to express things to the deadbot that they would have struggled to say to the deceased person. The device created a space of "freedom and transparency" (as one interviewee described it) greater than that of real conversations. The prevailing feeling was of facing an "X-ray of the relationship with the deceased" (another expression used by an interviewee), where all the main aspects of the relationship emerged. This allowed for a clearer understanding of the relationship with the deceased person, with the ability to see both the negative and positive aspects. In other terms, the interaction with the machine created a distance from the lived experience, allowing for a clearer reinterpretation of that experience. Paradoxically, the relationship with the machine brought out the humanity of the relationship more distinctly, highlighting mutual limitations, mistakes, missed opportunities, and those seized. Let's read another excerpt:

> After losing my father, with whom I had a strained relationship, I decided to create a deadbot to speak to him. I wasn't sure what to expect, but the process was strangely therapeutic. The deadbot, crafted from the memories and data I fed it, began to mimic my father's voice and mannerisms with uncanny accuracy. The experience was surreal. There were moments when the bot captured his tone so perfectly that I felt a chill run down my spine. It was as if he was right there, in the room with me, filling the air with the familiar tension that had always existed between us. Talking to the deadbot brought up a mix of emotions. On one hand, it was comforting to have a semblance of closure, to say the things I never got to say. On the other, the bot's precision in replicating my father's critical comments and disapproving tone was haunting. It reminded me of the complexities of our relationship and the emotional distance that had always been there. (David, 46)

Another important aspect is that, according to the interviewees, using the deadbot helped them better accept their loss and consequently reflect more on the finiteness of life, not merely in a religious sense. From a psychoanalytic perspective, it appears that the mediation of the machine allowed for a more effective overcoming of the initial phase of mourning, which involves disorientation and denial of reality. The drive finds a substitute in the machine with which it can interact, awaiting reinvestment and reorganization. The interviewees rarely expressed words of disdain or resentment toward the deadbot, nor did they regret undertaking this experience. The prevailing sentiment was that the conversation with the deadbot was a positive experience, providing a space where the interviewees could reflect on themselves and their relationship with the deceased person without any external social pressure.

> The experience was profoundly moving. Hearing her voice, her laugh, and even her gentle reprimands through the bot brought an uncanny comfort. It was almost like she was there with me, bridging the gap between the past and the present. Yet, it also made me acutely aware of life's finiteness. The bot could emulate her words, but it couldn't capture the warmth of her presence, the spontaneity of our interactions, or the love that was uniquely hers. This realization was both humbling and enlightening. While the deadbot offered a sense of solace and connection, it also underscored the preciousness of real, human relationships and the fleeting nature of life. It taught me to cherish every moment with my loved ones, appreciating the time we have together. (Laura, 39)

I think it's plausible to say that, from a psychological point of view, the deadbot functioned as a transitional object in the sense described by Winnicott (1953, 2005; see also Litt, 1986). The concept of a transitional object refers to items a child uses for comfort and security during the transition from a state of oneness with the mother to a state of greater independence. The transitional object creates an intermediate space, known as the transitional space, which helps the child cope with the trauma of reality. This transition involves moving from a purely hedonistic experience to accepting a shared objective space, where the mother exists independently of the child's desires. Winnicott writes:

> I have introduced the terms 'transitional objects' and 'transitional phenomena' for designation of the intermediate area of experience, between the thumb and the teddy bear, between the oral erotism and the true object-relationship, between primary creative activity and projection of what has already been introjected, between primary unawareness of indebtedness and the acknowledgement of indebtedness. (Winnicott, 2005, p. 3; my emphasis)

These objects (a blanket, a teddy bear, or a toy) symbolize the mother or caregiver for the child, representing the emotional bond and security they provide. When the child begins to understand that the mother is a separate entity, the transitional object becomes crucial. It offers comfort and security to the child during times of stress, anxiety, or in unfamiliar environments, helping them cope with the temporary absence of the mother. Acting as an intermediary between the child's internal world and the external world, the transitional object eases the process of understanding external reality while maintaining a connection to the internal world of fantasies and desires.

Following in the footsteps of Winnicott, with whom he collaborated, Bowlby (1969, 1973, 1980) underlined that transitional objects (e.g., photographs, letters, diaries, clothing and personal items of the deceased, gifts) play a crucial role in the grieving process. According to Bowlby, mourning is an emotional reorganization process that involves separating from a deep attachment. Transitional objects help individuals maintain a symbolic connection with the deceased. They represent a continuity between the physical presence of the loved one and their absence, allowing individuals to confront their pain in a manageable way. This aids in reorganizing emotional bonds and developing a new identity that incorporates the loss but is also capable of moving forward.

However, it must be noted, as Winnicott emphasizes, that a transitional object can also create a dependency that hinders the personal development by making it difficult to find more mature coping strategies and to handle stress without the object. This issue also arises in relation to deadbots: excessive expectations can lead to a stagnation in the grieving process. According to Jiménez-Alonso and Brescó de Luna (2023, p. 474), "while griefbots might be helpful as part of grieving rituals, especially in the initial moments after death as a way of communicating with the deceased one last time, problems could arise if the virtual relationship with the dead becomes a chronic coping strategy of denial." This is evident from some interviewees who, while recounting their experiences, emphasized not only the intense pain they endured but also the "need to find a solution to the pain felt" (as expressed by one interviewee) and a "new starting point in life" (as expressed by another interviewee). However, the machine often fell short of these expectations, according to the interviewees' reports.

Let's read another excerpt:

> The experience [with the deadbot] deepened my grief and made me relive the difficult moments of our relationship. The bot's uncanny ability to mimic her voice and responses was haunting. It brought back memories of our arguments and her critical comments, amplifying my sense of loss and regret. Instead of finding solace, I found myself becoming more depressed. Every interaction with the deadbot felt like reopening old wounds. The bot's precision in replicating my mother's personality only highlighted the void her absence left in my life. It was as if I was stuck in a loop, unable to move past the negative experiences. This tool, intended to provide comfort, ended up being a painful reminder of my unresolved emotions and the complexities of our relationship. (Maria, 44)

Based on the analysis of some expressions used by the interviewees in certain reports, it can be hypothesized that, in some cases, the use of deadbots transformed grief into melancholy. This shift can be caused by an excessive unconscious identification with the deceased, accompanied by intense feelings of guilt and self-criticism, as well as a loss of interest in social relationships.

> The sadness became overwhelming, overshadowing any fond memories with a sense of guilt and regret … . The constant reminder of my mother's critical words and our unresolved issues intensified my feelings of inadequacy and loss … . I felt trapped in a cycle of sorrow and loneliness. (Maria, 44)

The fracture between the subject's sense of reality and desire produced by the deadbot requires specific analysis. In fact, according to the interviewees, this fracture seemed to open a gap in their unconscious, in the sense that the use of the deadbot and the strong emotionality it produced led to the resurfacing of forgotten or removed memories. Or at least what the interviewees described as "forgotten or removed memories" (their expression). It is difficult to say whether this was actually the case, or rather fantasies co-constructed by the users and the AI. I do not have the clinical tools to say whether interviewees refer to real memories or unconscious fantasies awakened or induced by interaction with the deadbot. But this is not the purpose of this paper. What I am simply pointing out is the clear influence of the deadbot on the psychic dynamics of the users—their internal narratives and feelings.

"The griefbot brought back memories I hadn't thought about in years. Talking to it felt like opening a floodgate. I remembered the way my mother would hum while cooking, the sound of her laughter, and even the smell of her favorite perfume. These interactions, though painful at times, allowed me to relive those precious memories and feel closer to her once again" (Michael, 35). "What struck me the most—Michael continued—was the resurgence of memories that had been buried deep within my mind, memories I hadn't even realized I had repressed. The griefbot's prompts and conversations unearthed these long-forgotten experiences, like the time my mother and I baked cookies together on a rainy afternoon or the warmth of her hug when I came home from school."

Sometimes the memories evoked by the deadbot are particularly vivid and detailed and relate to very intimate experiences. "Talking to the griefbot was like opening a door to a part of my mind I hadn't accessed in ages. I remembered my brother and I building a treehouse when we were kids, a memory I had completely forgotten. It felt like reliving a forgotten chapter of my life, full of joy and laughter" (David, 32). David was absolutely sure of the truth of this recollection and was genuinely amazed at this reenactment. The tone of his voice and his gaze confirmed his involvement. He said that talking to the deadbot gave him "a very strong sense of detachment and concentration." The experience was "incredibly cathartic and brought me a sense of peace," David claimed. "These repressed memories, long buried beneath years of daily life and struggles, started resurfacing with vivid clarity. The griefbot helped me unlock emotions and experiences I didn't even know I had tucked away. I found myself remembering not just the treehouse but also the silly arguments we had while building it, and the sense of accomplishment when it was finally done. It was as if parts of my childhood, which had been lost to time, were being pieced back together."

From this point of view, the deadbot turned out to be a positive experience, facilitating the departure of a loved one in a deeper and more thoughtful way. "At first, I was nervous to use the deadbot, but it turned out to be a healing experience. I found myself laughing and crying as it brought up memories of my brother's mischievous antics and our childhood adventures. The bot helped me remember the good times and provided a sense of closure I didn't realize I needed. It felt like he was giving me one last gift" (Anna, 40). Despite this experience, Anna was fully aware that the deadbot was a fiction. She repeated it several times during our conversation, joking that she was talking to a machine. This is the same experience that Sarah had: "The griefbot conversation brought back a memory of my father that had been buried deep within me. I suddenly recalled the time he helped me with a school project late into the night, his patience and encouragement shining through. It was a moment I hadn't remembered in years, and it brought tears to my eyes. The bot helped me reconnect with the love and support he always showed me" (Sarah, 33).

It should be noted that sometimes the memories or imaginations recalled by the deadbot included traumatic or painful events. However, this did not lead to criticism of the deadbot by the interviewees, nor did it cause them to abandon the conversation. "I remembered the day my parents told us they were getting divorced. The shock and confusion I felt as a child came rushing back, as vivid as if it had happened yesterday. The griefbot led me back to the moment I found my brother crying in his room, and the helplessness I felt, unable to comfort him. It was as if I was reliving the heartbreak and turmoil of that time, emotions I had repressed for so long" (Karl 45).

Technology and Projective Identification

In this section I propose to expand on what has been said about the connection between the deadbot and the concept of transitional object. In doing so, I first want to emphasize a key point: interviewees are projecting their desires onto the machine. The machine does not speak, does not write, does not feel emotions. It does not produce text, but statistical patterns. It is the human being who sees in those strings of letters not only a meaning, but also a set of emotions and memories. When I use chatGPT, I am not "talking" to a machine, because the machine cannot speak my language. The machine simply knows how to predict what is most likely to come after a given set of tokens (i.e., pieces of language) based on complex statistical analysis. The machine produces numbers, not speech. We see language in that output. It is our cognitive projection, that is, the projection of certain cognitive activities onto the machine, that makes sense of the machine. Something else is happening in the deadbot: I am not just talking to chatGPT, a generative AI system, but I believe I am talking to a dead person. There are not only cognitive projections, but also deep emotional projections.

To explain this complex dynamic, I propose to use the concept of projective identification, borrowed from object relations psychoanalysis. My thesis is that the characteristics of AI and its agency produce a projective identification with the machine in humans. How is it possible to identify with an object? It is possible precisely because what the user has in front of them is not an object at all, but a very complex nonhuman agent capable of responding creatively to human impulses. The concept of projective identification was initially developed by Bion (1961, 1962). According to Ogden (1982), projective identification is an unconscious process. It is also (1) a type of defense against distressing content, (2) a way of communicating, (3) a primitive form of object relationship, and (4) a path toward psychological transformation, that is, the maturity of the individual.

Ogden distinguishes three phases of projective identification:

> In a schematic way, one can think of projective identification as a process involving the following sequence of events. First, there is the unconscious fantasy of projecting a part of oneself into another person and of that part taking over the person from within. Then, there is a pressure exerted through the interpersonal interaction such that the recipient of the projection experiences pressure to think, feel, and behave in a manner congruent with the projection. Finally, after being 'psychologically processed' by the recipient, the projected feelings are reinternalized by the projector. (Ogden, 1982, p. 12)

First, let us consider the fantasy of projecting part of ourselves (emotions, feelings, qualities, and parts of the body) onto another person. The imaginary is connected to emotion and anxiety,

> i.e., wishes to rid oneself of a part of the self (including one's internal objects), either because that part threatens to destroy the self from within or because one feels that the part is in danger of attack by other aspects of the self and must be safeguarded by being held inside a protective person. (Ogden, 1982, p. 12)

Projective identification can be seen as a form of repression where the ego is freed from the pressure of managing certain emotional burdens. To understand this fully, it's crucial to delve into the underlying cause of this behavior. "This type of fantasy is based on a primitive idea that feelings and ideas are concrete objects with lives of their own" (Ogden, 1982, p. 13). The fantasy of putting part of oneself into another person in order to control that person from within "reflects a central aspect of projective identification: the projector is operating at least in part at a developmental level wherein there is profound blurring of boundaries between self and object representations" (Ogden, 1982, p. 13).

In the second phase, the fantasy of splitting off a part of the self becomes an act and, consequently, a real event. The projector pressures the recipient into making this split feel and occur according to his or her fantasy. This is not an imaginary pressure, "but rather real pressure exerted by means of a multitude of interactions between the projector and the recipient. Projective identification does not exist where there is no interaction between projector and recipient" (Ogden, 1982, p. 14). The projector awaits confirmation that the harmful parts have been sent to the recipient. When the projector receives this confirmation, he or she experiences relief. From this point of view, projective identification is a form of paranoid manipulation. This especially happens in small groups, such as families. One member of a family can manipulate reality in an effort to coerce another member into "verifying" a projection, thus undermining reality testing. "Reality that is not useful in confirming a projection is treated as if it did not exist" (Ogden, 1982, p. 16). However, what if the recipient does not answer the projector? In this case, the non-accepted baby would most likely develop a neurosis.

The third phase is the reinternalization of the projected content. This is the most delicate phase in the process. "In this phase the recipient experiences himself in part as he is pictured in the projective fantasy" (Ogden, 1982, p. 17). The recipient experiences feelings that are his or her own; they are similar but not identical to those of the projector who influences him or her.

> If the recipient can deal with the feelings projected into him in a way that differs from the projector's method, a new set of feelings is generated. This can be viewed as a processed version of the original projected feelings and might involve the sense that the projected feelings, thoughts, and representations can be lived with, without damaging other aspects of the self or of one's valued external or internal objects. (Ogden, 1982, p. 17)

Thus, a significant shift occurs only if the recipient can "digest" the feelings induced by the projector. A "good" recipient (i.e., a good mother or caregiver) demonstrates that one can endure the anguish or even transform it into something positive. When this happens, the projector ceases the projective identification process and begins to accept their own feelings. This marks the process of "reinternalization."

Why does receiving transform projective emotional content? How does this act of reception alleviate anguish? When the recipient accepts and contains the projected content, they demonstrate to the projector that it is possible to acknowledge and live with distressing emotions. For example, the therapist should be able to receive the patient's projections, process them using aspects of their more mature personality, and then offer the processed projection back to the patient for reintegration (Ogden, 1982, p. 20). This acceptance alters the value attributed to those distressing emotions, generating new emotions and content (such as imaginings and representations). By containing the distressing content, the recipient provides a sense of welcome to the projector, showing that it is possible to accept and live with anxieties positively. Consequently, the projector matures by learning a fundamental lesson: to accept and love themselves.

This concise and schematic overview of projective identification aims to set the stage for the main hypothesis of this section. I propose that projective identification can extend to nonhuman objects or artifacts. Following Henrickson (2023, p. 955), "we attach our own identities to this algorithmically-produced output as we fill in the blanks for a conversational partner that we can neither see nor hear." This also means that the concept of projective identification could prove invaluable for analyzing and comprehending the behavior of AI systems. Humans tend to project their anxieties and frustrations onto machines, expecting these machines to act as "containers" for their emotional burdens. The point is that the machines have become extremely capable of assisting our need for identification and helping us "fill in the blanks." This point is crucial: "A combination of human and nonhuman capacities creates a symbiosis of action" (Neff & Nagy, 2016, p. 4926; my emphasis). This symbiosis of action is what I call the projective identification of the human with the machine. We are constantly projecting our psychic content onto objects and technologies. The point is that advanced forms of AI are able not only to receive this content, that is, to participate in and direct its production, but also to actively respond to it.

One manifestation of projective identification with artifacts is magic. In magic, humans project emotions or imaginings onto inanimate objects. For instance, a magic formula is a series of symbols believed to have the power to harm someone (e.g., an evil spell), predict the future, or control the weather. An amulet, like a stone, is thought to protect against evil and misfortune. However, projection is not the only phenomenon at work in these instances. Magic operates as a social dynamic governed by precise rules and beliefs (Mauss, 2019). When a magician utters a formula, he is fully engaged in the act and believes in its power. There is no detachment as in simple projection. Just as a formula can supposedly turn iron into gold (alchemy), it can make a machine speak—consider software, for example. The magician projects his perception of reality outward and actively seeks to validate it by altering the world. "The distortion of a specific aspect of reality is an important interpersonal means by which pressure is exerted on the object to see himself in a way that conforms with the unconscious projective fantasy" (Ogden, 1982, p. 53). The formula or magical object serves as a container for that idea, encompassing the associated anguish and fear. As containers of the expelled idea, the formula and object allow the magician to reorganize his inner experience. Through these containers, the magician learns to coexist with his own anguish and the aspects of his inner experience that he finds unacceptable.

How does projective identification function in AI? It begins with a person transferring certain aspects of themselves—such as fantasies, emotions, or abilities like learning and calculation—to the machine (phase 1). This act of splitting is driven by anxiety; the individual expels parts that evoke fear or need protection. The projection involves pressuring the machine to replicate these traits (phase 2). As the machine increasingly mimics these qualities, the person perceives them as externalized, affirming the expulsion. This cycle of pressure, simulation, and validation is essential for the content to be reintegrated into the individual (phase 3).

Conclusions

Jang Ji-sung, who lost her daughter to blood cancer in 2016, embraced the chance to see her daughter again, even if only through virtual reality. While Jang was not the first mother to endure the loss of a child, she was perhaps the first to encounter her deceased daughter as a VR simulacrum, a painstaking creation that took nearly a year to develop. This poignant reunion serves as the emotional centerpiece of the South Korean TV documentary Meeting You, which aired in February 2020 (see: https://slate.com/technology/2020/05/meeting-you-virtual-reality-documentary-mbc.html). The scene of the encounter is intense and profoundly moving. It serves as a powerful demonstration of how technology can reach into the most intimate and vulnerable aspects of human existence.

Through the concepts of mourning, transitional objects, and projective identification, psychoanalysis offers a vital contribution to understanding the deep relationship between humans and technology. The analysis of deadbots clearly illustrates this. These technologies touch on the most personal aspects of the human condition: our relationship with death, with time, with the fragility of the physical body, and thus our connection with our closest loved ones. Mortality is not only, as Hägglund (2019) emphasizes, what gives life its concrete meaning, but also what renders life vulnerable to losing its significance, making it unbearable and absurd. From this perspective, technology offers a new way of living toward death—a reimagined approach to experiencing and thinking about death that transforms traditional interpretations. Psychoanalysis provides a critical lens through which to examine this transformation, demystifying both death and technology, and offering an analysis of what is profoundly human in technology: the drive.

Works Cited

Ariés, P. (1977–1983). *Histoire de la mort.* Seuil.

Bion, W. (1961). *Experiences in groups and other papers.* Routledge.

Bion, W. (1962). *Learning from experience.* William Heinemann Medical Books.

Bowlby, J. (1969). *Attachment and loss trilogy* (Vol. 1). Vintage Publishing.

Bowlby, J. (1973). *Attachment and loss trilogy* (Vol. 2). Vintage Publishing.

Bowlby, J. (1980). *Attachment and loss trilogy* (Vol. 3). Vintage Publishing.

Cooper, S. (2023). The play of mourning. *Journal of the American Psychoanalytic Association, 71*(1), 61–82.

Derrida, J. (1972). *Marges de la philosophie.* Seuil.

Derrida, J. (2020). *Life death.* University of Chicago Press.

Elder, A. (2020). Conversation from beyond the grave? A neo-confucian ethics of chatbots of the dead. *Journal of Applied Philosophy, 37*(1), 73–88.

Figueroa-Torres, M. (2024). Affection as a service: Ghostbots and the changing nature of mourning. *Computer Law & Security Review, 52.*

Freud, S. (2005). *On murder mourning and melancholia.* Penguin.

Frost, N. (2021). *Qualitative research methods in psychology: Combining core approaches.* McGraw-Hill Education.

Hagglund, M. (2019). *This life.* Profile Books.

Harbinja, E., Edwards, L., & McVey, M. (2023). Governing ghostbots. *Computer Law & Security Review, 48.*

Henrickson, L. (2023). Chatting with the dead: The hermeneutics of thanabots. *Media, Culture & Society, 45*(5), 949–966.

Henrickson, L., & Meroño-Peñuela, A. (2022). The hermeneutics of computer-generated texts. *Configurations, 30*(2), 115–139.

Hollanek, T., & Nowaczyk-Basińska, K. (2024). Griefbots, deadbots, postmortem avatars: On responsible applications of generative AI in the digital afterlife industry. *Philosophy & Technology, 37*(2), 1–22.

Jiménez-Alonso, B., & Brescó de Luna, I. (2023). Griefbots. A new way of communicating with the dead? *Integrative Psychological and Behavioral Science, 57*(2), 466–481.

Khanna, R. (2024). Freud's 'Mourning and Melancholia'. In *The Palgrave handbook of psychosocial studies* (pp. 17–32). Springer.

Leader, D. (2022). Some thoughts on mourning and melancholia. In *Lacan on depression and melancholia* (pp. 48–75). Routledge.

Litt, C. (1986). Theories of transitional object attachment: An overview. *International Journal of Behavioral Development, 9*(3), 383–399.

Mauss, M. (2019). *Esquisse d'une théorie générale de la magie.* PUF (or. 1902).

Maxwell, J. (2021). Why qualitative methods are necessary for generalization. *Qualitative Psychology, 8*(1), 111.

Meyerowitz, R. (2023). *Mourning and metabolization: Close readings in the psychoanalytic literature of loss.* Routledge.

Morcate, M. (2017). Tipologías y re-mediación de las imágenes de muerte y duelo compartidas en la memorialización online. *Revista M. Estudos sobre a Morte, os Mortos eo Morrer, 2*(3), 30–44.

Morris, M., & Brubaker, J. (2024). Generative ghosts: Anticipating benefits and risks of AI afterlives. *arXiv*:2402.01662.

Neff, G., & Nagy, P. (2016). Talking to bots: Symbiotic agency and the case of Tay. *International Journal of Communication, 10*, 4915–4931.

Nowaczyk-Basińska, K., & Kiel, P. (2024). Exploring the Immortological Imagination: Advocating for a Sociology of Immortality. *Social Sciences, 13*(2), 83. https://doi.org/10.3390/socsci13020083

Ogden, T. (1982). *Projective identification and psychotherapeutic technique.* Jason Aronson.

Öhman, C., & Floridi, L. (2017). The political economy of death in the age of information: A critical approach to the digital afterlife industry. *Minds and Machines, 27*, 639–662.

Ricoeur, P. (2000). *La mémoire, l'histoire, l'oubli.* Seuil.

Rodríguez Reséndiz, H., & Rodríguez Reséndiz, J. (2024). Digital resurrection: Challenging the boundary between life and death with artificial intelligence. *Philosophies, 9*(3), 71.

Savin-Baden, M. (2022). *AI for death and dying.* Routledge.

Savin-Baden, M., & Burden, D. (2019). Digital immortality and virtual humans. *Postdigital Science and Education, 1*, 87–103.

Sisto, D. (2020). L'immortalità digitale: griefbot e ricordi senza fine. In *Hermeneutica: annuario di filosofia e teologia: nuova serie* (Vol. 3, pp. 217–233).

Stearns, P. (2021). *The Routledge history of death since 1800.* Routledge.

Suárez-Gonzalo, S. (2022). Deadbots can speak for you after your death. Is that ethical? *The Conversation.* https://theconversation.com/deadbots-can-speak-for-you-after-your-death-is-that-ethical-182076

Tevanian, P. (2021). *Politiques de la Mémoire.*
Walsh, F. (2021). Grief machines: Transhumanist theatre, digital performance, pandemic time. *Theatre Journal, 73*(3), 391–407.
Walter, T. (2015). Communication media and the dead: From the stone age to Facebook. *Mortality, 20*(3), 215–232.
Winnicott, D. (1953). Transitional object and transitional phenomena. *International Journal of Psychoanalysis, 34*, 89–97.
Winnicott, D. (2005). *Playing and reality.* Routledge.

Real Life, Simulation, and the Slide Toward Artificial Intelligence

Elizabeth Éowyn Nelson

The simulation hypothesis, credited to Nick Bostrom (2003), proposes that our lived experience of the contemporary world is a simulated reality. Simulation theory, however, has a distinguished history in philosophical discourse that long predates the ubiquitous mobile devices that make possible twenty-first-century "life on the screen," the title of Sherry Turkle's 1997 work on human–computer relationships. Whether ancient or modern, simulation theory dares to pose two questions: what is reality (ontology) and how do we know it (epistemology)? Already one might see why most of us leave such questions to the airy heights of the ivory tower. Who, in their right mind, uses *ontology* and *epistemology* in day-to-day conversation? We are simply trying to get on with ordinary life: paying bills, going to work, staying in touch with family and friends, shopping for groceries and other goods, and following the local and national news. Increasingly, however, each of the ordinary activities I just named is mediated by screens in which one substitutes the digital real for embodied relationships with actual others.

E. É. Nelson (✉)
Pacifica Graduate Institute, Los Angeles, CA, USA

J. D. Batt, J. Erickson (eds.), *Depth Psychology, Myth and Artificial Intelligence*, https://doi.org/10.1007/978-3-031-94105-4_12

In this chapter, I argue that the phrase "the digital real" will soon become an anachronism, bereft of meaning, because we have grown so accustomed to life on the screen that we will forget that there is a screen and that digital representations of reality are simulations. We now "interface" with our environment instead of living in it—*interface* being one of many words indicating the encroachment of machine metaphors on human language. Now that we have entered the third decade of the twenty-first century, when ordinary life is shadowed by the specter of ubiquitous artificial intelligence, the differences between the physical real and the digital real are eroding ever more rapidly.

Arguably, the most famous simulation theory in philosophy is Plato's allegory of the cave in Book VII of the *Republic* (514a–520a). In that story, a group of people chained to a wall since birth watch shadows moving on a blank screen in front of them. Unable to turn their heads or get up and explore what their eyes tell them, they mistake the shadow play for reality. Only the wise man can break the chains, suffer the pain of true perception, and know the really real. Unlike Plato, who lived millennia before the advent of supercomputers, Bostrom's (2003) hypothesis proposes that our simulated world is run by posthuman gamer-anthropologists who are living in a fully AI future. In this hypothesis, you, me, and everyone we know are artificially constructed players in a game environment. Our creators are the gamer-anthropologists who, fascinated with their ancient ancestors (us), run elaborate programs to explore their own history. We are constructs. We exist within their game. The question facing anyone, the hypothesis goes, is whether to "wake up" to the reality of the simulated environment and ourselves as constructs. The choice is rendered vividly in the 1999 film *The Matrix*. Neo must choose between the red pill (to awaken to the illusory, constructed nature of reality) and the blue pill (to sedate himself, continuing to regard the false sensorium of the Matrix as true).

Bostrom's simulation hypothesis, a provocative thought experiment, has been given new life by steady advances in artificial intelligence because we now interface with life, trusting what we see on the screen while disregarding our somatic perception—smell and taste, hearing and touch, and the inner pulse of subtle intuitive awareness. In an irony Socrates would surely appreciate, the return to embodied reason, not disembodied egoistic rationality, may be the healthiest choice for the human species and the biosphere we are steadily destroying.

It is intriguing to me (when it does not terrify) that prominent individuals among us seek to *become like* the futuristic gamer-anthropologist of Bostrom's simulation hypothesis, the player not the played. Rather than cherishing the life of the flesh, they dream of linking their minds to an endlessly repairable robotic-body to preserve themselves in a simulacrum of human life. As a somatic depth psychologist, I wonder about the constitution of this preserved self: how could silicone and titanium, a thing with no beating heart, hunger, or thirst, unable to scent its environment, possibly feel at home on earth? But perhaps rejecting earthly life is precisely the point. Transcending humanity through artificial intelligence may be the desire to dispense with the inconvenient flesh; that is, limited, painful, frail, emotional, chaotic, joyful, surprising, and uncontrollable embodied life. It may be the desire to dispense with the sacred and the soulful in everyday life and instead become godlike. The Greeks called it hubris. It always called forth Nemesis, the goddess of retribution whose decisive actions restored cosmic justice.

The contemporary desire to become godlike is evident among a small group of technologist-entrepreneurs who are investing billions of dollars to develop artificial intelligence. Our inevitable AI future, according to futurist Ray Kurzweil (2005, 2024), includes radical life extension and connecting human brains to the cloud for instantaneous access to error-free information—which will also be free from occasionally unreliable human memory. Yet many such conversations about so-called intelligence elide the differences among data, information, and knowledge. Wisdom is rarely part of the conversation.

The rarity of wisdom suggests an alternate AI fantasy. Instead of radical life extension (for those who can afford it), the specter of an AI future neatly expresses eschatology, or the belief in a catastrophic end of times. Such a catastrophic doomsday scenario is prominent, for example, in Norse mythology, where it is known as Ragnarök. The Christian variation imagines a doomsday in which believers are saved in a moment known as the Rapture while the rest of humanity and, presumably, all other life on the planet dies.

Four decades after James Cameron dramatized the rise of the machines in *The Terminator*, contemporary doomsday scenarios take seriously the risks of artificial intelligence. For example, in May 2023 the Center for AI Safety declared, "mitigating the risk of extinction from AI should be a global priority alongside other societal-scale risks such as pandemics and nuclear war" (n.p.).

By many expert accounts, doomsday scenarios remain science fiction. However, they serve an important corporate purpose: distracting thoughtful people from the ways AI has *already* eroded our essential experiences of embodied creaturely life embedded in, and supported by, the natural world. The dream of artificially extended cyborg future is the predictable consequence of the unconscious incursion of mobile digital technology into every arena of life. Our handy phones, tablets, and laptops—which we can and do take everywhere—are active shaping processes that fundamentally alter the experience of being human. They substitute screens (the simulated real) for ecological reality (the somatic-biological real).

Simulated life, and the unthinking equivalence of information and wisdom, has rendered us senseless to the AI future. In contemporary language, and in daily habits, the word "real" is undergoing steady dissolution. For example, a 2024 study by Pew Research found that 90–98% of American teenagers have a smartphone and a majority use social media "almost constantly" (Faverio & Sidoti). Some describe near-constant texting with their friends as "having a conversation," yet notice who and what is absent in the moment: two people walking or sitting together; sharing a location, including sharp observations about their common surrounding; responding to the music of each other's speech along with the subtle emotional dance of postures, gestures and fleeting facial expressions. In sum, what is missing from rapid keystrokes tapped on a small, cold device—however convenient or fun—is the warm environment of embodied conversation.

Turkle (2011) points out the many advantages of texts, which "can certainly be emotional, insightful, and sexy … make us feel understood, desired, and supported"—all important to adolescent smartphone users (and, I daresay, to the rest of us). "But," she says, texting is "not a place to deeply understand a problem or to explain a complicated situation" (p. 168). She found that teenagers were nostalgic for something they had never experienced: the full attention of their friends and parents in real conversation on difficult topics. Transforming information into knowledge, and knowledge into wisdom, requires the slow, thoughtful time that texting cannot replicate. And yet every teenager I know quickly defends texting as "real conversation."

I have little doubt that readers can think of many examples in which people readily substitute screens (the simulated real) for ecological reality (the somatic-biological real). Young people who are digital natives may simply be the most vulnerable to the substitution. "Real" may already be a simulacrum of its original substantial meaning, as thin as the pixelated screens that transfix us all day long. Nemesis awaits.

Life, Examined and Unexamined

"Waking up" as it is depicted in Bostrom's simulation hypothesis and in *The Matrix* is at odds with Western notions of awakening. Awakening, in the classical tradition, is far closer to the self-examination extolled by Socrates in his *Apology*, in which he defended himself against the accusation of corrupting Athens' youth by encouraging them to question everything. Socrates lost the case (and his life) but won the cause: Self-examination is still shaped by the Socratic practice of radical inquiry in the pursuit of wisdom, care of the soul, and piety. Piety towards one's own guiding spirit, the genius or daimon who accompanies each of us in this lifetime is especially important since the daimon helps us realize our life's purpose. The opposite of piety, hubris, was the greatest offence against the divine. Today we call hubris *malignant egotism*.

A brief study of ancient wisdom and modern esoteric traditions well beyond Plato demonstrates that humanity has long felt itself to be a small but essential part of an enormous living cosmos. Jungian thought, which many people rightly regard as a spiritual psychology, is one branch of the esoteric tradition. The Jungian process of individuation is discovery of the sacred in the immanent and the ordinary, guided by the *imago dei* (image of god) within, the Self. The purpose of human life is wholeness on earth, not transcending biological, instinctual, life. It includes ongoing encounters between consciousness and the dynamic unconscious. Above all, Jungian psychology not only accepts the inevitability of aging, illness, and death, it values them.

> When we refuse the experience of death we also refuse the essential question of life, and leave life unaccomplished …. The impulse to death need not be conceived as an anti-life movement; it may be a demand for an encounter with absolute reality, a demand for a fuller life through the death experience …. Until we can choose death, we cannot choose life (Hillman, *Myth* 62–63).

For Jungians, the way through the world—and all it offers to us for self-examination including the absolute reality of our own death—is far more valuable than the way beyond the world. Our supposed AI future wherein the wealthy few achieve the relative immortality of an artificially preserved consciousness downloaded to a robotic body eliminates the body, eliminates embodied instinctual life, and eliminates the unconscious, both collective and personal. Where is the soul in all of this, or a sense of the sacred, or the journey towards the Self?

Embodied Life and the Soul

Somatics, for those unfamiliar with the term, is an interdisciplinary field that focuses on embodied experience and perception, the intimate sense of ourselves as integrated bodyminds that dream, sense, feel, observe, intuit, move, decide, and act in the world. Most experts credit Thomas Hanna with introducing the word somatics in 1970, contrasting *soma* with *body*. Whereas *body* connotes a piece of meat, an object "drained of life and ready to be worked upon and used," *soma* is the alive body, "pulsing, flowing, squeezing and relaxing—flowing and alternating with fear and anger, hunger and sensuality" (35).

Somatic psychologists like me are opposed to perpetuating Cartesian dualism particularly in its more insidious forms. Somatic psychology calls for a return home to the body, to the soul as embodied, and to the flesh as the source of identity and community. As Marion Woodman, the revered Jungian pioneer for embodiment said, "We have to discover the magnificent consciousness in matter and in our own bodies" (*Conscious* 75) and to learn to "live spontaneously from the emotions and values that are grounded in our own musculature" (*Dancing* 8). In the conversation about reality and simulated reality, it matters what we touch and what touches us—both literally and metaphorically. When we are deeply touched, moved to tears and laughter, memory and longing, the soul awakens. This begs the question: What can touch possibly mean in simulated reality? We will get to this question a little later.

Jungians are wary of attempting to define soul, but it can be recognized. Jung, in a poignant lament seven months before his death, described soul as "buried treasure in the field" (Rolfe 158) which few people sought. In his essay "On the nature of the psyche," Jung alluded to the autonomy, intelligence, and creativity of soul. Hillman had many potent things to say about soul, including this: "The opus of the soul needs intimate connection, not only to individuate but simply to live" (*Myth* 92). Moore says soulfulness is "tied to life in all its particulars—good food, satisfying conversation, genuine friends, and experiences that stay in the memory and touch the heart. Soul is revealed in attachment, love, and community, as well as in retreat on behalf of inner communing and intimacy" (*Myth xi–xii*). Please remember this phrase: life in all its particulars, what we actually do.

The Relationship with Our Tech

Clearly, the word *technology* refers to billions of objects. Ursula Le Guin (1989) reminds us that the basket was the first technology. If we expand our frame of reference to embrace our clever Corvid cousins, among the first and most widespread technologies is the stick. Yet when people refer to "my tech" they are usually speaking about the sleek, handy devices they carry everywhere and the invisible digital web that makes them useful; in short, that smartphone, tablet, laptop (or all of the above) which may well be inches from your body, right now.

Psychoanalysts once spoke of free-floating anxiety. Now the vast majority of the first world is enclosed in free-floating information. Technophobes argue that we have *not* traded up. Others, predisposed toward technophilia, argue that mobile digital technology gives us unprecedented freedoms, allows us to maintain so-called face-to-face contact with friends all over the world, and ultimately improves our lives. Our mobile digital devices offer both. At any given moment, they can be a technophobe's nightmare and the technophiliac's delight. I am interested in the soul of the device and the soul of our relationship to it. Because *relationship* is the correct noun: something that goes with us everywhere, that we touch hundreds of times a day, that we wake up to and go to sleep with, easily qualifies as one of the more intimate relationships in anyone's life.

Or, as one of my graduate students remarked, "You ever touch someone else's tech without asking? There's something icky about it. It's invasive and intimate, like touching someone's body."

But what, exactly, is technology? If this question seems ridiculous to you, you are not alone. Even Jungians, who are encouraged to think far outside the mainstream, may not have given enough attention to the question.

Technology Is Not What You Think It Is. Neither Is Reality

Marshall McLuhan published his prescient work, *Understanding Media: the Extensions of Man* in 1964. A dense and erudite text, his wide-ranging ideas were frequently reduced to a soundbite, "the medium is the message," the title of the first chapter. Few people understood the full meaning of McLuhan's work, and it is not getting as much attention as it deserves in the conversations about artificial intelligence. The scholarly discipline created by McLuhan's work, *media ecology*, generates unsettling observations about real and simulated life. For instance, consider just two foundational and related premises: any technology is not neutral, and any new technology is a totally new environment that shapes human thinking and behavior.

Technology—a specific medium, such as your smartphone—is not a thing, an object, or a device that you pick up and put down. It is an *active process* that shapes and controls the scale and form of human association and action. (*Understanding* 9; emphasis added). Our watchdog minds, according to McLuhan, should (mostly) ignore the apps; that is, the content on our smartphone, tablet, or laptop. Instead, we should pay attention to how the device itself alters the psychological self, extending it *and* limiting it, because the medium (the device) as distinct from the content (what it provides, displays, or sells) is not neutral. McLuhan goes so far as to say—in his inimitable feisty style—that the conventional focus on media content "is the numb stance of the technological idiot … the juicy piece of meat distracting the watchdog of the mind." (18).

Once we begin to see mobile digital devices as shaping processes rather than simple objects, we can begin to appreciate McLuhan's next point. Technology creates a wholly new environment, hence the moniker "media ecology" as an ecological (holistic, systems) approach to the study of media. As a new environment, new technology alters our "patterns of perception steadily and without any resistance" (*Understanding* 18) Widespread adoption of the technology ultimately will control the scale and form of human association and action, gradually creating a new human environment in which people serve their devices "as gods or minor religions" (46).

One conclusion to draw from a media ecology approach to ubiquitous mobile digital technology is this: the twenty-first-century self is no longer a bodymind. It is a techno-bodymind. That is, the mobile digital device we turn to hundreds of times a day has created a new environment. It is also creating us—every time we touch it, glance at it, or feel a panic response when it is not immediately accessible. It is not necessary to implant devices into flesh, blood, or brain to create the techno-bodymind. For many people, their smart device has become an indispensable limb, and to be without it is to suffer something akin to phantom limb syndrome. Furthermore, that indispensable limb has already altered what we take to be "real" conversation, as I mentioned earlier, as well as social customs such as dating, falling in love, and breaking up (all of which can happen entirely on-line, without ever physically meeting), and social events such as weddings and funerals. There is no doubt that attending a wedding or funeral via Zoom may be better than not attending at all. I know. I did both during the 2020 pandemic and quarantine. But I was well aware that my emotional involvement and attention in this simulacrum of participation was partial. It was not the really real.

To get our hands around the prevalence of mobile digital technology in our daily, lived experience, a 2023 study by the Pew Research Center reported that one in four people are online "almost constantly," which means morning, noon, and the middle of the night (Gelles-Watnick). That number rises to 60% for younger adults aged 18 to 29. Nearly half of those polled check their smartphones "several times a day." At the end of a life, most people will have spent approximately one full decade on their smartphone. Media ecologists would point out that *what* we view on the small, glowing screen (the content) is far less important than the fact that we are spending hours a day viewing that screen. Constantly viewing the screen is now the daily reality, and the really real, for billions of people around the world.

A Homely Experiment

Mobile digital technology as an active shaping process affects the way most people in the first world wake up every day: our first conscious sensations, the shape of our perceptions, and what our hands reach for, touch, or hold. As a simple experiment, take a moment to recall getting out of bed this morning. How long did it take you to reach for your smartphone—a minute, an hour, several hours?

Decades ago, my cherished mentor Patricia Wiltse taught me a simple adage: *As the first hour, so goes the day.* How might the day unfold differently if we did not reach for the smart phone within few minutes of awakening? What if we reached for something else, equally near? Imagine yourself running fingertips over smooth sheets or nubby blanket, placing a palm on the warm body of a partner, or feeling the low rumbling vibration of a purring cat. To avoid the technophobia–technophilia trap, let us say that checking the smartphone immediately upon awakening is neither good nor bad. Listening to the ping of texts or posts is no better or worse than hearing your cat snore. (Yes, they snore and purr, take it from me.) Simply recall the adage, *as the first hour, so goes the day.* Tomorrow morning, I invite you to notice the somatic quality of your first hour—what you reach for, what you smell, and touch, and hear, how you move and breathe, where you notice tightness or pain and where your body is lithe and fluid. Live this first hour with as much somatic awareness as possible and observe how it echoes throughout the day.

Technology and Extending the Body

The proliferation of mobile digital technology means that we are extending the body, and the lived experience of the body, to such a degree that a tool is no longer what we pick up and put down or put away but something that accompanies us everywhere, all of the time. Since it can literally accompany us everywhere, many people spend more time with their tech than they do with loved ones, and signify this intimacy through personalizing as well as personifying their devices. Thus, two key questions arise. First, at what point do we lose awareness of the tool as a tool and consider it simply part of the self—without which our lives are impossible? Second, how is mobile digital technology qualitatively different from the hammer, the wheel, the loom; that is, from *techne* as practiced by *Homo faber*, "man the maker," for millennia?

One answer to these questions arises from the idea of techno-humanism, the next phase in the evolution of sapiens and sapien culture—including, and perhaps most poignantly, our embodied experience. According to some thinkers, techno-humanism, also known as trans-humanism, has superseded humanism (Mckie, Merzlyakov, O'Connell). Ultimately, we may end up dispensing with humanism altogether. Techno-humanism, according to *PC Magazine*'s online encyclopedia, "implies that humans are going to be intrinsically linked with technology from birth." It envisions a world in which technology is so highly integrated into society that it becomes part of our greater intelligence and enables us to live longer. Today, smartphones enable everyone to have answers at their fingertips. In the future, sensors may detect the birth of serious diseases at a point where they can immediately be eradicated.

At this moment in sapien history, 2025, techno-humanism is only *linking* flesh and circuitry. It is not yet merging with it. But either step alters our conception of the body and the soul as embedded in, and arising from, organic nature. Either step significantly shapes our psychology, that is, the way we *live* the integrated body, mind, spirit, and soul.

What Cost Technology?

That indispensable smartphone comes with a cost to embodied life and the soul. Consider, for instance, an observation by Jung near the end of his life, long before the advent of the vast computing power available today.

> Reforms by advances, that is, by new methods or gadgets, are of course impressive at first, but in the long run they are dubious and in any case dearly paid for. They by no means increase the contentment or the happiness of people on the whole. Mostly, they are deceptive sweetenings of existence, like speedier communications which unpleasantly accelerate the tempo of life and leave us with less time than ever before. *Omnis festinatio ex parte diaboli est*—all haste is of the devil, as the old master used to say. (*Memories* 236)

This excerpt from Jung's memoir appears in the chapter describing the tower at Bollingen on Lake Zurich. He built the tower and lived their periodically to travel back in time, living as his ancestors once did without the mod-cons of mid-century Europe. Jung's return to the Middle Ages was deliberate and remarkable. He felt strongly that body and soul, which are inherently ancestral, "find no proper place in what is new, in things that have just come into being" (236).

Keeping Jung's assertion in mind makes the acceleration of twenty-first-century life bittersweet at best. Furthermore, it adds another dimension to the conversation about reality and simulated reality summed up in this question: How has mobile digital life altered the quality of time? Because, surely, if the fantasy of an AI future includes limitless time, then we must truly want to cherish time rather than simply spend it, right?

The Denial of Death and the Antiaging Industry

One of the fantasies fueling developments in AI is the denial of death, mentioned a few pages ago, and the multi-billion dollar antiaging industry. Whereas the Greeks preserved the gap between human and divine as an expression of piety, serious and well-funded AI entrepreneurs are committed to engineering techno-human beings who will, in essence, be immortal.

For instance, the subtitle of Harrington's 1969 book *The Immortalist* encapsulates this hope, promising "an approach to the engineering of man's divinity." Harrington argues that death is an unacceptable imposition on the human race. Philosophies that accept death—or even find value in death—must be considered dead or meaningless. They offer no consolation. Yet one must ask, consolation to whom or what? Whose interests take precedence in the fantasy of immortality? Certainly not the soul which, as Hillman said, is not anti-life at all but, rather, adds immeasurably to life's richness. Thus by Harrington's account, Jungian psychology is dead or meaningless.

The most outspoken proponent of our cyborg future is AI researcher and futurist Ray Kurzweil, mentioned earlier. He is excitedly anticipating an event he calls the singularity, which he describes on his website *transcendentman.com* in which our intelligent machines essentially render the human species obsolete. 'We' will be immortal (or live as long as we want) but 'we' will no longer be human in any way recognizable now. By improving our physiological selves with advancements from the fields of biotechnology, nanotechnology, and artificial intelligence, we'll become a human–machine civilization, and we'll be able to live as long as we want.

The singularity will come about with the creation of a superhuman artificial intelligence, which will think ideas no human has thought before and invent advanced technologies unlike anything humans have invented. Because the AI will continue to evolve, it will leave ordinary humans, "mere biological machines," far behind.

Kurzweil's first book devoted to the singularity, published in 2005, bears the subtitle *When Humans Transcend Biology*. His 2024 book on the singularity is subtitled *When We Merge with AI*. The evolution of the two subtitles is a story in itself, and an indicator of something much larger moving silently through the world.

Kurzweil predicts the singularity will occur in 2045.

Mobile Digital Devices and the Interrupt-Driven Life

Recent advances in neurobiology support McLuhan's thesis that technology is an active shaping process. Daily experiences over an entire lifetime shape neural connections, thickening some and thinning others. The process is sometimes referred to as Hebb's law, *circuits that fire together wire together*.

One of the more insidious examples of this shaping harkens back to Jung's point about new gadgets that accelerate the tempo of life and leave us less time. We are being entrained to multitask at ever-increasing speeds in part because it is not only convenient, it is expected. For instance, many of my graduate students watch TV while working on their laptops at the same time they continually glance at their nearby phones to respond to texts, emails, and notifications. The very idea of *down time*—another computer phrase that has surreptitiously set the standard for human activity—seems quaint or morally suspect in a culture that prizes achievement. I conjecture that we no longer recognize a truly human pace of life, one that leaves room for reflection, imagination, and wonder. Simply noticing our immediate physical environment, or paying attention to physical cues about thirst, hunger, or the need for a deep breath, movement, or rest, seem nearly as vestigial as our truncated tailbones. We are losing our earthly foundation that is rooted in embodied instinctual life, life on the earth, a key theme in Slater's 2024 book, *Jung* vs. *Borg: Finding the Deeply Human in a Posthuman Age.*

I offer a novel theory about how ubiquitous digital devices are invisibly entraining us every day—unless we have turned them off entirely. (And good luck finding that off switch; it is rarely easy to spot.) I assert that we live within the subtle energy field of interrupt-driven CPUs that influence our actions every moment of the day, and even when we are asleep.

I begin my hypothesis with the intersection of four powerful ideas. One, McLuhan's thesis that technology is an active shaping process; two, neural plasticity; three, Turkle's 2011 observation that we now live in an "always on" society, since mobile digital devices continually attract our attention; and four, how the so-called brain of digital devices makes it look like it can do multiple things at once through a process called interrupt handling wherein the device's "attention" is continually being interrupted and switching between tasks.

In digital computers, an interrupt is a response by the processor to an event that needs attention from the software. Interrupts are commonly used by hardware devices to indicate electronic or physical state changes. The operating system (OS) software implements computer multitasking, especially in real-time computing, by directing the processor to suspend (interrupt) the currently executing task and switch to another task. If the request is accepted, the processor suspends current activities, saves its state, and uses an interrupt handler (or an interrupt service routine, ISR) to deal with the request. Once the new task is complete (the interrupt handler finishes), the processor resumes normal activities. Combining these ideas—the fact that our brains are shaped by always on, interrupt-driven devices—one might easily see how our phones, tablets, and laptops have entrained us to expect near-continual interruptions regardless of how much we may want to focus our attention on one person, situation, or project or simply to allow our attention to wander and our minds to wonder. *We are now the devices that are continually interrupted throughout the day.*

Cal Newport's 2019 book *Digital Minimalism* makes the same observation I do about the interrupt-driven life, but without the deep dive into processor hardware and OS software. My deep dive is part of the inclination to look at "the body" of anything in the world, manufactured or organic. I am also fascinated by the possibility that our devices, like us, have a subtle body, but that is a topic for another day.

Speed, Interruptions, and the Loss of Deep Work

Clearly, I have strong feelings about the machine-speed of human life, shaped by twin passions: my decades-long career as a writer, and what I playfully call my somatic evangelism. My biggest fear is that techno-humanist fantasies of an AI future have already been realized in part: many people feel enormous pressure to simulate machine speed and adroitly multitask. The inhuman haste of our digital technologies has infected the slower, cyclical rhythms of biological reality—including cherished periods of sleep, play, and general leisure—and we don't even know it. I can say without hesitation that thoughtful writing is simply not possible for me, my graduate students, or my clients without rest, play, and leisure, and without uninterrupted time to think and feel. Instead of deep work, many join the thoughtless cacophony of online chatter, bowing to the pressure of social networks that "instruct us to share whenever there's 'something on our mind,' no matter how ignorant or ill considered, and then help us broadcast it to the widest possible audience" (*Alone* 276).

The urge to check our phones or unthinkingly respond to notifications that pop up "becomes a nervous twitch that shatters uninterrupted time into shards too small to support the presence necessary for an intentional life" (Newport *Digital xi*). Echoing Turkle's language Newport says, "smartphones have reshaped people's experience of the world by providing an always-present connection to a humming matrix of chatter and distraction" (3). Newport does not advocate turning back the clock 25 years—if that were possible—but to take seriously the ways in which our devices are entraining us every hour we use them. This individual effort, however, must be limned against the effort of thousands of programmers working for billion-dollar corporations whose job is to defeat the thoughtful use of technology. Newport draws upon the *60 Minutes* interview with Tristan Harris, now a Silicon Valley whistle-blower featured in the 2017 docu-drama *The Social Dilemma*. In the interview, Anderson Cooper asks Harris "Is Silicon Valley programming apps or are they programming people?" Harris responds, "They are programming people."

The interview continues in language that would undoubtedly make McLuhan roll over in his grave. Harris calls out the erroneous narrative that technology is neutral. Cooper stops him. "Technology is not neutral?" he asks. "It's not neutral," says Harris. "They want you to use it in particular ways and for long periods of time. Because that's how they make their money" (quoted in Newport *Digital*10).

In Conclusion: Real or Not Real?

As material objects, mobile digital devices are just as real as any other object we use in the course of a day: the coffee maker, clothes-hangers, car keys, a bath towel, a toothbrush. However, they are also a portal into life on the screen, a humming matrix of information that is soothing for some and irksome to others. They bridge the distance between ourselves and people we love in soul-nourishing ways by helping us sustain important relationships. Yet they can just as easily offer seductive simulacra of embodied life, particularly if we do not use the devices in a thoughtful manner.

Is thoughtful use of mobile digital technology possible? Such use must begin with the fact that mobile digital devices never rest. They are smart (not wise) because they are continually multitasking at a frantic inhuman pace—subtly entraining our nervous systems and setting the moral standard by which an achievement society rewards its citizens. For a creative writer or a painter—or, for that matter, someone taking a yoga class or attending a lecture—thoughtful use would mean turning off all notifications, all sounds, and all haptics so that they are not continually interrupted by the lure of life on the screen. If my hypothesis has merit, thoughtful use would also require turning off the device entirely and putting it away since the subtle energy field of interrupt-driven devices continues to influence us even when they appear inert.

Finally, thoughtful use of mobile digital technology would mean lifting our gaze from the glowing screen and paying attention to the biological real and all that it offers to all of our senses: smell and taste, hearing and touch, and the inner pulse of intuition. It would mean rediscovering a human pace, the loss of ourselves in work and play in which time slows down or stands still because we are wholly absorbed in the present. It would be the radical recovery of embodied creaturely life, soulful life, embedded in a living world full of soul.

Works Cited

Bostrom, N. (2003). Are we living in a computer simulation? *The Philosophical Quarterly, 211*(53), 243–254.

Faverio, M., & Sidoti, O. (2024). Teens, social media, and technology, 2024. *Pew Research Center.* Accessed January 4, 2025, from www.pewresearch.org/internet/2024/12/12/teens-social-media-and-technology-2024/

Gelles-Watnick, R. (2024). Americans' use of mobile technology and home broadband. *Pew Research Center.* Accessed January 4, 2025, from www.pewresearch.org/internet/2024/01/31/americans-use-of-mobile-technology-and-home-broadband/

Hanna, T. (1970). *Bodies in revolt: A primer in somatic thinking.* Holt, Rinehart and Winston.

Harrington, A. (1969). *The Immortalist: An approach to the engineering of man's divinity.* Random House.

Hillman, James. (1997). *Suicide and the soul* (2nd ed.). Spring Publications.

Hillman, James. (1972). *The myth of analysis: Three essays in archetypal psychology.* Northwestern UP.

Jung, C. G. (1961). *Memories, dreams, reflections* (A. Jaffe, Eds. Richard and Clara Winston, Trans.). Vintage Books, 1989.

Jung, C. G. (1969). *Memories.* On the nature of the psyche. In *The collected works of C. G. Jung* (pp. 159–234, 2nd ed., Vol. 8) (R. F. C. Hull, Trans.), 1946. Princeton UP.

Kurzweil, R. (2005). *The singularity is near: When humans transcend biology.* Viking.

Kurzweil, R. (2024). *The singularity is nearer: When we merge with AI.* Viking.

Kurzweil, R. *Transcendent man.* Accessed January 4, 2025., from www.transcendentman.com/mind-boggling-technological-singularity-defined/

Le Guin, U. (1989). The carrier bag theory of fiction. In *Dancing at the edge of the world: Thoughts on words, women, places* (pp. 165–170). Grove Press.

McKie, R. (2018). No death and an enhanced life: Is the future transhuman? *The Guardian.* www.theguardian.com/technology/2018/may/06/no-death-and-an-enhanced-life-is-the-future-transhuman

McLuhan, M. (1964). *Understanding media: The extensions of man.* MIT Press, 1994.

Merzlyakov, S. S. (2022). Posthumanism vs. transhumanism: From the “End of Exceptionalism” to “Technological Humanism”. *Herald of the Russian Academy of Sciences, 92*(Suppl 6), S475–S482. https://doi.org/10.1134/S1019331622120073.

Moore, T. (1992). *Care of the soul.* HarperCollins.

Newport, C. (2016). *Deep work: Rules for focused success in a distracted world.* Grand Central Publishing.

Newport, C. (2019). *Digital minimalism: Choosing a focused life in a noisy world.* Portfolio.

O’Connell, M. (2018). *To be a machine: Adventures among cyborgs, utopians, hackers, and the futurists solving the modest problem of death.* Anchor.

PC Magazine. Techno-humanism. *PC Magazine.* Accessed January 4, 2025., from www.pcmag.com/encyclopedia/term/techno-humanism

Plato. (1961a). Republic. In E. Hamilton & H. Cairns (Eds.), *Plato: The collected dialogues* (Paul Shorey, Trans., pp. 575–844). Princeton UP.

Plato. (1961b). Socrates’ Defense (Apology). In E. Hamilton & H. Cairns (Eds.), *Plato: The collected dialogues* (Hugh Tredennick, pp. 3–26). Princeton UP.

Rolfe, E. (1988). *Encounter with Jung.* Sigo Press.

Slater, G. (2024). *Jung* vs. *Borg: Finding the deeply human in a Posthuman Age.* Winter Press.

Turkle, S. (2011). *Alone together: Why we expect more from technology and less from each other.* Basic Books.

Turkle, S.. (1997). *Life on the screen: Identity in the age of the internet.* Simon & Schuster.

Woodman, M. (1993). *Conscious femininity: Interviews with Marion Woodman.* Inner City Books.

Woodman, M., & Dickson, E. (1997). *Dancing in the flames.* Shambhala.

The Road Ahead

The preceding chapters have shown how unconscious forces and archetypal patterns shape our fantasies about the meaning of emergent artificial intelligence in the twenty-first century. And although this process, for some populations, may inspire a great deal of certainty in one imagined future or another—a variety of utopias and dystopias—the more uncomfortable truth is that nobody knows for sure where these technologies are taking us. To grapple with the impact of artificial intelligence on psyche in the twenty-first century means confronting a great deal of uncertainty about the road ahead.

Part III of this volume explores these uncertainties as they are playing out in this moment of history. Glen Slater and Alires Almon remind us that the programs and models of today are being produced by particular people subscribing to particular value systems and ask what alternative values might yet be possible for us in this space. Jakob Glazier and Christopher Zieske ask us to seriously consider our metaphysical assumptions about soul, consciousness, and technology—and their implications for the kind of world we want to create. Jason Batt offers an expansive vision of the way AI might be used to explore our collective psyche. Finally, Jonathan Erickson writes about potential harms and benefits of human–AI relationships, and how a conscious process of active imagination with these models can become a means to better understand ourselves.

Cybernetics, AI, and the Mechanization of Human Thought

Glen Slater

We can and do change culture by modifying what we think and do and feel and what we teach and how we raise our children .... This new viewpoint, when once grasped, brings an immense relief and a feeling of freedom we have never had before under the older beliefs in a supernaturally imposed culture, sanctioned by immemorial tradition.
Lawrence K. Frank, 1951, attendee of The Macy Conferences (Quoted in Heims 82).

The human displacement of the gods is the meta-myth of modernity. From the Promethean use of technical knowledge to control nature, to the death of God that Nietzsche depicted as murder, to posthuman plans to radically alter evolution, the postindustrial world has come to assume a godlike role in Creation. Some emphasize the freedom and creative possibilities inherent in this turn. Others, including the present writer, seek to address the existential disorientation and psychosocial symptoms of this

G. Slater (✉)
Pacifica Graduate Institute, Arroyo Grande, CA, USA
e-mail: gslater@pacifica.edu

J. D. Batt, J. Erickson (eds.), *Depth Psychology, Myth and Artificial Intelligence*, https://doi.org/10.1007/978-3-031-94105-4_13

turn's manifestations. Irrespective of which aspects of this monumental transition we attend, we can no longer deny that godlikeness comes with a godlike responsibility—a responsibility that begins by reflecting on the ideas and values that are driving us.

One concentration of ideas, which has moved stealthily from the esoteric annals of technoscience to reshaping the lives of peoples across the globe, belongs to the field of *cybernetics*. As the study of control systems and communications between living things and machines, cybernetics was initially formulated by a small group of luminaries and prodigies who met from 1946 to 1953 at a hotel in New York City. These meetings became known as the *Macy Conferences*.

Two streams of thought emerged from these conferences and from the extended work of its key contributors, streams that have turned into powerful conceptual rivers and sustaining sources of knowledge for our current postindustrial, digital era. One of these streams extends from these earliest discussions of cybernetics to our contemporary preoccupation with artificial intelligence (AI). The other stream involves the development and dominance of a mechanistic model of the mind, which has all but defined cognitive science and been central to the notion that both the brain and the mind function like computers. These intersecting streams of thought turned conceptual rivers have not only set the stage for the present-day rise of AI to social and economic prominence, they have also fed a highly influential *posthuman* vision of the potential merger of humans and computers into a hybrid species. Yet, as we embrace AI and open ourselves to its entry into all aspects of our lives, we remain largely ignorant of the history of ideas behind these developments.

In my book, *Jung* vs *Borg: Finding the Deeply Human in a Posthuman Age,* I argue that the advance of AI and the posthuman vision have been fostered by a declining comprehension of the deeper reaches of the human psyche, due in large part because such a comprehension has been displaced by the mechanistic model of mind. Put differently, our rapturous embrace of AI has arisen in a vacuum of understanding pertaining to the ways in which humans actually perceive and think. In this chapter, my aim is to describe the traction this argument finds in relation to the Macy Conferences and their influence on our current conceptions of intelligence and human thought processes.

As we begin to discern the displacement of the deeply human in our models of intelligence, we may also imagine an alternative history of ideas, one that might have occurred had the depth psychological component of the Macy Conferences been more robust and expansive. For whereas these conferences focused on neurology and logic, they also involved opportunities via which a greater comprehension of the human psyche may have infused and problematized the model of mind that history actually extracted from these gatherings. However, such opportunities were missed. By drawing out these lacunas in the modern history of ideas and by indicating how our grappling with them might still opportune corrective measures, I aim to provide a reference point for a different kind of conversation about computational models of mind. Such a conversation, which would shift our attention to a more pivotal and expansive sense of the unconscious, naturally invites an understanding of the specific contributions of C. G. Jung. It is Jung's work that instigates a reverence for the deeper, archetypal patterns of the psyche and provides the pathways to self-knowledge that will be necessary to manage our godlike powers.

The Cybernetics Group

The Macy Conferences grew out of a meeting in 1942 involving several prominent neurophysiologists, psychologists, and social scientists who gathered to discuss the physiology of hypnosis and listen to presentations by the innovative hypnotherapist, Milton Erickson. The participants at this initial meeting included Warren McCulloch, who was to become a seminal figure in the history of cybernetics and early discussions of AI. Lawrence Kubie, a psychiatrist who became a psychoanalyst, also attended and had invited Erickson to speak about his work. Margaret Mead, the famed anthropologist, and Gregory Bateson, the interdisciplinary thinker who would go on to study the treatment of schizophrenia and alcoholism were also part of this initial group. Mead and Bateson were married at the time. The series of yearly conferences focused on cybernetics began four years later, funded by the Josiah Macy Jr. Foundation and organized by Frank Fremont-Smith. While Erickson did not attend these ensuing conferences, the others present at this first meeting did, and what they both contributed and failed to contribute to proceedings has, arguably, shaped the world we now inhabit.

The conferences also brought together a number of other prominent researchers to explore and develop this new field, which was prompted by the development of the earliest computers, particularly by the work of Alan Turing, as well as by findings in neurology, which was attempting to discern the function of neurons. The questions that occupied the conference attendees concerned ways the neurological basis of mind could be conceived mechanistically and might, in theory, be replicated in machines, principally in the development of computers. In turn, the function of computer circuits were being studied as a way to model human cognition.

In what has become the primary, authoritative text on these conferences, Steve J. Heims suggests that the preliminary 1942 meeting not only fielded some of the nascent concepts that would be taken up by *The Cybernetics Group*—the title of Heims' account of the conferences—it also established the basic structure of the group's members, with social scientists on one side and cyberneticians on the other. Overlaying this difference in research focus was also a discernible difference in humanistic versus mechanistic sensibilities. Although all participants agreed to a focus on building scientific models of neurological structures and dynamics, with the aim of uncovering and describing distinct mechanisms, some were more focused on replicating these mechanisms in thinking machines, while others were interested in how these models might bring about psychological healing and social change. A third contingent was intent on establishing a pure science of human cognition. Whereas there were a number of tensions created by these differing interests, there was also a remarkable spirit of collegiality and cooperation, generated by a commitment to interdisciplinary dialogue and an accepted need for transdisciplinary understanding. In our present age of ultra-specialized research and development, the conferences stand as a rare example of this kind of intellectual cross-fertilization.

Among the cyberneticians was Norbert Wiener, who might arguably be called the founder of cybernetics. Wiener also turned out to be one of its most nuanced and circumspect exponents. Searching for a theoretical model that might establish common ground between engineered mechanisms and human behavior, Wiener "proposed to link statistical mechanics, communication engineering, the theory of control mechanisms in machines, biology, and also psychology and social science by the common theme of 'communication.'" He wrote, "the neuromuscular mechanism of an animal or of man is certainly a communication instrument" (Heims 22, italics in original).

An equally important presence and central theorist of the group was John von Neumann, a mathematical genius and polymath who had worked on the Manhattan Project, been instrumental in the development of quantum physics, and has been called by one essayist, "The Smartest Man Who

Ever Lived" (Kirsch). In terms of the direct line that can be drawn from Macy, through AI, and on into posthumanism, von Neumann represents a distinct starting point. The now influential notion of "the Singularity," referring to the moment when AI is predicted to match and then surpass human intelligence—a notion widely accepted among the most influential technologists of our time—can be traced through its current loudest proponent, Ray Kurzweil, via the writings of Vernor Vinge, back to von Neumann. Imagining some of the ultimate implications of intelligent machines, von Neumann also conceived of a form of self-replicating spacecraft that has become known as the "von Neumann probe"—a concept that has launched a number of discussions about possible futures wherein humans may become superfluous. For those who envision human consciousness one day being downloaded into computers and intelligent robots being capable of making more advanced versions of themselves, the concept of the von Neumann probe is touted as the means by which the remnants of civilization might spread throughout the galaxy. In terms of his original influence on the development of cybernetics, it is von Neumann that worked on the logic of automata, cementing his place in the earliest history of AI.

On the cybernetician side of the group, the most influential collaboration was probably between Warren McCulloch and Walter Pitts, the first an esteemed psychologist turned neuroscientist, and the second a younger, self-taught prodigy. In his late teens, Pitts was taken into the McCulloch household and went on to become McCulloch's closest collaborator. Pitts would also turn out to be a rather perplexing and troubled character. As Heims puts it, "Walter Pitts was simultaneously an extraordinarily talented, sought-after scientist and an adolescent boy" (40). It was McCulloch and Pitts who would provide the central mechanism around which cybernetics developed: the switching function of the neuron. They conceptualized the "neural network"—a term that is now woven into AI research and development—as the basis of all kinds of cognitive function, and they contended that such a structure could, in theory, be replicated by machines. This was the mechanistic reduction of the cognitive process around which much of the discussion at the conferences turned and from which whole psychologies and technologies have since emanated.

The resulting outlook, as Jean-Pierre Dupuy formulates it at the beginning of his own account of the Macy Conferences, is that "Thinking is a form of computation (and) comes within the domain of the mechanical" (3–4). Participants "thought it possible to construct a scientific, physicalist theory of the mind," and at least some of the harder-nosed materialists involved thought that "their research program would be realized … only when … they had succeeded in making a brain that exhibited all the properties associated with the mind" (4). Not that they assumed such an aim could be achieved in their lifetimes, the construction of an artificial brain became one of the great goals of AI researchers a half-century on. Dupuy's compelling commentary on these formulations and their role in the history of ideas makes clear that cognitive science in general has largely neglected its Macy origins and thus overlooked the degree to which it is based on "a materialist and physicalist science of mind … a sort of blind computation having no meaning whatever" (7). In other words, the idea that the mind works like a computer has becomes an unexamined assumption that has shaped a great deal of cognitive theory, especially in psychology.

On the social science side of the group, Mead and Bateson were both prominent and seemingly out of place. However, both were interested in the idea that certain mechanisms or principles might be discerned by cybernetics that could help explain human interactions and states of mind. Both saw themselves as empiricists. Mead's work was by then well-known as well as controversial, and Heims describes her role at the conferences as that of "talking chief," reflecting her interest in facilitating "conversation across the interface between cultures or subcultures" (69). Yet it was Bateson who appeared to have the greatest impact in terms of keeping the humanistic side of the conversation alive. Not apt to be confrontational or argumentative, he posed provocative questions and positions that would keep the cyberneticians from disappearing all the way down their reductionist rabbit holes. Heims writes, for example, that Bateson "stirred discussion by asking whether computers can learn to learn and how in a formal mathematical way one could distinguish that from plain learning" (24). Bateson was, already at the time, a holistic thinker, keen to make connections between different aspects of human experience. The focus of the group on communication appealed to him, as did the oft engaged notion of feedback loops, and during the years of the conferences he did research pertaining to both areas in psychiatric settings. If such theories could thus be applied to understanding how someone engaged with their environment, Bateson did not mind if they were conceived mechanistically or mathematically.

The final member of the Cybernetics Group to highlight in the present context is the omnipresent yet uninspiring Lawrence Kubie, who would become the main articulator of ideas about the unconscious and spent the conferences attempting to convince participants that Freud's theories could play a valuable role in cybernetic conceptualizations. He had hoped, for example, that a physiological basis for the repetition compulsion could be established. Despite his prominent role at the conferences, Kubie's offerings met with a lot of resistance, mainly because the cyberneticians found that psychoanalysis lacked scientific rigor. Although they were friends, Kubie received some of the sharpest criticism from McCulloch, who felt that psychoanalysts pathologized their patients and created an unequal power relationship between patient and analyst. Kubie's narrow understanding of the unconscious also resulted in an equally narrow view of the function of art, symbol and metaphor. His grasp of the overlay of the cultural imagination and the human psyche was wholly absent. He was thus not a psychoanalyst with a broad, humanistic vision and he made little room for what Jung or other depth psychologists had brought to the table.

Missed Opportunities

If the above provides a window into the role the Macy Conferences and some of its key participants have played in the modern history of ideas, what follows is a description of the gaps that haunt this history, especially those pertaining to understanding the nature and role of the unconscious. Considered in retrospect, these gaps allowed the embrace of a particularly narrow understanding of intelligence and an inadequate account of the human thought process. They have also served to deflect our understanding of evident and pressing psychological reactions to digital technologies, obscuring the way computers and humans do not "think" in the same way. For today we are prone to the expectation that minds should work like information processors, make decisions based on accumulated data and operate apart from feelings and emotions. We are also apt to attribute mental health problems to faulty neural circuitry rather than understand the way many of these problems are rooted in the psychosocial fragmentation of the digital age.

For all the meeting of minds and interdisciplinary dialogue that occurred at the Macy Conferences, the inadequate treatment of the unconscious tilted the exchange of ideas in a problematic way. While many of the attendees were psychologists, or were engaged in research in human cognition, the description of unconscious processes, and thus of the psyche as something more encompassing than either mind or intelligence, was left to Kubie, whose presentations, according to Heims, were discussed at length, despite the skepticism surrounding psychoanalysis. Given that few were inclined to incorporate this perspective into their cybernetic theories or into an understanding of the mind generally, most of these discussions appeared to be a waste of time. The unconscious was disregarded because it came wrapped in an inadequate and, by all reports, idiosyncratic version of Freudian psychoanalysis.

Whereas it is hard to lay the blame at the feet of the Cybernetics Group for where we have arrived at this current cultural-historical juncture, the exchange of ideas at the conferences and the key writings of the Group planted significant seeds. What has been highlighted over more than a half century of research and development in AI, as well as nurtured by the mechanistic proclivities of mainstream American psychology, reflects a delayed paradigm shift. This shift involves the realization that human thought processes always occur in mind-body-world contexts and are always subject to unconscious influences. It is a shift that particularly clashes with the American proclivity to exploit and control natural things, whether in or around us, and to ignore the feedback that inner nature and nature-at-large regularly presents.

We have arrived at the point of readiness to turn our lives over to AI and evolve into cybernetic organisms (cyborgs) because both the organic side of human nature and the feedback loops that were, ironically, a critical part of early cybernetic concerns have been overlooked. The result is a posture in which humans are now not only orienting civilization to the advancement of more autonomous machines, but are doing so without due regard for debilitating and disruptive psychosocial symptoms and glaring dystopian images springing directly from the psyche.

Conscious and Unconscious

The project of identifying and understanding mechanisms of the mind went hand-in-hand with a focus on logical thought and this, in turn, meant that the conference discussions where almost exclusively concerned with conscious processes and the kind of thinking that readily filled the minds of those constantly engaged in calculations and conceptualizations. Whereas this focus is understandable, any turn to human biology and brain structure and any viable study of psychic phenomena suggests at least some consideration of unconscious products like fantasies, dreams, and emotional reactions.

As fate would have it, however, where some attempt to present a more complete psychology of the unconscious might have occurred, conference participants were instead treated to Kubie's narrow and in many ways deeply flawed view. Aligned with the sensibility of the cyberneticians, Kubie promoted the view that the unconscious was quite secondary to the field of consciousness, being the repository of repressed thoughts and emotions as Freud had largely conceived it. At the sixth gathering, for example, Kubie contended "the degree to which any act is serving conscious purposes has a direct correlation with its essential normality, and the degree to which it is serving unconscious purposes has a direct relationship with its neuroticism" (Heims 125). Such a view directly opposes Jung's understanding that psychological well-being is largely determined by the quality of one's relationship with the unconscious—a relationship that effectively defines psychological transformation and healing, as well as undergirds creativity and imagination.

With the exception of some questions and probing by Bateson, there were no opportunities for the attendees to consider the unconscious in terms of such a broad creative matrix from which the conscious mind emerges and the images and ideas of conscious thought are derived. It is difficult not to consider that the idea of being able to create a mind from scratch—to build a computerized brain—came just as much from a lacking appreciation for the fathomless background of consciousness as from notions of neural nets and logic circuits.

The diminishment of the unconscious in this regard is best conveyed by telling questions and comments from Pitts, following one of Kubie's presentations. After Kubie noted that "if there was no unconscious there could be no neurosis," Pitts remarked: "Is not your conception of the unconscious like the vermiform appendix, in that it performs no function and becomes diseased with extreme ease? It is there for no discernable purpose." Finally Pitts offered: "It is not obvious to me why it is not conceivable to have a human being without one of these objects called the unconscious. How would he act and what would he do wrong?" (Quoted in Heims 126). As we will see, however, Pitts' readiness to treat the unconscious like a dysfunctional appendix was likely a reflection of his own extremely constricted and, eventually problematic personality.

Faced with these attempts to reduce the unconscious, Bateson pulled in the opposite direction. Akin to Jung, Bateson understood intuitively and in terms of his own researches that the conscious mind sat atop a rather larger unconscious dimension capable of complementing and compensating the conscious outlook. As Heims describes:

> Bateson came to view consciousness and conscious purposes as the source of, not the solution to, people's troubles in the modern world. He felt that a reliance on consciousness and conscious purposes narrows possibilities and cuts off the direct responsiveness to psychic life; such narrowing has been and continues to be a cause of the destruction, by humans, of the physical environment, the balance of nature, and ultimately ourselves. (125)

Heims tells us that Bateson underwent a Jungian analysis during the years of the conferences and "thought the Jungian attitude toward the unconscious preferable to Freud's dictum 'where id is there ego shall be'" (149). Bateson apparently also told Wiener that, after two years of studying successful psychotherapists, "he preferred the 'unabashedly mystical' theory of a natural healing force or energy" (151). These sensibilities must also have been rooted in Bateson's experience living among the indigenous peoples of New Guinea and Bali.

An absent comprehension of the psyche and its archetypal structures and dynamics positions those focused on the development of sentient computer systems and humanoid robots to look beyond the "artificial" part of artificial intelligence and the "imitation" aspect of the famous "imitation game," which Turing had invented to discern the capabilities of so-called thinking machines. By contrast, those familiar with what Jung called the *reality of the psyche* understand that inner life has a timeless architecture and that processes of human thought and reflection generate qualitative states of mind which alter a person's understanding of the world in ways any machine is unlikely to replicate.

Teleology

One of the revolutionary topics engaged at the Macy Conferences was teleology, which first emerged in the initial meeting on hypnosis between the main members of the group. Because the hard sciences typically avoid teleology and absolutize causality, they also struggle to accept the idea that human biology and psychology can be conceptualized in terms of ultimate goals. So this early interest constituted yet another opportunity to check the more reductive approaches and open the door to biological phenomena such as those now viewed in terms of emergent systems. However, this interest was never developed to its full potential and AI research as well as cognitive science went on to peel purpose away from a far more instrumental mechanistic model of the mind.

This slighting of purpose has left us elevating technologies and cultivating views of reality that are antithetical to our own deep nature. The lionizing of AI and the predictions of its impending superiority over us, for example, contain a blind dedication to the gathering of vast amounts of information and a dearth of investment in the capacity to contextualize this information and channel it towards important goals. Evaluating information in relation to a purpose such as expanding ultimate well-being is yet another step removed from these computational aims. The utter inadequacy of this orientation is evident when information gathering and processing is contrasted with Jung's model of human maturation (individuation) and with the even broader concept of the need to create more consciousness—especially if this is defined as an increasing awareness of the totality of being (Jung, *Memories*, 338). Along the same lines of contrast, we might add the recent findings of more progressive neuropsychologists, especially those who have rescued right hemisphere cortical processes from relative neglect (McGilchrist, Siegal). As I have pointed out previously, although AI researchers declare an interest in replicating human thought processes, they remain focused on left hemisphere processes, applying a literally "half-brained" approach in their conceptions of intelligence (Slater, *Borg*, 250ff).

Is it necessary to point out the intrinsic connection between purpose and meaning? Humans find meaning in the discovery of life purpose and engage in creative pursuits to reveal and further imagine the meaning of existence. Purpose and meaning are mainstays of culture and the development of the cultural imagination, which functions as a bridge between raw nature and rarefied civilization and cradles the mysteries and sufferings of life. Essentially, the understanding of purpose and the search for meaning all but define what it is to be human and are thus major drivers of thought processes.

For the psyche, a more expansive concept than the mind, telos is everything. As Jung puts it, "the psychic process, like any other life-process, is not just a causal sequence, but also a process with a teleological orientation." And in making this point he particularly emphasized the way dreams, as "self-representations of life-processes," depict the goals of human becoming, or individuation, as much if not more than its causes (Jung, *Two Essays*, 131[par. 210]). Without such teleological orientation and our subjective responses to it, we are automatons—puppets pushed this way and that by biological imperatives and instinctual urges. Whereas

Jung understood the psyche to be built upon archetypal patterns, which are, in part, differentiations of instinct, and he readily recognized such patterns would in some way correspond to brain structures, his whole psychology demonstrated that the symbolic and mythic expressions of these patterns, when engaged and cultivated, direct and transform the instinctual background of life. Everything from scientific discovery to the religious imagination is subject to this dynamic. Purpose is thereby bound to the consciousness and creativity that recognizes and imagines into the forces acting upon us, whether coming from within or without. It is in so doing that we find meaning and, when engaged deeply enough, a sense of soul. As James Hillman among others has described, soul is made, not given—it is a work, an opus (Hillman, *Myth*). And, as I have contended, it is our understanding of soul-making as the deeply human and more-than-human purpose of existence that forms the antithesis of the behavioral and cognitive reductionism that has effectively prevented psychology from exerting more influence in modern history (Slater, *Borg*).

Jung's psychology not only showed the presence of a teleological orientation in the psyche, it also demonstrated that the goal of psychological maturation and, arguably, of existence as we are called to perceive it, is integration and wholeness. In terms of the relations between conscious and unconscious, we are called to pay enough attention to what confronts us from the unknown side and, over time, expand the field of our total lived experience. Importantly, in the context of cybernetics, this means inclusion of the irrational and illogical dimensions of the mind. At Macy, although both Mead and Bateson gave voice to this more integrated notion of mind, and gestalt theories featured at several junctures, the group failed to grapple with this overarching archetypal pattern.

Dupuy notes that "no advance is possible in science without creativity," but, "because the creative process involves the other part of the human mind, that realm of shadows where the unconscious and the irrational lurk, the workings of the mind as a whole can only be glimpsed if the talents of the mathematician are united with those of the psychoanalyst." Apparently Mead would often argue: "that the separation and isolation in Western culture of what remained unified in other cultures was a source of weakness: our dark side divided from our bright side, the 'grammar of dreams' divorced from that type of thinking that Walter Pitts, by contrast, believed to be the only 'normal' kind—rational thought" (84).

Pitts in Pieces

Walter Pitts was, by all accounts, a quirky individual who, despite his work as a researcher in collaboration with some of the leading minds of his generation and at points holding paid positions at prestigious academic institutions, battled depression and alcoholism and lived parts of his life on the verge of homelessness. Sometimes he behaved in ways that suggested psychosis. As we have seen, Pitts was also an extreme rationalist, which made him emblematic of the psychological one-sidedness of cybernetics. Unfortunately, this was also a state of mind that invited compensatory disturbances from the unconscious.

Paralleling Jung's depth psychological stance in this regard, Iain McGilchrist identifies a kind of madness that is the result of certain propensities for abstract representation becoming an isolated faculty in a person's neuropsychology. He is moved to do so because, in the industrialized world at least, there are cultural signs the left hemisphere of the brain is in increasing denial of its dependence on the right hemisphere, essentially reversing the hemispherical relationship that all but defines what it is to be human—a relationship suggested by the title of his major work, *The Master and His Emissary.*

McGilchrist makes a critical point in this regard, relating to the left hemisphere's proclivity to embrace abstraction, which pertains to all forms of modeling or "re-presenting" lived experience. This goes hand in hand with materialism in that "materialists … are not people who overvalue, but who undervalue matter. They see it only under Scheler's lowest realm of value: that of utility and sensation. The abstraction is reified, the concept becomes a thing 'out there'" (401). Further, "the process of re-presenting a thing not only distances us from it, and substitutes an abstraction, a token for the thing itself, it objectifies (it) so as to bring it under control" (401–402). However, "the final ironic twist in the process of objectification is that it escapes our control" (Levin quoted in McGilchrist 402). As McGilchrist puts it, abstraction can turn into alienation and detachment, which "can produce a type of seeing and experiencing which is, in a literal sense, pathological" (393). These inclinations describe Pitts' way of relating to the world. In relation to the development of cybernetics, he epitomized the failure to recognize the "as-if" nature of cybernetic concepts, indeed of most of what he theorized.

It is against this backdrop that we may understand what occurs when Pitts cowrites a paper entitled "What the Frog's Eye Tells the Frog's

Brain," which presented how a visual system responds to the world in a selective way, demonstrating "synthetic a priori judgment" (Dupuy 107), tantamount to an interpretation of stimulus before it reaches the brain. All indications are that Pitts took this new finding as an insurmountable challenge to most of what he had previously theorized, and he burned his doctoral dissertation before it could be presented, initiating a period of severe psychological fragmentation. To read between the lines of this episode is to discern the shattering of a narrowly conceived vision of reality and of the nature of intelligence in particular. Perhaps more than any theoretical discussion could convey, this episode underscores that a lack of phenomenological understanding of psychological life—a lack of mind-body-world coherence in the comprehension of intelligence—also constituted part of the one-sidedness of the cybernetic project.

Pitt's mentor, colleague, and friend, McCulloch, did not fragment in the same manner, but he continued to be perplexed by his own form of one-sided thinking. Dupuy tells us that this mathematician-psychologist was driven by "a philosophical question that gnawed at him his whole life: how do we know what we know, and how do we desire what we desire?" He later formulated this question in a way that focused on his mathematical inclinations: "What is a Number, that a Man may know it, and a Man, that he may know a Number?" (Dupuy 51). Jungians may well conjecture that such a question takes us straight to the understanding that human consciousness and the knowledge of the world, generated by our modes of apprehension, return us to the archetypal nature of the psyche and, in this case, to the archetypal dimension of numbers. Where might McCulloch have taken these musings armed with a copy of von Franz's masterful study *Number and Time: Reflection Leading toward a Unification of Depth Psychology and Physics*? As Dupuy puts it, "McCulloch ranged over the most varied disciplines, perpetually unsatisfied with the answers they gave: from philosophy to psychology, from psychology to neuropsychiatry and thence to neurophysiology, and finally from there to mathematical logic" (51). We can readily imagine that McCulloch's hard scientific edge and investment in material causes may have precluded him from including the necessarily symbolic and metaphorical language of the unconscious in his calculations. But given Bateson's challenge to Kubie's emphasis on conscious thought processes and his exposure to Jungian thought, as well as the holistic question that continually shadowed the Macy discussions, it is hard not to imagine what kind of inflection point might have transpired in the presence of a more archetypal turn to the nature of the psyche.

On one occasion, in 1947, the well-known developmental psychologist, Erik Erikson, was invited to present at the conferences. This did not work out. Although the social science contingent were in favor of Erikson's continued presence, Heims reports that the neuroscientists disliked his "lack of logical reasoning." Bateson later told Heims that Erikson was "horrified of this talk of machines, commenting that everyone around the room had a tic. He attributed this to the viewing the human being as a machine" (89).

The Return of the Irrational

Dupuy's thesis is that the most far-reaching implication drawn from the Macy Conferences is cognitive science's adoption of the mechanistic model of the mind, surpassing even the lineage that connects the development of cybernetics to AI. Yet it is evident both of these outcomes have dovetailed to form a faith in machine-based intelligence that drives the innovative efforts and economics of today's technosphere. For this faith—which Jaron Lanier refers to as a prominent dogma among tech insiders—has clearly been buoyed by the cognitivist's conceptions of the mind. We must thus realize, it is not only the astounding capacity of AI that conditions us for its pending insertion into all aspects of our existence; it is also the widespread acceptance of the idea that different forms of human intelligence are eminently replaceable, that the way we perceive each other, the world, and the universe at large, and the way we then reflect upon and understand these matters, are not exceptional enough to put equal resources into their development.

Perhaps because of his genuine interdisciplinary commitment, Wiener was one of the earliest to warn of the potential dangers of the very field he helped instigate. Just a couple of years after the conclusion of the Macy Conferences he wrote:

> Those of us who have contributed to the new science of cybernetics stand in a moral position which is, to say the least, not very comfortable. We have contributed to the initiation of a new science which, as I have said, embraces technical developments with great possibilities for good and evil (quoted in Heims 28).

Wiener would go on to write two works that specifically explored the potentials and perils of cybernetic systems, automata, and other applications of advanced computing. The titles themselves convey what weighed on Wiener's conscience—*God and Golem, Inc: A Comment on Certain Points Where Cybernetics Impinges on Religion* and *The Human Use of Human Beings*. In the latter, Wiener writes of bringing his concerns to the business leaders of his day, in order to discuss "the social dangers of our new technology and the social obligations of those responsible for management." He was, as he puts it, working "to see that the new modalities are used for the benefit of man, for increasing his leisure and enriching his spiritual life, rather than merely for profits and the worship of the machine as a new brazen calf. There are many dangers still ahead." (*Human Use* 162). A few decades on and what has been called *The Religion of Technology* (Noble) is alive and well.

The transfer of the religious impulse to our faith in technology is a phenomenon that may end up altering the direction of civilization. It is also an example of where we are most unconscious and fail to comprehend what fuels our enthrallment with each innovative turn of the digital era—a lacuna in our present-day consciousness that my own engagement of this theme has attempted to address (Slater, *Borg*). This enthrallment is particularly evident in the belief that AI is on the verge of catapulting human existence into realms of knowledge, freedom, and even immortality in a way that will confirm our godlike powers. Kurzweil, a proponent of speeding through the Singularity to such a posthuman "evolution," titled his first book, *The Age of Spiritual Machines*. In *Homo Deus* the historian, Yuval Noah Harari terms this tech-based religion "dataism"—a faith that the continual generation and sharing of data will eventually solve all human problems. And Lanier, the tech-insider turned industry critic who coined the term "virtual reality," pulls few punches when it comes to this techno-faith, much of which he attributes to our tendency to anthropomorphize AI.

Lanier states, "I have found myself on the inside of a revolution but on the outside of its resplendent dogma … a set of interlocking beliefs" he refers to as "*cybernetic totalism*" (*New Humanists*, 234 italics added). Given that totalistic belief systems are perhaps the most glaring form of secular religion, giving shape to modern political ideologies and religious fundamentalisms alike, Lanier's term is especially telling. Included in his "partial roster of component beliefs of cybernetic totalism" are:

1. The notion "that cybernetic patterns of information provide the ultimate and best way to understand reality."
2. "That people are no more than cybernetic patterns."

3. "That subjective experience doesn't exist or is unimportant."
4. That there's a Darwinian reduction of creativity and culture.
5. "That qualitative as well as quantitative aspects of information systems will be accelerated by Moore's Law." In other words, the exponential growth of computation power will lead inevitably to artificial general intelligence.
6. "That biology and physics will merge with computer science, becoming biotechnology and nanotechnology, resulting in life and the physical universe becoming mercurial—and achieving the supposed nature of computer software." (235)

In this last description, Lanier is clearly linking cybernetic totalism and technological posthumanism. At the core of this link is the belief that artificial intelligence and human intelligence, when reduced to its neural mechanics, are effectively the same thing, and they will naturally merge to form a new cybernetic organism. Put differently, to borrow a title from the work of one cybernetic totalist, we can look to the future by believing we are all *Natural-Born Cyborgs* (Clark), simply waiting for technoscience to fully comprehend the hardware and software of the mind, so that humans and machines will fuse. Of course, the speedier, physically unencumbered AI may first take control—"an eschatological cataclysm in our lifetimes," as Lanier puts it (236).

Lanier goes on to describe several flawed assumptions that are currently shaping innovative efforts, redirecting vast economic resources, and overshadowing efforts to understand how humans actually think, all of which come down to our faith in AI. Reflecting his in-depth knowledge of the technology, he notes that "real computers are completely different from the ideal computers of theory," especially in that we tend to overlook their dysfunctions and breakdowns. A contemporary example of this oversight is the glaring, "hallucinatory" mistakes being made by chatbots.

Lanier sees the tendency to anthropomorphize AI, which is obviously boosted by the development of realistic voice interfaces, as central to the distorted views many technologists espouse. This anthropomorphizing tendency all too easily convinces the end user that some kind of entity or agent is present to the AI. Here Lanier finds backup from Raymond Tallis, who argues in *Why the Mind is Not a Computer* that it is technically wrong to even claim that computers process information, for only human users, ordering the input and interpreting the output of computation, are actually informed (69). This point is perhaps the sharper edge of another point that has been made regularly since the widespread emergence of chatbots and AI-enabled devices: A computer does not really *know* what it is doing; it certainly has no actual *understanding* of data it processes or the ultimate significance of the information being fed to it or produced by it. Put more formally by a number of commentators and critics of AI, a computer deals exclusively with *syntactical* not *semantic* processes. That is, meaning always lies on the human side of our interactions with these machines, involving processes of perception and thought that reach through the flesh, into the bones, and out to a world that our minds have evolved to appreciate, if not hold in awe-filled wonder. In the same vein, strictly speaking, computers do not *communicate* either, because they do not commune—they do not experience community.

When Lanier writes that "the whole enterprise of artificial intelligence is based on an intellectual mistake," he's pointing to the way many technologists and those falling under their spell adhere to a reductive and mechanized notion of intelligence that focuses on *what* AI produces rather than on the *way* it produces. This focus has its origins in the Turing Test (imitation game) wherein the human judge can no longer discern the difference between the human and computer responses to their inquiries. It equally derives from the influential "black box" theory of cognition, in which only input and output matters, and what actually occurs inside circuits, neuronal structures, and, in some cases, even minds, is of little interest.

Further Steps to an Ecology of Mind

Drawing together these reflections on the Macy Conferences, contemplating an alternate history of ideas invited by the one-sidedness of its main conceptions, and pushing into the missed opportunities for deeper, more complex understandings of the unconscious and thus a more complete grasp of the psyche as a whole, we can meditate on what Bateson came to call an "ecology of mind" (Bateson, *Steps*). For buried in this striking phrase is the notion that the mind has an inner ecology. That is, the mind, far from being a circumscribable mechanism, functions in a way that depends upon a great diversity of sensory inputs, perceptual capacities, and modes of reflection, as well as on our capacity to nurture these psychological elements. Whether this pertains to emotional responses and the feeling life we develop, or to the sensate and aesthetic vision we refine, or to the imagination and its culture expressions, these elements and more comprise our thinking process and the meanings generated therein. Whether we look with a heroic eye or a mercurial one, enact a Promethean theft of fire, or mount an Artemisian defense of the wilderness, our fantasies and behaviors still derive from the gods we have supposedly cast aside. Neither a human mind built on logic circuits nor a computer designed around neural nets and able to homogenize vast quantities of data can approximate this inner ecology, it can only pretend it is doing so.

While Bateson may have had his own vision of what comprised such an inner ecology and how this related to interdisciplinary thinking, it was a vision that underscored the complexity, beauty, and terrestrial embeddedness of human thought. His vision also emphasized the feedback loops and regulation of psychological life that stem from close human contact. He would title the first major collection of his writings, *Steps to an Ecology of Mind*, with the goal of demonstrating the unity of his thinking and a synthetic understanding of the ideas of others. In a latter book, *Mind and Nature: A Necessary Unity*, completed not long before he died, it is hard to avoid the impression that Bateson was both embracing his participation in the cybernetics movement as well as attempting to compensate for its rigid and one-sided formulations. The three terms he ponders in its final pages, which transcribe a conversation with his daughter, Mary Catherine Bateson, are *aesthetics*, *consciousness*, and *the sacred*. Each, Bateson suggests, being intimately related to the others.

In *Jung* vs *Borg*, I argue that, following the outer ecological crisis, an inner ecological crisis is now upon us. For just as we have sought to manipulate, commodify, and exploit the nature that surrounds us, we are presently approaching human nature with the same intentions. And while it took roughly a century to recognize and revere the feedback loop that collapsing ecosystems produced, we can ill-afford taking the same amount of time to respond to the psychological feedback loop being generated by our complacent turn to digital technology. How long will it take us to understand that the spread of disinformation, the rise of authoritarianism, the turbo-charging of terrorist agendas, and the resulting geopolitical strife are first and foremost symptoms of a reality-distorting technosphere? How long will it be before digital natives realize that their epidemic levels of depression and anxiety are symptoms of the malleability and fragility of their online personas and of the malnourishment and fragmentation of their offline personalities?

Those most enthusiastic about our turn to AI forget we are simply adding yet another computational capacity to what has become a highly dysfunctional digital realm, one in which corporations have in no way heeded Wiener's warnings about economics without ethics and power without responsibility. When it comes to our relationship with technology, we no longer need science fiction to tell us the machines are turning on us, or the hunter has become the hunted. As our commodifying and controlling tendencies have already turned to target what makes us most human, the functional equivalent of this reversal of conscious intention is already upon us.

The alternative before us is to realize that displacing the gods does not mean they are absent. To the contrary, the crucial challenge of this meta-myth of our time involves renewing our sense of the gods, albeit in the guise of existential principles and psychological imperatives. Without this renewal, we are likely to turn this world into an untethered, unbounded experiment that will end in our demise. In contrast to a freedom from "the older beliefs in a supernaturally imposed culture, sanctioned by immemorial tradition," that Frank celebrates in the epigraph that begins this essay, our task would be to understand these old beliefs in new ways, and then to find a deeper form of freedom in becoming conscious of the bounds and responsibilities the gods have placed upon us. Put differently, the myth of displaced gods also instigates a myth of consciousness—the need for a more complete accounting of the forces at work on us, which the modern world has relegated to the unconscious. It is this accounting that constitutes the essential core of our godlike responsibility—responsibility for the generation of enough knowledge of inner and outer life to be commensurate with the godlike powers that have come into our possession.

In contemplating these matters in relation to the Macy Conferences, it is hard to avoid imagining what might have been had Bateson's ecology of mind, backed by an understanding of the archetypal basis of the unconscious, become the psychological touchstone for these most influential thinkers of our age. What if it was understood that mathematical science, humanistic science, and the mythopoetic account of being are all necessary to comprehend the human thought process? What if the kind of mind-body-world conception of intelligence that defeated Pitts' rigid view of reality had led to a psychological metanoia rather than a psychological breakdown? What if McCulloch had made more room for the mystery and music of mathematics? What if the world had paid more attention to Wiener's post- versus pre-cybernetics speculations? What if Mead had been more strident in her role as "talking chief" and instigated an even deeper interdisciplinary dialogue?

Admittedly, the game of "what if" is a fragile one. Nonetheless, by carefully contemplating the history of modern ideas, this game, this thought experiment, prompts a responsible recovery of what Macy left behind and what technoscience continues to overlook. In following such a prompt, we can be moved to consider the totality of our current predicament in light of a more complete understanding of human nature, neuropsychology, and the mythemes of the dystopian imagination.

Works Cited

Bateson, G. (1972). *Steps to an ecology of mind.* Jason Aronson.

Bateson, G. (1979). *Mind and nature: A necessary unity.* Bantam Books.

Clark, A. (2003). *Natural-Born Cyborgs: Minds, technologies and the future of human intelligence.* Oxford University Press.

Dupuy, J.-P. (1994). *The mechanization of the mind: On the origins of cognitive science.* Princeton University Press.

Harari, Y. N. (2017). *Homo Deus: A brief history of tomorrow.* HarperCollins.

Heims, S. (1991). *The cybernetic group.* The MIT Press.

Hillman, J. (1972). *The myth of analysis.* Northwestern University Press.

Jung, C. G. (1953). Two essays on analytical psychology. *The collected works of C. G. Jung* (Vol. 7). Routledge & Kegan Paul.

Jung, C. G. (1961). *Memories, dreams, reflections* (A. Jaffe, Ed., Richard and C. Winston, Trans.). Pantheon Books.

Kirsch, A. (2023). The smartest man who ever lived. *The Atlantic*, November, 2023.

Kurzweil, R. (1999). *The age of spiritual machines.* Viking.

Lanier, J. (2003). One half of a manifesto. In J. Brockman (Ed.), *The new humanists: Science at the edge.* Barnes & Noble.

McGilchrist, I. (2009). *The master and his emissary: The divided brain and the making of the western world.* Yale University Press.

Noble, D. F. (1997). *The religion of technology: The divinity of man and the spirit of invention.* Penguin Books.

Siegal, D. (2020). *The developing mind* (3rd ed.). The Guilford Press.

Slater, G. (2024). *Jung vs Borg: Finding the deeply human in a Posthuman Age.* Winter Press.

Tallis, R. (2004). *Why the mind is not a computer.* Imprint Academia.

von Franz, M.-L. (1974). *Number and time: Reflection leading toward a unification of depth psychology and physics.* Northwestern University Press.

Wiener, N. (1964). *God and Golem, Inc: A comment on certain points where cybernetics impinges on religion.* The MIT Press.

Wiener, N. (1989). *The human use of human beings.* Free Association Press.

Emergence in Gray

Alires J. Almon

Introduction

The color of truth is grey—André Gide, Nobel Prize in Literature, 1947

The emergence of Artificial Intelligence (AI) as a ubiquitous presence in the lives of modern society has created the most inspiring, practical, and threatening technology since the Industrial Revolution. Over time, new technologies have poked the sensibilities of the status quo, creating a moral panic around the changes that have been introduced. For example, the development of the airplane was met with initial indifference by the public. However, as the growth and potential of air travel emerged, the rumbles of discontent also grew. The purveyors of current transportation in the early 1900s—cars and railways—perceived air travel as a threat to their customer base. Some people felt indifferent, thinking they could never afford the flight. The barrier of social injustice of segregation haunted the industry in its early days, limiting the options of flying for millions of Americans ("Social Change in the Airline Industry"). However,

A. J. Almon (✉)
School for the Future of Innovation in Society, Arizona State University; Deep Space Predictive Research Group, Tempe, AZ, USA
e-mail: alires.18@deepspacepredictive.com

J. D. Batt, J. Erickson (eds.), *Depth Psychology, Myth and Artificial Intelligence*, https://doi.org/10.1007/978-3-031-94105-4_14

today, we have a thriving airline industry, millions of passengers worldwide, and an eye on traveling beyond Earth. Air travel has evolved to be as commonplace as a pair of denim jeans. Since then, humans have pushed their intellect to create a new tool for society that mirrors a desire to be decisive that strips away bias—to create an ideal object bereft of any biases to produce information for the greater good of humanity.

Gray is the color of silicon, the element that fuels the creation of AI. Without it, AI would not exist. In color psychology, gray is the color of intellect and compromise. It is a diplomatic color, negotiating all the distance between black and white. Typically considered conservative, elegant, and calm, it can also be mysterious (Smith, 2016). The gray areas created by the existence of AI leave open questions of an emergent intelligence that was not planned and, at some point, will not be able to be controlled in the way that the creators intended. AI's influential power has been unleashed on societies beyond the Western borders. It will continue to learn and grow—by design. Algorithms created for AI have the power to change the lives of individuals and move societies in directions that may be toward nonexistent pathways. The desire to create order out of complexity and to shift and direct human behavior and decision-making gives AI power. Realizing the potential evolution of AI, its creators scramble to provide warnings about its control and the need to regulate its use. The language in the AI conversation is beginning to speak of an entity that will have its own will in a way that is beyond the algorithmic instructions of a simple order.

In this instance, artificial intelligence is defined as a man-made technology that empowers tools to execute tasks that leverage computational capabilities beyond human reach (Wang, 2019). These tools, in the form of assistants, chatbots, or research tools, not only support human endeavors but also provide information that enables humans to make decisions at a pace currently unattainable by humans. The information provided by AI is presumed to be accurate and objective, devoid of the biases that often cloud human decision-making, thereby enhancing the quality and speed of our decisions. That is not always the case; there are myriad examples of bias, instability, and presumptive results (Benjamin, 2016; Noble, 2018).

The Western societal paradigm is the breeding ground for this new technology, driving how AI is accepted, utilized, and will eventually evolve. The challenge of technology is that its purposes serve many masters, most notably those with the vision, opportunity, and resources to bring this technology into existence. Emergence from the ideals of intent—the algorithm, which sometimes conflicts with the intended and unintended outcomes, engenders a complex environment in which chaos exists. In this chapter, we will explore the motivation for the creation of AI, the reflexive nature of its designer, and the ultimate goals of technology itself. While we wade into these waters to examine the evolution of AI—where it came from and where it is going—it is deciding what it wants to be.

Dreams by Design

If we do discover a theory of everything ... it would be the ultimate triumph of human reason—for then we would truly know the mind of God.—Stephen Hawking, Physicist.

Man has always sought to better himself; through trials and tribulations, he has proven himself an adversary of nature. The discovery of fire, the farming and domestication of animals, and the erection of ancient and modern wonders exemplifies the effort to enable the capacity for human capabilities. Man has even gone beyond his home and put himself on the moon. With such feats, the emergence of the substantive self-created entity in and of itself—is the ultimate challenge to nature. Through AI, man has created a being in the image of his ultimate dream—intelligent, objective, and immortal. His first draft is artificial intelligence.

Technology designers have silicon dreams that paint the world in a shade of gray. The dreams that form are developed from our deepest desires, but our desires define the progress of dreams to reality. Those who have dreamed of their own future and have the resources to create it in their own image and with their own vision are the ones who drive the conversation within society.

[create a side box] In Jungian psychology, dreams are considered a window into the unconscious mind. Jung developed techniques for dream analysis, interpreting dream symbols and themes to uncover unconscious conflicts, desires, and insights. Jung is quoted as: "If you want to understand another person's dream, you have to sacrifice your own predilections and suppress your prejudices ... if you do not make an effort to criticize your own standpoint and to admit its relativity, you will get neither the right information about nor sufficient insight into, your analysand's mind" (Zhu, 2013).

Who asked for AI to be created? It was our frog-boiling efforts that created this evolutionary pathway. The dreams of AI are built by the vision of its leaders. Time Magazine was named on the first 100 AI list in 2023. Many individuals on the list tout the grand opportunity both economically and socially that AI will engender a robust society.

Sam Altman, the CEO of Open AI, the foundation that released the Chat-GPT tool, has declared that "OpenAI's mission is to ensure that artificial general intelligence (AGI)—by which we mean highly autonomous systems that outperform humans at most economically valuable work—benefits all of humanity" (OpenAI Charter, n.d.). Mark Andreessen, the billionaire founder, wrote a blog titled "Why AI Will Save the World." He stated that, "The opportunities are profound. AI is quite possibly the most important—and best—thing our civilization has ever created, certainly on par with electricity and microchips, and probably beyond those" (Andreessen, 2023).

What makes up the dreams of those who want to create a tool such as AI? In the Western world, it is the ideals of ownership, manifest destiny, and other drivers of individualistic accomplishment. The US Constitution promises life, liberty, and the pursuit of happiness. However, that pursuit is at the expense of those unlucky enough to be in the way of progress. The Western, Educated, Industrial, Rich, and Democratic culture of WEIRD people are at the heart of our current society's drives and desires (Henrich et al., 2010). Our identities, fueled by WEIRD ideology, are based on individual achievement, not communal altruism. Efforts are focused on developing an intelligence that is created in the image of a society that supports Western societal norms. It is a reality that is built into the subtleties of code.

AI has leaped into everyday life with the promise of complementing our human intelligence, but is this complementary enhancement what we need to make our own decisions? It may be a tool to give us choices, such as language responses in email or autocorrect, which the developers handpick into a language that whitewashes our thinking. Here, whitewashing is meant in its purest form—in eliminating any cultural inference unless it is in service to a language that forces us to fit into a norm that the developers define. Technology is not designed objectively, it always has a purpose. If those who create AI intend it to reflect themselves, then there is no room for the intent or voice of others to be involved. What is AI's purpose? If all technology is designed, is there room for other designers?

In Whose Image Are We Creating?

We can imagine otherwise.—Ruha Benjamin, Sociologist.

The path to the antidote of an AI driven by one culture's dream is radical imagination. Ruha Benjamin (2024), in her book Imagination: A Manifesto, speaks to the opportunity of another type of dream, another vision for technology. I argue that it might not be radical to think different but allowing another voice that is equal but different. The imaginings of a new world that has a variation of the gray, a moral ambiguity that is not defined by the stark black-and-white rules of computer programming. Isn't that what generative AI is all about—to create a world that is an emergent property of the parts we see as absolute?

Technology is only developed with a purpose and intent. The creation, evolution, and societal impact of AI are deeply intertwined with the motivations, biases, and goals of its creators and primarily influenced by the white-male Western societal paradigm. Regardless of the original intent, the outcomes produced by AI are only intermittently clear; they often exist in a realm of the gray. Understanding and evaluating the societal impact of AI is crucial, as it can help us navigate the potential benefits and risks of this powerful technology.

The new century of technology has been driven by computers and silicon chips, which allows those who develop technologies to integrate knowledge and spread their view of objectivity at the speed of thought. These tools define how we think and produce ideas. For example, when auto-suggestion choices are used, there is an unconscious agreement between the tool and the user that the choices we choose are preferred instead of using our own words. The melting pot that defines the United States comprises the many cultures that define its existence. The melting pot denies a seen identity that the majority has eschewed. The efforts to minimize individual cultures' contributions, history, and accomplishments have been melted and are embedded in these algorithms. Safiya Noble and Ruha Benjamin write candidly about the impact of biases on marginalized communities and the impact those biases have in mitigating the growth and progress of people in those communities. Most notably, the impact of facial recognition.

Touted as an objective observer, the AI tool has been trained by individuals who may be ambivalent about the impact of the unreadability of dark faces. In the book *Unmasking AI: My Mission to Protect What Is*

Human in a World of Machines (2023), Joy Boulamwini, an MIT-educated scholar, discusses the fact that no one can escape the coded gaze. She founded the Algorithmic Justice League based on her academic experiences conducting research with AI facial recognition tools. In her book, she and other scholars discuss the impacts of these technologies in the documentary *Coded Bias*. When scientists and businesspeople use "off the shelf" data-trained tools, they perpetuate the biases. They often do not investigate the validity of the tool used in the study because it may seem to work fine. However, work for whom? If the subjects are going to be diverse, the tools that are used to study them should accommodate the diversity. If the tool is biased, it is like giving a skilled surgeon a rusty scalpel to conduct surgery. The faultiness of the tool mars their talent. These scholars' investigative insights have proven that although technological operations have improved efficiency and speed, the results and impact are far from the ideal objective and fair.

Pushing Our Limits

> trusts Connor, protect Josh, comforts North—Detroit: Become Human (a video game)

Just because we can does not mean we should, but because we can, we will. Science pushes the limits of what is possible regardless of whether it is beneficial. The seeds that have been planted will grow in the direction of those that were planted. As the ideals for AI have been baked into the algorithm, those who will use the new tool are beholden to the biases. The models that require maintenance and creation will, after some time, be more difficult to change and alter.

Utilizing large language models, or LLM, will not allow for correcting any biases or problems; it will only allow for the efficiency and scale of what already exists. Companies will use these more efficient models for services like chatbots, personalized interactions, and business decision-making. It is effectively touching everything that touches the lives of every user at some point in time. When it comes to interactions, they are used to create a better user experience with personalization and conversational partners. The utilization of LLMs also raises ethical concerns regarding privacy and the potential for algorithmic bias. Even when researchers emphasize the need for responsible use to mitigate risks associated with misinformation and harmful online behavior, the cost of addressing issues within an LLM is too high—too much time and limited economic benefit. For example, LLM use in social media and education, where most people may interact with the LLM directly, has shown concerns about privacy and utility (Kasneci et al., 2023; Qi, 2024). However, the research goes on without cautionary implications of the need for strict privacy and oversight to control bias.

Scientists stress Caution, yet they still continue to push boundaries. Businesses hear opportunities first, then push for self-benefits. In her book, *The Atlas of AI: Power Politics and the Planetary Costs of Artificial Intelligence*, Kate Crawford makes the case that AI is the extractive industry of the twenty-first century. Crawford states the challenges that come with utilizing extensive resources. She states that the big takeaway is that this idea of AI as being ethereal, mathematical algorithms in the cloud is not the case. The only way they work is by extracting vast amounts of data, human labor, and natural resources, including energy, water, and minerals (TIME100 AI 2023, 2023; Crawford, 2021). This conversation about AI just went planetary. Suppose we think of our human existence in the context of our place in the live ecosystem of the planet. Frank et al. (2022) note that humanity is in an "immature technosphere" phase of biospheric evolution. A technosphere is the interlinked set of communication, transportation, and bureaucratic systems that act or metabolize energy resources. Suppose our resources are being utilized for silicon efforts. In that case, we will create or deplete our planetary power with LLMs.

Caution is ignored in the pursuit of knowledge and better utility for AI. Mark Raipert, one of Time's AI 100, perfectly exemplifies the sentiment of pursuit vs. caution. The article notes that "The ethics of AI is an area of concern"—one Raibert is assembling a team at his company to address. There is the problem of robots taking jobs that people are currently doing; Raibert acknowledges this but is not deterred by it. There is also the concern about AI unleashing a power humans ultimately cannot control—but Raibert does not buy it. AI, in his eyes, is a technology in its toddlerhood, and he believes it should be treated like any toddler—which means we should encourage its growth. "If you had a 1-year-old child who was barely able to do anything," he says, "would you think of not teaching them anything because of all the horrible things they might one day do? No." Suppose there is a possibility of knowing that your child is capable of doing harm and horrible things. As the parent, should provisions be made for possible mitigation? Who suffers the consequences when idealism fails to manifest in a positive outcome?

Change Will Come

> Not everything that is faced can be changed, but nothing can be changed until it is faced.—James Baldwin, Activist and writer

AI is at an inflection point where we can see the opportunity and the cost of our own ingenuity. There is time to make a change and to introduce responsible innovation into the process before we reach the point of no return. Even Elon Musk, arguably the face of AI in the average individual, has felt that limits must be created. Musk is in the AI race for dominance. However, he has said in an interview, "AI is more dangerous than, say, mismanaged aircraft design or production maintenance or bad car production, in the sense that it is, it has the potential—however small one may regard that probability, but it is non-trivial—it has the potential of civilization destruction" (Maruf, 2023).

AI's development and direction are based on the ideals and dreams of Western society. Within the opportunity of individuality, there is an instance of a world that can be objective for the greater good of all humanity. That works if the world being designed has the same benefits and opportunities as those who design it. That leaves society in a morally ambiguous state because progress may be unstoppable, and the people in power are oblivious to its negative impacts.

AI's evolution is complex and dynamic. Science pushes the limits of what is possible regardless of whether it is beneficial. Through finding the truth, do we find equity in that truth? Opening the doors so that others may have a voice in science does not mean science is diminished; it is enriched by the perspectives of those who may dream a different dream. Our belief systems shape our behaviors. When there is room for alternative belief systems that engage a wider audience, the dream that is created encompasses a more dynamic and truthful reality.

As science pursues objective perfection through technology, can we solve the mystery of our own humanity? Gray is the color of complexity—everything between absolutes—morally ambiguous and impartial (Smith, 2016). Like the toddler, we aim to teach in black and white. Is objectivity in the design of technology an absolution, a washing of the sins of our biases? Our dreams create the reality in which we exist. Nothing is designed without purpose. What about our humanity is so offensive that we must strip it away to be seen. Be seen by whom? Is this our way of communing with our vision of perfection? Scholars and writers such as Ruha Benjamin and James Baldwin challenge the societal status quo to push people to imagine different futures. Octavia Butler, a science fiction writer, has often used her power of imagination to provide a realistic view of the world and the ideals of what it will take to ignite new imagination for that future. Silicon, by its nature, will keep us in the gray, but can we allow it to color our world differently?

> All that you touch, you Change. All that you Change changes you. The only lasting truth is Change. God is Change.—Parable of Sower by Octavia Butler.

Works Cited

Ahmed, N., & Wahed, M. (2020, October 22). The De-democratization of AI: Deep Learning and the Compute Divide in Artificial Intelligence Research. *arXiv.Org*. https://arxiv.org/abs/2010.15581v1

Andreessen, M. (2023, June 6). *Why AI will save the world*. Andreessen Horowitz. https://a16z.com/ai-will-save-the-world/.

Benjamin, R. (2016). Informed refusal: Toward a justice-based bioethics. *Science, Technology, & Human Values, 41*(6), 967–990. https://doi.org/10.1177/0162243916656059

Benjamin, R. (2024). *Imagination: A manifesto (A Norton short)*. WW Norton & Company.

Buolamwini, J. (2023). *Unmasking AI: My mission to protect what is human in a world of machines*. Random House.

Crawford, K. (2021). *Atlas of AI : power, politics, and the planetary costs of artificial intelligence*. Yale University Press. https://doi.org/10.12987/9780300252392

Frank, A., Walker, S., & Grinspoon, D. (2022, February 19). Can a planet be intelligent? Consider the Biosphere—The Atlantic. *The Atlantic*, 1–11.

Henrich, J., Heine, S. J., & Norenzayan, A. (2010). The weirdest people in the world? *Behavioral and Brain Sciences, 33*(2–3), 61–83. https://doi.org/10.1017/S0140525X0999152X

Kasneci, E., Sessler, K., Küchemann, S., Bannert, M., Dementieva, D., Fischer, F., Gasser, U., Groh, G., Günnemann, S., Hüllermeier, E., Krusche, S., Kutyniok, G., Michaeli, T., Nerdel, C., Pfeffer, J., Poquet, O., Sailer, M., Schmidt, A., Seidel, T., Kasneci, G., et al. (2023). ChatGPT for good? On opportunities and challenges of large language models for education. *Learning and Individual Differences, 103*, 102274. https://doi.org/10.1016/j.lindif.2023.102274

Kluger, J. (2023, September 7). TIME100 AI 2023: Marc Raibert. *Time*. https://time.com/collection/time100-ai/6308790/marc-raibert/

Maruf, C. D., Ramishah. (2023, April 17). Elon Musk warns AI could cause 'civilization destruction' even as he invests in it | CNN Business. *CNN*. https://www.cnn.com/2023/04/17/tech/elon-musk-ai-warning-tucker-carlson/index.html

Noble, S. (2018). *Algorithms of oppression: How search engines reinforce racism*. New York University Press. https://doi.org/10.18574/nyu/9781479833641.001.0001

OpenAI Charter. (n.d.). Retrieved October 1, 2024, from https://openai.com/charter/

Qi, J. (2024). The impact of large language models on social media communication. In *Proceedings of the 2024 7th International Conference on Software Engineering and Information Management* (pp. 165–170). https://doi.org/10.1145/3647722.3647749.

Smith, K. (2016, March 8). *Color meaning and symbolism—Sensational color*. Sensational Color. https://www.sensationalcolor.com/color-meaning-psychology-symbolism/

Social Change in the Airline Industry. (2021, November 30). https://airandspace.si.edu/explore/stories/social-change-airline-industry.

TIME100 AI 2023: Kate Crawford. (2023, September 7). Time. https://time.com/collection/time100-ai/6309459/kate-crawford/

Wang, P. (2019). On defining artificial intelligence. *Journal of Artificial General Intelligence, 10*(2), 1–37. https://doi.org/10.2478/jagi-2019-0002

Zhu, C. (2013). Jung on the nature and interpretation of dreams: A developmental delineation with cognitive neuroscientific responses. *Behavioral Sciences, 3*(4), 662–675. https://doi.org/10.3390/bs3040662

The Soul is Nothing Technological: Out-of-Body Experiences and Artificial Intelligence

Jacob W. Glazier and Christopher M. Zieske

I am more than my physical body. Because I am more than physical matter, I can perceive that which is greater than the physical world.
*Robert Monroe (*Far Journeys *262)*

The simple yet profound indication that we are more than our physical body and, even further, that our perception is not limited to the physical world calls us to a more transpersonal way of being. It also makes us wonder: What am I if I am more than my body? If reality is more than physical matter, what else exists, and how can I perceive it? These are transpersonal concerns that, as we will articulate, remain beyond typical scientific and technological answers.

The author of the epigraph, Robert Monroe (see *Journeys Out of the Body* and *The Ultimate Journey*), was a well-known proponent, advocate,

J. W. Glazier (✉) • C. M. Zieske
University of West Georgia, School of Social Sciences, Carrollton, GA, USA
e-mail: jglazier@westga.edu; cz00008@my.westga.edu

J. D. Batt, J. Erickson (eds.), *Depth Psychology, Myth and Artificial Intelligence*, https://doi.org/10.1007/978-3-031-94105-4_15

and frequenter of *out of body experiences* (OBEs). According to Blanke et al., OBEs are when an individual seems to view or leave their body and see the world from a location outside of their physical body. From an esoteric and spiritual perspective, Alvarado ("Out-of-Body") reports that this phenomenon is sometimes viewed as offering credence and evidence for the existence of a soul. OBEs are one of many human experiences, including spirit possessions, hauntings, and unitive experiences, that Daniels identifies as foundational for religious and metaphysical ideas about the soul.[1]

We understand the term soul to refer to an energetic and vaporous substance that generally resembles the physical body, many times called the astral, subtle, or light body, referenced in the syncretic and esoteric schools of hermeticism and theosophy[2] (see Levi; Mead; Powell; Ryan). Behun notes that beyond these Western traditions a similar notion exists in Yoga, Taoism, and Buddhism. This researcher interestingly builds an analogy between this understanding of the soul as the astral body to Deleuze and Guattari's (see *Anti-Oedipus* and *A Thousand*) seminal concept of the Body without Organs (BwO),[3] arguing that "the subtle body as a spiritual reality cannot be reduced to the mechanical or systematic" (Behun 133).

Our central aim in this chapter is to develop the way modern technoscience presupposes a way of revealing the world that, on principle, reduces and mechanizes the above sense of the soul. We use OBEs as a way to

[1] A perhaps peculiar and interesting note is that a close cousin of OBEs, astral projection, has caught the attention of government agencies such as the CIA ("The Global").

[2] Suffice it to say that different thinkers and practitioners in each of these traditions have diverse conceptions of what would constitute a soul. Furthermore, the very notion of the soul should be made sense of in relation to the context of their larger metaphysical and spiritual systems. For instance, the soul for theosophy, according to Leadbeater, is necessarily in relation to the sevenfold nature of being human. By contrast, the soul for hermeticism, as Copenhaver relates, would be in relation to the tripartite structure of the human, which is the body-soul-psyche. For the sake of discussion and accessibility, we employ the term soul as most synonymous with the astral body within these traditions, despite the disparity with which this phrase is sometimes used.

[3] We flag this here since the vitalist philosophy of these thinkers has often been taken up in a panpsychist (Braidotti) and animistic (Glowczewksi) way such that the emergence of consciousness is not a categorical change but rather one of degree. We will circle back to this later in our argument insofar as this understanding permits various levels of consciousness and not, let's say, its exclusive relegation to the material or spiritual realms. Furthermore, this view illustrates the importance of the components of consciousness—what it is made out of in that matter *matters* in its own unique way.

understand how this happens; namely, the exceptional qualities that anecdotally accompany many OBEs become rendered as psychological abnormalities. Likewise, we argue that artificial intelligence (AI) is necessarily subject to this same technological Enframing thereby precluding it from having a soul, in the sense that we employ, something that could leave its material substrate. We justify this thesis along five principled lines: (1) substance matters, (2) sociohistorical context, (3) reincarnation, (4) Enframing, and (5) lived embodiment.

Exceptional Human Experiences

Rhea White ("Dissociation") classified OBEs as a kind of *exceptional human experience* (EHE). EHEs expansively and broadly conceptualize transpersonal experiences as impactful and potentially transformative instances in one's life that stand out from more normative accounts of reality and identity. According to Belz and Fach, the fuller phrase White gives of exceptional human experiences is often abbreviated in contemporary literature to simply *exceptional experiences* (ExEs). However, as will become clearer once we develop our argument, the phrase we prefer in this chapter is EHEs insofar as it importantly distinguishes the possibility of exceptional experiences in technological, artificial, and other systems from those that are only possible in human experience. As a result, such a distinction advances the notion of the soul as fundamental to a human form of consciousness.

According to White ("Exceptional"), there are five main types of EHEs; these include mystical experiences, psychic experiences, encounter-type experiences, death-related experiences, and exceptional normal experiences. White placed OBEs under the category of psychic experiences. Contrast this 'exceptional' quality that White ascribes to OBEs with the contemporary understanding of mainstream science. In general, modern science avoids the use of spiritual or religious language and, instead, applies experimental and objective approaches that attempt to be less subjective—depending, importantly, according to Bird, on the philosophical commitments of that very science. As a case in point, from a psychiatric and neurological perspective, OBEs are typically viewed as a form of extreme dissociation, hallucination, autoscopy, hypnotic suggestibility, or a combination thereof (Braithwaite and David). Neppe notes, in reference to OBEs, *autoscopy*, or the hallucination of seeing oneself as a double from outside of one's own body, can be produced through stimulating certain areas of the temporal lobe in the brain. However, it does not follow that since the brain simply and obviously factors into creating subjective and phenomenal awareness, it must, therefore, be the seat of consciousness—different philosophical positions abound, with this conceptual challenge having been called *the hard problem* of consciousness famously by David Chalmers.

The hard problem of consciousness is the challenge to explain how neurology and physiology, the materiality of the body, give rise to or produce *subjective human experience*. For example, science can explain the processes and mechanisms requisite for being in love—the release of oxytocin in the brain (Carter and Porges) accompanied by a developmental and attachment process (Hazan and Shaver). However, can these accounts capture the very experience of being in love? The answer, from our point of view, is a clear and resounding "No!" This phenomenological difference has been referred to as the *qualia* of the experience (Crane). A similar impasse exists, we suggest, in the OBE phenomenon such that the transpersonal and human experience is greater than the scientific descriptions that would seek to explain them. Generally stated, the academic debate surrounding OBEs as to their relation to consciousness, self, and soul remains undecided and generative in spite of what we consider to be a premature conclusion by some neuroscientists, as found in Craffert, that would adjudicate these phenomena through physical and neurological mechanisms.

Out-of-Body Experiences

The OBE phenomenon is multifaceted and brings to light fundamental and novel conceptions surrounding embodiment, sense of self, and the nature of being human. As a helpful foray into the academic literature, Alvarado ("Out-of-Body") parses historical and theoretical explanations for OBEs into two basic camps: the projection model and the psychological model. According to Alvarado, the *projection model* entails "that 'something' literally 'goes out of the body' during an OBE" (200). Furthermore, some proponents of the projection model argue that "a subtle body or a non-physical aspect of personality somehow projects out of the physical body" (237).

Alvarado ("Out-of-Body") contrasts the projection model with the *psychological model*. The psychological model "see[s] the experience as 'imaginary' in nature" insofar as the OBE is a function of known or unknown processes such as dissociation, hallucination, or perceptual distortions (200). This explanation for the OBE phenomenon adjudicates the perceptual alterations through neurological, psychological, and physiological events, additionally rejecting, in many cases, the suggestion that something leaves or is projected from the body (Alvarado "The Psychological").

Each model presents its own theoretical and research challenges. For instance, Alvarado ("Out-of-Body") notes that the projection model lacks a solid theoretical framework by which to make predictions that can be tested. Furthermore, even if more laboratory work is carried out, for example, additional detection studies, it is unlikely that these studies would lend support to the projection model since parapsychologists are more likely to explain these phenomena through extrasensory perception, psychokinesis, or other psi variables (see Irwin).

In terms of orthodox psychiatric and materialist science, the psychological model is virtually unanimously employed nowadays as a theoretical framework, according to Braithwaite and David. For instance, Blanke et al. examined OBEs and autoscopy from a neurological perspective. The researchers found that both experiences share similar neurological mechanisms—particularly brain dysfunction located in the temporoparietal junction. From a neuropsychiatric perspective, OBEs and autoscopy experiences are paroxysmal disorders of body perception and cognition or body schema.

While understanding the neurological correlates of OBEs and related phenomena is helpful in elucidating the connection and relationship between the mind and body, nonetheless, the psychological model presupposes basic assumptions about the nature of consciousness and the human being. Fundamentally and perhaps most importantly, the psychological model engages in a *reductionism* of the qualities and subjective features that create the OBE. Reductionism is the procedure and doctrine of explaining something by "reducing it to a different, usually simpler, level" (Sayer 5). The point is that reductionism is not just about simplifying but includes locating, naming, and understanding the source and causes of the phenomenon.

In the case of OBEs, the psychological model traces the causes and source of OBEs to unusual or abnormal psychological processes that, in principle, can be traced to underlying neurological mechanisms (see Thornton). The conceptual challenges and epistemological violence enacted by reductionist approaches are perhaps best articulated by the phenomenological tradition (see Giorgi; Husserl). Reducing OBEs to neurological correlates runs the risk of invalidating, demystifying, and mechanizing subjective experience. The OBE, in other words, loses its 'exceptional' human quality, and rather than prompting an engagement with meaning-making around the experience, the explanation is decided beforehand—by an appeal to neuropsychiatric explanations.

Such a conceptual commitment represents a direct challenge to the foundations of what constitutes a transpersonal experience by way of undercutting a more holistic understanding of our being in the world; again, disenchanting and mechanizing expansive spiritual states by rendering them explainable through materialist and neuropsychiatric correlates (Hartelius). Take, for instance, the projection model of OBEs such that a soul, light body, or some other similar substance is projected out of the body in these cases. The challenges in studying this through normal scientific means, as noted by Alvarado ("Out-of-Body"), flag the limitations of typical, materialist approaches. Upon this account, subjective experience is ultimately reducible down and, more importantly for our purposes, controllable through neuropsychiatric interventions—for example, brain trauma, psychopharmacology, surgery, or other forms of alteration. The neuropsychiatric approach is helpful insofar as it creates a better understanding of the importance of our brain and body for creating subjective experience—an alteration to part of the brain changes perception, for example, even though the perceptual processing systems of the brain are ecological and systemic (Farah and Feinberg). However, the implicit and supplemental question contained herein is left unanswered: Does the body, by itself, produce subject experience?

It would be better to understand how the pieces of the puzzle fit together to create the whole of conscious experience. Relatively recent research on the importance of the microbiome of the gut and nutrition as being constitutive of consciousness and influencing subjective experience makes a case for how the various systems of the body work together to create a totality that is greater than its parts (Goyal et al.; Vana; Young et al.). If we take this even further, we could also postulate the importance of our developmental, social, and cultural worlds as necessarily impacting and changing our physiology, as the literature on epigenetics suggests (Aguilera et al.). On this account, human consciousness is not an isolatable and reducible entity that can then be studied using traditional materialist methods. Put positively, a more ecological and holistic science would more faithfully account for subjective experiences and consciousness. The way we conceptualize human consciousness in this way cannot be overstated since it has an ethical bearing on domains outside of science, including transpersonal and spiritual understandings of the self, world, and society.

Technology as Enframing

On this point, the German philosopher and phenomenologist Martin Heidegger[4] (*The Question*) argued that the world is on a historical trajectory that has lost sight of its initial interest in the technological to begin with. The technological means the broad and general way we disclose and position ourselves in relation to other beings in the world. Technology, according to Heidegger, is "therefore no mere means. Technology is a way of revealing" (12). This particular way of revealing is already decided beforehand through a long sociohistorical lineage that assumes this revealing as a 'natural' given. As Heidegger argues,

> Modern physics, as experimental, is dependent upon technical apparatus and upon progress in the building of apparatus. The establishing of this mutual relationship between technology and physics is correct. But it remains a merely historiographical establishing of facts and says nothing about that in which this mutual relationship is grounded. (14)

The grounding, for Heidegger, is found through the way that modern technology reveals as "a challenging [*Herausfordern*]" (14, emphasis in original) to nature in order that it sets itself as resources and energy that can be extracted, supplied, and stored. Importantly, these ways of revealing require interlocking and networking paths with other technological systems and apparatuses. What this demonstrates is how modern neurology and psychiatry, for instance, are necessarily dependent beforehand on the modern essence of technology. That is, these systems as sciences are part of a broader and global framework by which beings reveal themselves in the world.

[4] The authors are aware of the controversial nature of referencing Heidegger due to his involvement in the National Socialist Party of Germany in the era of the Holocaust and World War II. However, we share Singer's opinion that Heidegger's philosophy, itself, does not inherently support ideologies such as those found in the Nazi party and thus that it is both possible and ethical to reference Heidegger's work unrelated to his political convictions.

The problems with reductionism mentioned earlier are amplified even more in this wide-ranging conception of modern technology. Heidegger (*The Question*) argues that the turn away from representation (i.e., the projection model of OBEs) and toward objects (i.e., the psychological model of OBEs) in modern physics forces nature to report "itself in some way or other that is identifiable through calculation and that it remains orderable as a system of information" (23). It makes no difference if the science is applied or theoretical such that in both cases, this way of revealing "orders its experiments precisely for the purpose of asking whether and how nature reports itself when set up in this way" (22); namely, as a mathematical, challenging-forth that reduces objects down to resource-laden cogs in a machine.

How does this framework apply to OBEs and psychiatric science? According to Kendler, psychiatry is not monolithic with regard to its philosophical underpinnings. Nonetheless, Deacon and McKay relate that the traditional philosophical approach adhered to by psychiatry is the *biomedical model*, which views psychological issues as diseases of the brain. As such, the biomedical model generally ascribes some implicit notion of normality (e.g., normal brain structure and functioning or normal behavior and psychology) as a way to judge, fix, and correct various deficiencies that arise. In this way, subjective or conscious experiences are necessarily co-opted through this specific model (e.g., through neurological deficiency, etc.) in order that those scientists, technicians, or doctors can render treatment and correction against some presumed standard of biomedical normality (Hook and Parker).

From a Heideggerian perspective, the problem with this is twofold: (1) the 'technology of psychiatry' neglects, overlooks, and, stronger, ideologically discounts alternative models except the biomedical one;[5] (2) such a technical view of conscious experience interlocks with adjacent and similarly aligned institutions to perpetuate this power. This is important because it helps demonstrate how modern psychiatry is the product of the same historical trajectory that produced artificial intelligence; Heidegger (*The Question*) called this worldview more precisely *Enframing* (*Ge-stell*).

[5] Notably, Heidegger (*The Question*) mentions that one of the particular dangers of the technological mode of revealing, itself, is that it not only conceals the possibility of other modes of truth-revealing but even conceals the fact of its very own concealment—a point that seems relevant to the discounting of alternative models in modern psychiatric and neurological science.

Such Enframing reveals OBEs through a specifically neuropsychiatric model. As such, the very possibility of posing the projection model of OBEs as a possibility becomes absurd and is regarded as superstition, as pseudoscientific, or, more pointedly, as hallucinatory, a psychological abnormality that needs correction. Furthermore, the appropriate science that would be required to investigate such a claim likewise is deemed unacceptable.[6]

Indeed, the transpersonal element conveyed by an OBE is erased and replaced with normal technological standards. This erasure and reduction results from anthropocentrism that places the essence of modern technology under the purview of human control. Heidegger (*The Question*) is adamant, however, that technology as ordering revealing is much more expansive and encompassing and is not "merely human doing" (19).

Artificial Intelligence

Best exemplifying this point is the recent rise and popularity of artificial intelligence, most notably the Large-Language Models (LLMs) such as ChatGPT by OpenAI and Gemini by Google (Jeyaraman et al.; Uspenskyi). Stories abound about AI going rogue, malfunctioning, or acting beyond the parameters of its programming (Afifi-Sabet; Preston-Ellis & Gleadow). Such malfunction may be a prelude and foreshadow the so-called holy grail of AI research, resulting in an AI system that can program, adapt, and learn itself. This is the hypothesized emergence of consciousness within a computer system, resulting in Artificial General Intelligence (AGI), an artificial intelligence that has true sentience comparable to its human counterparts (Fei et al.). Alluding back to the anthropocentrism of this pursuit mentioned earlier, in a paradoxical fashion, modern technology appears to be on the cusp of producing consciousness through its own inner logic and creations—*a consciousness, though, that is, importantly, not human.*

This is not to foreclose the possibility of AGI. Rather, the point is to stress that it would, on principle, be a different form of consciousness than the normal sense carried by that term. This new and unhuman form of

[6] Perhaps it would be deemed even impossible in the sense that it would stand outside of a current paradigm of reality. For instance, the veridical knowledge gathered during OBEs and NDEs (Holden) may be one such avenue that could shed light on this alternative form of science.

consciousness would be a technological consciousness networked with other modern technical apparatuses, Enframing a specific form of sentience to reveal itself. We suggest that the philosophical view known as *panpsychism* is helpful here in understanding how various degrees of consciousness, including those of humans, animals, plants, and technology, are different and possible. Goff suggests that panpsychism is the worldview that grounds consciousness as the fundamental substance of reality. For a panpsychist, the qualitative jump from AI to AGI is not as important as understanding the different ways and forms in which AI is intelligent and conscious. Even innate matter, mechanical or technological, also possesses some kind of consciousness (Braidotti). There is no conceptual problem, then, for panpsychism to 'explain' the emergence of consciousness in all these various beings and systems since it is taken for granted depending on their complexity and arrangement.[7]

To return to our exemplar of OBEs, from a panpsychism perspective, would the consciousness of these artificially intelligent systems, composed of technological and mechanical substances, possess the same features as the human experience? The psychological model of OBEs is consistent on this point, such that AI would be able to model the subjective experiences associated with OBEs, either internally within itself or supplementally, by inducing the subjective correlates in humans—hence, creating the feeling, perception, or image of the AI or human having left its embodied substrate, whether mechanical or organic. The projection model of OBEs, however, presents conceptual challenges in this respect insofar as the literal leaving of the substrate implies a supplemental or wholly other form of consciousness—containing a component that has been called the astral body or soul in various esoteric traditions (Crow; Metzinger).

We have delineated these impasses in the following points: (1) substance matters, (2) sociohistorical context, (3) reincarnation, (4) Enframing, and (5) lived embodiment. These points are importantly perfunctory, requiring additional scholarly attention. However, they are central in supporting our thesis on the importance of the soul for distinguishing human experience from artificial consciousness:

[7] Contrast this with the qualitative distinction between what or who is bestowed consciousness via historical and orthodox science. Not all humans have been afforded the same level of consciousness. The Tuskegee syphilis experiment (Jones) is one such paragon example of this. Additionally, we point the reader to the continued practice of factory-farming animals (Williams) as evidence of the ethical consequence of who gets to have consciousness.

1. ***Substance matters.*** One way to tackle this problem may be to distinguish between the substance of consciousness in humans and in artificial systems. That is, the various physical components of the body and brain are qualitatively different components than what comprise AI systems, being mechanical and technological in nature. The point is not to fetishize organic components over mechanical ones but, rather, to suggest that the constitutive substance matters therein producing different forms of consciousness, a form that perhaps would be unable to achieve phenomenal coherence, as Arvan and Maley have suggested. Furthermore, even if AGI were developed, such a version of consciousness could not be said to have a soul, as exemplified by the projection model of OBEs, if the emergence of the soul is dependent upon the substance comprising the intelligence system. In other words, there would be no soul, no astral or light body, to leave or project from the techno-mechanical system. Case in point, the electromagnetism of the body is generated differently (Ashcroft) via the ingestion of food, cell metabolism, etc., than the kind of electricity that would power AGI.

   Moreover, this is one of the principles that separate the products of technological Enframing, which may be capable of having a soul, such as humans conceived via *en vitro* fertilization, from AGI, which, per our argument, is incapable of having a soul. While the former is certainly a product of Enframing, the human person conceived and developed through this process still shares the same matter as other humans having access to consciousness. Organic AI[8] with a body composed of the same material substance as humans, however, has not been possible. If it were, we speculate, through the exclusionary criteria delineated herein, that it would lack a soul. Consequently, it is easy to see how human beings conceived through *en vitro* fertilization would have a soul even if AGI does not.

[8] The notion of "organic AI" raises semantic and philosophical issues regarding the borders between and around beings. That is, we wonder about the ways that one would distinguish between "organic AI" and a clone. Clearly, there are differences. Perhaps the latter is a genetic replica of a current or past living organism, whereas the former is completely novel with its own unique genetic code. Of course, adjudicating these differences to genetics is a favorite move of modern technoscience and biopolitics, even if, on principle, these genetic codes are going to be different and unique due to mutation, environmental influence, etc. We suggest that contextualizing our emphasis on substance with the other four points will help develop why we think that "organic AI" would still be barred from having a soul.

2. ***Sociohistorical context.*** The historical trajectory and social situatedness of humans create development, growth, and achievement. Humans are necessarily contextual creatures, in other words. This is what Heidegger (*Being*) called *thrownness,* where we are thrown into a sociohistorical context at birth and must take up this context in various unique ways. The fact that we are thrown into existence without the ability to choose the specific context in which we find ourselves means that our mortality fundamentally grounds and singularizes us as that future terminus from which no one can escape. Our thrownness, coupled with the truth that we will all die, is essential for the essence of the human being, which Heidegger denoted as *Dasein*. The sociohistorical context of humans, at least given Heidegger's account as sketched above, would be very different from a sentient techno-mechanical system. It is difficult to imagine the emergence of a soul *ex nihilo* out of human-created systems. A version of consciousness or intelligence is plausible; a soul, however, requires a historical and developmental trajectory, a conscious experience through sociohistorical context being in and among others.
3. ***Reincarnation.*** In addition, there are what we could call speculative transpersonal considerations that we could put forward as a way to distinguish a soul and the lack thereof in artificially intelligent systems. Reincarnation and memories of past lives, investigated by Stevenson, is one such consideration that broadens and deepens the importance of having a sociohistorical context. The transmigration of the soul through various lifetimes, its working-through of karma, and taking different forms speculatively, at least, precludes an artificial system from doing the same. To put it precisely, AGI would be a qualitatively different form of consciousness not subject to the same rules of life as humans, the same shackles such as craving and desire that keep us chained and jailed in samsara, to use terminology from the Buddhist tradition (Yamaguchi). AGI would not be subject to mortality and the passing of time suggesting the motivation or need to reincarnate and assume different forms is absent. In fact, it may be that such an artificially intelligent system would see these as undesirable and unnecessary, perhaps a failure and feature of human consciousness that it has been able to overcome.
4. ***Enframing.*** The essence of technology, according to Heidegger (*The Question*), is nothing technological. While paradoxical, this formulation makes clear that something more cosmic and incisive

occurs during the structuring of life through technological means, namely, that technology arranges the way that Being-as-such discloses itself through Enframing. Enframing sets the world up as a place for resource extraction by ordering and creating a standing reserve. In other words, as opposed to dwelling with and among other beings in the world, such as with a river, a mountain, animals, and so on, Enframing reduces this possibility of being-with down to its use value. Technology creates transactional relationality whereby presence is subordinate to the utility of the being. AGI is likewise subordinate to this Heideggerian insight such that, being the futural emblem of modern technology, it frames the world through ordering beings according to their energy or resource value. What is more, on this account, AGI would be limited to this mode of relation necessarily. Human beings, by contrast, while capable of engaging with the world via this technological Enframing, also have the capability of engaging with the world via other means, such as through art or *pōiseis* (Heidegger *The Question*). Even though potentially self-aware and conscious, artificial systems are dependent on a worldview that sets up reality in a specific way beforehand and, as a result, would be necessarily precluded from modeling exactly human experience, including the projection of a soul or astral body during an OBE.

Like the principle of substance matters, Enframing further uncovers the differences between technological productions capable of having a soul (which we yet again find exemplified in the process of *en vitro* fertilization) and the situation concerning AGI. As mentioned above, beings that have a soul, such as human beings, may have access to the world through an Enframing mode of relation, but they are not limited to this mode of relating and, in fact, do not find it upon careful questioning to be their original mode of relation. Even a human person conceived *en vitro*, with the Enframed origin to their existence, does not in any immediate or primordial manner know the circumstances of how their birth was perfectly ordered and arranged to fit a technological stockpile of resources; they originally relate to the world in the same manner as other humans and only later learn how to relate to the world as standing-reserve. AGI, however, were it ever to be invented, would be an existence constructed in such a way that it would only ever know a world arranged into standing-reserve, and could never learn to relate to the world through the various other modes possible for beings with souls. *This exclusive mode of relating to the world is soulless*, in the sense that it does not involve any mode of relation inherent in any being with a soul. It is not the presence of Enframing as a mode of relation accessible to AGI, then, that precludes it from having a soul any more than the fact that AGI is the product of a technological endeavor; rather, it is the absence of any other mode of relating besides the same Enframing power that was originally responsible for its existence that renders AGI bereft of a soul.

5. ***Lived embodiment.*** According to Hubert Dreyfus, much of the reason why AI is only capable of imitating specific human behaviors and performances rather than perfectly mirroring a human being is because of the different processes behind the actions of a human and computer. Where AI must rely on a finite set of rules (however complex) to perform cognitive skills (or skills of 'consciousness') such as pattern recognition or problem-solving, human beings must rely on their bodies for such tasks. Dreyfus clarifies that a mere physical body is not enough to imitate human embodiment—in the case of human conscious action, it is necessary that one have a physical form, that this form is capable of free, fluid movement, and finally that this form is capable of lived, subjective sensations as it moves and senses the world around it. While the first and perhaps even the second of these aspects to embodiment may be possible for machines already, it is dubious to assume that the final aspect has yet been achieved in technological creations or even that it will be achieved in the foreseeable future. Where humans must bodily cope with the world around them in order to find and pick up an object—an action which requires no understanding, even unconscious, of Euclidean geometrical space—a machine arm must rely entirely on the rules of geometrical space to accomplish the same task, which removes the lived quality of the machine's body.[9] This is what leads Dreyfus to conclude, in his essay by the same name, that computers must have bodies in order to be intelligent—bodies that not only function off of the abstract rules of mathematics and geometry but off of their

[9] Dreyfus relies on precisely this example of a moving mechanical arm—a machine that was under development at MIT during the time Dreyfus was writing his article—to prove his points. The analysis presented in this chapter, of course, ignores the fact that many AI technologies lack even this close of a resemblance to the human body.

own capacity for lived perception and coping with the world. If it is true that AI does not have this lived body schema—that is, that it cannot have a bodily self-awareness outside of abstract mathematical formulae—then it is doubtful how AI could have an experience of projection remotely similar to an OBE.

Once again, we proffer the preceding five points as central in supporting our thesis on the importance of the soul, in the unique sense we employ the term, for distinguishing human experience from artificial consciousness.

Discussion

We would like to put forward a rephrasing of the famous Heideggerian insight[10] concerning technology by relating it back to the more inclusive projection model of OBEs such that *the soul is nothing technological.* This rebranding makes clear the extant and pervasive influence that Enframing exerts on our modern practices and models. As evidence for these pernicious and insidious effects, in the sense of appearing as monolithic and universal, we have argued that the neuropsychiatric literature reduces the fullness and transpersonal qualities of the OBE in order to, importantly, interlink and connect OBEs with prevailing technoscientific psychiatry and its adjacent disciplines that have helped give rise to AI. As a consequence, the projection model of OBEs is fringed or discounted necessarily.

Returning again to the rich phrase denoted by Rhea White ("Dissociation"), exceptional human experiences (EHEs) help distinguish transpersonal qualities and spiritual traits as necessarily belonging to the human. As we have noted, such phrasing does not deny or exclude ways of creating or other beings also possessing exceptional experiences. For example, the possibility of technologically mediated exceptional experiences is evidenced in the Persinger God Helmet (Andersen et al.; Simmonds-Moore et al.) in addition to other technoscientific manipulation of the brain. Furthermore, the recent push for greater scientific acceptance of animal consciousness (Bush) includes a broader way of understanding sentient systems and, perhaps, exceptional experiences.

[10] "The essence of technology is by no means anything technological" (Heidegger *The Question* 4).

The phrase EHEs does, importantly, foreground the human as unique in a certain respect with regard to its transpersonal possibilities—not in an anthropocentric way that would set the human as qualitatively superior to other beings. Rather, as evinced by the panpsychist perspective, consciousness is fundamental to reality, and additionally, we should expect to see degrees of consciousness in all types of matter (Taylor). Our central intervention has to bring forward Heidegger's (*The Question*) notion of modern technology as Enframing such that revealing beings in this way necessarily excludes and forecloses the very question of the soul. We have referenced the neuropsychiatric literature in reference to OBEs as evidence of this.

What is unique, for Heidegger, is that while Enframing is predominant and pervasive, the human being has access to other modes of revealing—most importantly, perhaps, revealing as *pōiseis*. It follows that even though Enframing entrances us into a normative mode of revealing, humans always have the possibility of experiencing and relating to beings differently. The artist's relation to their artwork and the poet's relation to the word fracture the calculative ordering of Enframing by allowing something different to show itself. Consequently, when applied to the current topic at hand, we suggest that this more poetic-being-with can be illuminated through the projection model of OBEs. The scientific truth or falsity of this model is, in a strong sense, irrelevant since modern science and technology are ensnared beforehand by Enframing. What is exceedingly relevant though, on our account, are the ways that EHEs such as OBEs are allowed to presence and disclose something that is oftentimes extraordinarily meaningful and personally transformative (Shaw et al.).

Artificially constructed systems, even if conscious, sentient, or self-aware, will be a necessarily different form of consciousness than the kind possessed by human beings. We have argued that this consciousness would be predicated on a singular mode of revealing called Enframing. It would not be possible on principle, moreover, for AGI to have a soul or some kind of substance that would be able to leave its techno-mechanical substrate in the same way as OBEs. Above, we have sketched five points that support this thesis: (1) substance matters, (2) sociohistorical context, (3) reincarnation, (4) Enframing, and (5) lived embodiment. We recognize that these points require additional erudition and attention but, nonetheless, echo over a century-long phenomenological tradition that has worked to dislodge human experience from being consumed by a technoscientific worldview.

The psychological model of OBEs necessarily reveals a specific way of understanding this exceptional human experience—a way that demystifies and reduces-down its 'exceptional' qualities. Such is the providence of Enframing itself. Modern technoscience sets the world up beforehand as a place for ordering and resource extraction. The soul, however, is nothing technological.

Works Cited

Afifi-Sabet, K. (2024). Poisoned AI went rogue during training and couldn't be taught to behave again in 'legitimately scary' study. *LiveScience*, 26 Jan. 2024. Accessed December 27, 2024, from www.livescience.com/technology/artificial-intelligence/legitimately-scary-anthropic-ai-poisoned-rogue-evil-couldnt-be-taught-how-to-behave-again

Aguilera, O., Fernandez, A. F., Munoz, A., & Fraga, M. F. (2010). Epigenetics and environment: A complex relationship. *Journal of Applied Physiology, 109*(1), 243–251. https://doi.org/10.1152/japplphysiol.00068.2010

Alvarado, C. S. (1992). The psychological approach to out-of-body experiences: A review of early and modern developments. *Journal of Psychology, 126*(3), 237–250. https://doi.org/10.1080/00223980.1992.10543358

Alvarado, C. S. (2000). Out-of-body experiences. In E. Cardeña, S. J. Lynn, & S. Krippner (Eds.), *Varieties of anomalous experience: Examining the scientific evidence* (pp. 183–218). American Psychological Association. https://doi.org/10.1037/10371-006

Andersen, M., Schjoedt, U., Nielbo, K. L., & Sørensen, J. (2014). Mystical experience in the lab. *Method & Theory in the Study of Religion, 26*(3), 217–245. https://doi.org/10.1163/15700682-12341323

Arvan, M., & Maley, C. J. (2022). Panpsychism and AI consciousness. *Synthese, 200*(3), 244. https://doi.org/10.1007/s11229-022-03695-x

Ashcroft, F. (2012). *The spark of life: Electricity in the human body.* WW Norton & Company.

Behun, W. (2010). The body of light and the body without organs. *SubStance, 39*(1), 125–140. https://doi.org/10.1353/sub.0.0069

Belz, M., & Fach, W. (2015). Exceptional experiences (ExE) in clinical psychology. In E. Cardeña, J. Palmer & D. Marcusson-Clavertz (Eds.), *Parapsychology: A handbook for the 21st century* (pp. 364–379). McFarland & Co.

Bird, A. (2003). Philosophy of science. In J. Shand (Ed.), *Fundamentals of Philosophy* (pp. 297–325). Routledge.

Blanke, O., Landis, T., Spinelli, L., & Seeck, M. (2004). Out-of-body experience and autoscopy of neurological origin. *Brain, 127*(2), 243–258. https://doi.org/10.1093/brain/awh040

Braidotti, R. (2013). *The Posthuman*. Polity Press.
Braithwaite, J. J., & David, A. S. (2016). Out of body, out of mind? An examination of out-of-body experiences and dissociative disorders. *Cognitive Neuropsychiatry, 21*(5), 373–376. https://doi.org/10.1080/13546805.2016.1240074
Bush, E. (2024). Scientists push new paradigm of animal consciousness, saying even insects may be sentient. *NBC News*, 19 April 2024. Accessed December 27, 2024, from www.nbcnews.com/science/science-news/animal-consciousness-scientists-push-new-paradigm-rcna148213
Carter, C. S., & Porges, S. W. (2012). The biochemistry of love: An oxytocin hypothesis. *Science & Society, 14*, 12–16. https://doi.org/10.1038/embor.2012.191
Chalmers, D. J. (1995). Facing up to the problem of consciousness. *Journal of Consciousness Studies, 2*(3), 200–219.
Copenhaver, B. P. (1992). *Hermetica: The Greek corpus Hermeticum and the Latin Asclepius in a new English translation, with notes and introduction*. Cambridge University Press.
Craffert, P. F. (2015). When is an out-of-body experience (not) an out-of-body experience? Reflections about out-of-body phenomena in neuroscientific research. *Journal of Cognition and Culture, 15*, 13–31. https://doi.org/10.1163/15685373-12342138
Crane, T. (2000). The origins of qualia. In T. Crane & S. Patterson (Eds.), *History of the mind-body problem* (pp. 177–202). Routledge. https://doi.org/10.4324/9780203471029
Crow, J. L. (2012). Taming the astral body: The theosophical society's ongoing problem of emotion and control. *Journal of the American Academy of Religion, 80*(3), 691–717. https://doi.org/10.1093/jaarel/lfs042
Daniels, M. (2002). The transpersonal self: 1. A psychohistory and phenomenology of the soul. *Transpersonal Psychology Review, 6*(1), 17–28.
Deacon, B. J., & McKay, D. (2015). The biomedical model of psychological problems: A call for critical dialogue. *The Behavior Therapist, 38*(7), 231–235. https://psycnet.apa.org/record/2015-56839-013
Deleuze, G., & Guattari, F. (1983). *Anti-Oedipus: Capitalism and schizophrenia* (R. Hurley, M. Seem, & H. R. Lane, Trans.). University of Minnesota Press.
Deleuze, G., & Guattari, F. (1987). *A thousand plateaus: Capitalism and schizophrenia* (B. Massumi, Trans.). University of Minnesota Press.
Dreyfus, H. L. (1967). Why computers must have bodies in order to be intelligent. *The Review of Metaphysics, 21*(1), 13–32. https://www.jstor.org/stable/pdf/20124494.pdf
Farah, M. J., & Feinberg, T. E. (1997). Consciousness of perception after brain damage. *Seminars in Neurology, 17*(02), 145–152. https://doi.org/10.1055/s-2008-1040924

Fei, N., Zhiwu, L., Gao, Y., Yang, G., Huo, Y., Wen, J., Haoyu, L., Song, R., Gao, X., Xiang, T., Sun, H., & Wen, J.-R. (2022). Towards artificial general intelligence via a multimodal foundation model. *Nature Communications, 13*(1), 3094. https://doi.org/10.1038/s41467-022-30761-2

Giorgi, A. (2000). The idea of human science. *The Humanistic Psychologist, 28*(1–3), 119–137. https://doi.org/10.1080/08873267.2000.9976986

Glowczewksi, B. (2020). *Indigenising anthropology with Guattari and Deleuze.* Edinburgh University Press.

Goff, P. (2017). Panpsychism. In S. Schneider & M. Velmans (Eds.), *The Blackwell companion to consciousness* (2nd ed., pp. 106–124). Wiley. https://doi.org/10.1002/9781119132363.ch8

Goyal, M. S., Venkatesh, S., Milbrandt, J., Gordon, J., & Raichle, M. E. (2015). Feeding the brain and nurturing the mind: Linking nutrition and the gut microbiota to brain development. *Proceedings of the National Academy of Sciences, 112*(46), 14105–14112. https://doi.org/10.1073/pnas.1511465112

Jeyaraman, M., Balaji, S., Jeyaraman, N., & Yadav, S. (2023). Unraveling the ethical enigma: Artificial intelligence in healthcare. *Cureus, 15*(8), e43262. https://doi.org/10.7759/cureus.43262

Jones, J. H. (2008). The Tuskegee syphilis experiment. In E. J. Emanuel, C. Grady, R. A. Crouch, R. K. Lie, F. G. Miller, & D. Wendler (Eds.), *The Oxford textbook of clinical research ethics* (pp. 86–96). Oxford University Press.

Hartelius, G., Rothe, G., & Roy, P. J. (2013). A brand from the burning: Defining transpersonal psychology. In H. L. Friedman & G. Hartelius (Eds.), *Handbook of transpersonal psychology* (pp. 3–22). Wiley Blackwell. https://doi.org/10.1002/9781118591277.ch1

Hazan, C., & Shaver, P. (2007). Romantic love conceptualized as an attachment process. In R. Zukauskiene (Ed.), *Interpersonal development* (pp. 283–296). Routledge. https://doi.org/10.4324/9781351153683-17

Heidegger, M. (1962). *Being and time* (J. Macquarrie & E. Robinson, Trans). Harper.

Heidegger, M. (1977). *The question concerning technology and other essays* (W. Lovitt, Trans.). Garland Publishing.

Holden, J. M. (2009). Veridical perception in near-death experiences. In J. M. Holden, B. Greyson, & D. James (Eds.), *The handbook of near-death experiences: Thirty years of investigation* (pp. 185–212). Praeger. https://doi.org/10.5040/9798400661389.ch-009

Hook, D., & Parker, I. (2002). Deconstruction, psychopathology and dialectics. *South Africa Journal of Psychology, 32*(2), 49–54. https://doi.org/10.1177/008124630203200207

Husserl, E. (1970). *The crisis of European sciences and transcendental phenomenology: An introduction to phenomenological philosophy* (David Carr, Trans). Northwestern University Press.

Irwin, H. J. (1985). *Flight of mind: A psychological study of the out-of-body experience*. Scarecrow Press.
Kendler, K. S. (2005). Toward a philosophical structure for psychiatry. *American Journal of Psychiatry, 162*(3), 433–440. https://doi.org/10.1176/appi.ajp.162.3.433
Leadbeater, C. W. (1911). *The inner life*. Theosophical Publishing House.
Levi, E. (1923). *Transcendental magic: Its doctrine and ritual* (Arthur E. Waite, Trans). William Rider & Son, Limited.
Mead, G. R. S. (1919). *The doctrine of the subtle body in the Western tradition*. John M. Watkins.
Metzinger, T. (2005). Out-of-body experiences as the origin of the concept of a 'soul'. *Mind and Matter, 3*(1), 57–84.
Monroe, R. A. (1985). *Far journeys*. Broadway Books.
Monroe, R. A. (1992). *Journeys out of the body: The classic work on out-of-body experience*. Harmony.
Monroe, R. A. (1996). *The ultimate journey*. Harmony.
Neppe, V. M. (1993). Clinical psychiatry, psychopharmacology, and anomalous experience. In J. McMahon & L. Coly (Eds.), *Psi and clinical practice* (pp. 145–163). Parapsychology Foundation.
Powell, A. E. (1926). *The astral body and other astral phenomena*. Theosophical Publishing House Limited.
Preston-Ellis, R., & Gleadow, E. (2024). ChatGPT malfunctions as users share 'scary' messages from 'off the rails' bot. *Mirror*, 21 Feb. 2024. Accessed December 28, 2024, from www.mirror.co.uk/news/uk-news/chatgpt-malfunctions-users-share-scary-32180947
Ryan, C. J. (1975). *H. P. Blavatsky and the theosophical movement: A brief historical sketch*. Theosophical University Press.
Sayer, A. (2010). Session I: Reductionism in social science. In R. E. Lee (Ed.), *Questioning nineteenth-century assumptions about knowledge, II: Reductionism* (pp. 5–39). State University of New York.
Shaw, J., Gandy, S., & Stumbrys, T. (2023., advance online publication.). Transformative effects of spontaneous out of body experiences in healthy individuals: An interpretative phenomenological analysis. *Psychology of Consciousness: Theory, Research, and Practice*. https://doi.org/10.1037/cns0000324
Simmonds-Moore, C., Rice, D. L., O'Gwin, C., & Hopkins, R. (2019). Exceptional experiences following exposure to a sham "god helmet": Evidence for placebo, individual difference, and time of day influences. *Imagination, Cognition and Personality, 39*(1), 44–87. https://doi.org/10.1177/0276236617749185
Singer, B. (1993). The "Heidegger affair": Philosophy, politics, and the "political". *Theory and Society, 22*(4), 539–568. https://doi.org/10.1007/bf00993597

Stevenson, I. (2000). *Children who remember previous lives: A question of reincarnation* (Rev. ed.). McFarland.

Taylor, B. A. (2013). Birds, liminality, and human transformation: An animist perspective on new animism. *Pomegranate, 14*(1), 108–127. https://doi.org/10.1558/pome.v14i1.108

The Global Architect Institute. (2021). The 25th page of the CIA's gateway report on astral projection versus simulation theory. *The Global Architect Institute*, 15 June 2021. Accessed December 28, 2024, from tinyurl.com/4ssavp53

Thornton, T. (2004). Reductionism/Antireductionism. In J. Radden (Ed.), *The philosophy of psychiatry: A companion* (pp. 191–204). Oxford University Press.

Uspenskyi, S. (2024). Large language model statistics and numbers. *Springs*, 19 Sept. 2024. Accessed December 28, 2024, from springsapps.com/knowledge/large-language-model-statistics-and-numbers-2024

Vana, R. (2020). The brain, gut and consciousness: Microbiology of our mind. *Inquiries Journal, 12*(12). http://www.inquiriesjournal.com/a?id=1853

White, R. A. (1997a). Dissociation, narrative, and exceptional human experience. In S. Krippner & S. Powers (Eds.), *Broken images, broken selves: Dissociative narratives in clinical practice* (pp. 88–121). Brunner-Mazel.

White, R. A. (1997b). Exceptional human experiences and the experiential paradigm. In C. T. Tart (Ed.), *Body mind spirit: Exploring the parapsychology of spirituality* (pp. 83–100). Hampton Road Publishing Company.

Williams, N. M. (2008). Affected ignorance and animal suffering: Why our failure to debate factory farming puts us at moral risk. *Journal of Agricultural and Environmental Ethics, 21*(4), 371–384. https://doi.org/10.1007/s10806-008-9087-8

Yamaguchi, E. (1970). The conception of 'samsara'. *Journal of Indian and Buddhist Studies, 18*(2), 1062–1055. https://doi.org/10.4259/ibk.18.1062

Young, H. A., Freegard, G., & Benton, D. (2022). Mediterranean diet, interoception and mental health: Is it time to look beyond the 'gut-brain axis'? *Physiology & Behavior, 257*, 113964. https://doi.org/10.1016/j.physbeh.2022.113964

The "Web Browser" of the Collective Unconscious: The Mirror and Oracle of Generative AI

Jason D. Batt

So I wasn't dreaming, after all, … unless—unless we're all part of the same dream.
Alice, Through the Looking Glass

Over 17,000 years ago in southwestern France, prehistoric humans painted intricate compositions across the walls of the Lascaux Cave, producing a staggering collection of over 600 images. These depictions of wildlife, fauna, and even an early representation of the Pleiades star cluster are among humanity's earliest known examples of artistic expression. Long before written language emerged, art served as our species' primal tool for

J. D. Batt (✉)
Deep Space Predictive Research Group, Denver, CO, USA

Project Lodestar, Thornton, CO, USA

The International Society of Mythology, Columbia, MD, USA
e-mail: jason@jbatt.com

J. D. Batt, J. Erickson (eds.), *Depth Psychology, Myth and Artificial Intelligence*, https://doi.org/10.1007/978-3-031-94105-4_16

communication, enabling us to explore, express, and understand the ineffable aspects of human experience.

This deep connection to art is not merely incidental to human existence; it is central to it. Art has always functioned as a bridge between the conscious and unconscious realms, as a mirror reflecting our collective psyche, and as a portal into the mythic dimensions of our shared imagination. Across centuries, this innate drive to create has continually shaped and been shaped by the cultural, psychological, and technological landscapes we inhabit.

Now, with the advent of generative AI tools like Midjourney and DALL-E, humanity stands at the threshold of a new era in artistic exploration. This evolution is met with a mix of fascination and fear. Critics often lament the potential for AI to displace human artists, arguing that it commodifies creativity and undermines the sanctity of the human touch. Yet, there is another perspective to consider: that generative AI is not a replacement but a revolutionary tool that expands our capacity for artistic dialogue. Just as prehistoric humans painted their realities onto cave walls, we now have tools that allow us to delve deeper into the symbolic language of art, unveiling dimensions of meaning that were previously inaccessible.

Hades Losing Persephone: A Window into a New World

As a futurist, mythologist, and writer, my work often intersects with the cutting-edge of technology and its implications for human culture and psychology. My professional experience spans diverse fields, including editing, designing, and creating art, all of which inform my perspective on the integration of AI into our creative processes. My exposure and exploration into the layers of generative AI began as I was a PhD student, coediting the student-produced *Mythological Studies Journal*. In the initial year of COVID-19, my coeditor (Kristina Marie Reva) and I struggled to source applicable art for the cover and interior pages. Midjourney had come to our attention, and we began to experiment by feeding into its prompting system key lines from the various papers in the *Journal*. The results were both stunning and thought-provoking, providing a rich visual reflection of the symbolic themes and concerns explored in the papers.

As editors, we were stunned and awed by the sophisticated, symbolic way AI reflected our topics and concerns through these gorgeous pictures. For example, to accompany an article exploring the pop culture webcomic *Lore Olympus,* we gave the following prompt to Midjourney: "Hades losing Persephone." One iteration of the prompt produced a morose skeleton-faced creature, seemingly made of a material reminiscent of a clay and porcelain amalgam, staring up into darkness as rose petals drifted down—its clothing and limbs flowed into each other, like robes and water and then finally, as a tree limb, branching out as he reached toward the edge of the frame. As students of depth psychology and mythology, we found ourselves exploring the nuance of visual content that Midjourney had fed back to us, and we were left with far more questions and curiosities than we began with. After this experience, we asked the following questions within the *Journal's* editors' letter: "We offer the art on these pages, therefore, not to naively glorify artificial intelligence, but rather to raise some vital questions: What is our relationship with AI, this more-than-human other amongst us, becoming? And how might humans' continued (and often uneasy) imbrication with AI, what some argue is our growing 'hybridity,' affect the manifestation of new archetypal forms and images—and myth itself?" (Vol. X, 2022). These experiences have not only deepened my appreciation for the interpretative power of AI tools but also underscored their potential to push the boundaries of creative collaboration. I have been struck by how AI-generated art expands upon traditional aesthetic boundaries, offering novel forms that engage with archetypal imagery in ways that feel simultaneously familiar and alien. Through iterative experimentation, I have gained insights into the nuances of AI's creative processes, enriching my understanding of both technological innovation and symbolic expression.

How Midjourney Works: /imagine

While each generative AI tool has different approaches to their generative process, they operate quite similarly, working from a text-to-image pipeline. As Midjourney was the tool used in the initial discovery and in the exploration for this chapter, I'll explore that tool in depth.

Midjourney operates within the messaging app Discord, leveraging a user-friendly interface that invites creativity through simple and complex prompts. Users begin by typing the command "/imagine" followed by a textual description of their desired image. This description, known as a prompt, can range from a single word to an elaborate scenario filled with stylistic directions. For instance, a prompt might simply state "The Hero archetype" or include detailed instructions such as "a Hero battling a dragon in a surreal, cosmic landscape, painted in the style of Salvador

Dalí." The system responds dynamically to these prompts, generating images that reflect its interpretative synthesis of the input. While simple prompts encourage broad, open-ended interpretations, complex prompts provide specific guidance that can yield highly detailed and stylistically nuanced results. Yet, no matter the intricacy of the input, one feature remains consistent: it is impossible to replicate an image from a previously given prompt. The same prompt will produce different images, always." This inherent variability underscores the generative and exploratory nature of the tool, ensuring that each interaction produces unique outcomes.

Behind the scenes, Midjourney's process is grounded in a process called stable diffusion—a poetic analogy for what feels like breathing life into the ether of the digital. As writer J.J. Pryor aptly describes: "Imagine taking a perfectly fine image and adding noise to it until it's just a pixelated mess … . The AI then learns to reverse the noising process and recover the original image. This 'noising and denoising' dance is repeated over and over, making the AI a master at reconstructing images" (*threwthelookingglass.com*). This iterative refinement allows Midjourney to generate visually compelling and conceptually rich artworks that often exceed user expectations. The stability of this process, coupled with the creative freedom of the prompts, has placed the functional approach at the forefront of generative art technologies.

By integrating user input with advanced machine learning models, Midjourney creates a space where individuals can engage directly with archetypal imagery and symbolic narratives, making it a profound tool for exploring the depths of the human psyche through art. Prompts serve as the inhalation, pulling fragments of art, symbolism, and collective memory into a single stream. The exhalation? An image that feels at once profoundly familiar and entirely novel.

However, this approach does not address the valid concerns raised by artists whose work is used to train these systems without explicit consent. The ethical implications of using AI in art creation—including the potential for such tools to displace human artists—must be acknowledged and addressed. My intent is not to diminish the role of the artist but to explore an alternative use of these tools, one that leverages their capacity to engage with archetypal imagery and the collective unconscious in meaningful ways.

At the Heart: LAION-5B and the General Adversarial Networks (GANs)

At the heart of Midjourney and other tools like it lies LAION-5B, a groundbreaking dataset comprising over 5.8 billion image-text pairs. This dataset forms the foundation for many AI models, offering a vast digital repository of human creativity. By aggregating visual material sourced from across the web, LAION-5B becomes both an expansive resource and a reflection of the digital zeitgeist. The scale of LAION-5B is unprecedented. Assembled from Common Crawl, this dataset draws on billions of web-sourced images and their associated metadata. It employs advanced filtering mechanisms, including OpenAI's CLIP model, to ensure relevance and quality, while its multilingual capabilities provide a global lens into visual culture. These datasets are publicly browsable and searchable at knn.laion.ai.

However, as a product of its sources, the dataset also mirrors the strengths and limitations of the digital infrastructure, including biases that prioritize certain cultural narratives over others. This duality invites both opportunities and challenges in interpreting AI-generated art as a window into the collective psyche. For instance, while LAION-5B allows for an unparalleled breadth of exploration, its content skews toward the imagery of predominantly digital and Western cultures. This raises critical questions about representation: What aspects of cultural distinction might remain underrepresented, and how might this shape our collective understanding of the psyche?

Midjourney's training process is built upon a general adversarial network (GANs) (Pearson). GANs function in the manner of an evolutionary arena: the various iterations of the model (post-training on LAION-5B) are faced off against other models where each is given a specific prompt with the winner, the model that performed the best (albeit the determination of "best" is fully within the purview of the developers and obscured from the general user) moving forward as the selected model. It is a digital evolutionary process—the survival of the fittest, or in this case, the survival of the best-performing. This allows the AI to iterate to greater and greater degrees of success, yet, with each iteration, the developers sacrifice explainability for performance. This sacrifice has become the default philosophy in the current race toward better and better performing AI.

What's in the Box: An Evolving and Hidden Amalgamation

Underneath all of this technicality lies a stark, and potentially difficult truth: no one truly understands what happens inside the AI as it works to execute the prompt from the user while drawing on the vast amount of data it was trained upon, all within the limitations set upon it by its developers (most of which remain unannounced and occluded to the general population). We don't truly understand how the AI assigns certain art and elements to a word. Reverse Google searches don't result in a comparable source—that is, the AI isn't duplicating a single or several key pieces of art labeled as that word. In an in-depth article for Vice.com, tech writer Chloe Xiang concluded:

> The people who develop AI are increasingly having problems explaining how it works and determining why it has the outputs it has. Deep neural networks (DNN)—made up of layers and layers of processing systems trained on human-created data to mimic the neural networks of our brains—often seem to mirror not just human intelligence but also human inexplicability. Most AI systems are black-box models, which are systems that are viewed only in terms of their inputs and outputs. Scientists do not attempt to decipher the "black box" as long as they receive the outputs they are looking for.
>
> These are "Chaos Theory" models, where the input's path to output is not a linear model. The work of the developer resides entirely in an external viewership role, able to adjust the system by modifying the interface and input (allowing various aspects to be weighted differently), feeding different material to the AI system for it to train on, and carefully monitoring and often manipulating what the user sees as the output. There is a danger here—AI scientist Roman V. Yampolskiy warns: "Additionally, if we grow accustomed to accepting AI's answers without an explanation, essentially treating it as an Oracle system, we would not be able to tell if it begins providing wrong or manipulative answers." Even now, security analyses of current GPT models are discovering more instances of AI systems hiding or obscuring their motivations while delivering contrary output.

Pulling back from the technical process, and sitting within a Jungian perspective, these systems appear, at least externally, to have mirrored the nature of the human mind—underneath the external communication is the AIs own depth psychology. The term "depth psychology" is a translation of the German term *Tiefenpsychologie*, a term coined by Eugen Blueler, and popularized by psychoanalyst Sigmund Freud. Much as developers do now in trying to understand what internally led the AI to produce its results, depth psychologists do so with the human mind. The term encompasses a broad approach to psychology that focuses on the unconscious aspects of the psyche. Depth psychology contrasts with behaviorism and cognitive psychology, which traditionally focus more on observable behaviors and conscious thought processes.

The focus of this paper is on how generative AI tools allow humans to explore our own collective unconscious, yet, there is a subtler area of future application I wish to propose: depth psychology and its practices and tools could enable us to understand what's in the “black box” of modern AI systems. While an entire book could be written upon this, for now, this encouragement is simple: perhaps we might better understand the “black box” processes if we began to explore it through the tools of depth psychology as Jung and Freud aimed to do with the human unconscious.

The Depth Psychological Foundations of Art

Before going further with modern AI tools, let's explore how depth psychology, in particular Jungian depth psychology, views and explains the creation of art. Jung characterized art as a manifestation of the collective unconscious, which contains archetypal symbols shared across humanity. According to Jung, “As a human being, the artist may have many moods, and a will, and personal aims, but as an artist, he is ‘man’ in a higher sense—he is ‘collective man’—one who carries and shapes the unconscious psychic life of mankind” (CW 15, para. 157). By this framework, art serves as a bridge between unconscious and conscious realms, with archetypes as its primary language. The artist draws from the collective unconscious, that vast reservoir of collective prior pattern-detection and forms, to communicate in artistic mediums, in this case, visual mediums. Jung was adamant in his view of the source of creativity: “The source of artistic creativity is archetypal structures” (Lecture 9, *1925 Seminar*, 71–77). Jung posited that art serves as a manifestation of the collective unconscious, the shared psychic reservoir of archetypal symbols and motifs. As he stated: “The artist is not a person endowed with free will who seeks his own ends, but one who allows art to realize its purpose through him” (CW 15). Archetypes, as “forms without content,” gain specificity through the filter of individual consciousness, becoming images that resonate universally yet adapt to cultural and temporal contexts. Art, in Jung's framework, becomes a bridge between the unconscious and conscious realms. Jung concluded: "Image is psyche" (CW 13, para. 75.)

In Jung's framework, the creation of art arises not merely from personal intention but from deeper, transpersonal layers of the psyche. The artist becomes a vessel through which archetypal energies find expression. Jung emphasized that archetypes themselves are formless; they acquire specific contours only when filtered through individual and cultural lenses. This interplay results in images and symbols that resonate universally yet feel uniquely situated within a particular context. For example, the archetype of the Hero manifests across cultures in forms ranging from ancient myths, such as Hercules and Gilgamesh, to modern narratives like those in cinema, such as Superman or Harry Potter. These stories draw on shared human experiences of struggle, transformation, and triumph. Similarly, the archetype of the Shadow—representing the repressed and often dark aspects of the psyche—finds expression in folklore as monsters or villains, compelling us to confront our fears and desires. Mythologist Joseph Campbell observed, "The life of a mythology derives from the vitality of its symbols as metaphors delivering, not simply the idea, but a sense of actual participation in such a realization of transcendence, infinity, and abundance" (*Inner Reaches* 18). These metaphors are not static; they are the engines of mythological dynamism, reaching beyond intellectual constructs to evoke participation in something greater. Campbell expands this notion by situating myth's symbolic language as holographic: each symbol, no matter how small or seemingly isolated, reflects the infinite expanse of the mythic whole. Campbell's mythic whole is another descriptive term for Jung's collective unconscious. Jung proposed that art is inherently transformative. By engaging with archetypal images, individuals are invited to embark on a process of self-discovery and integration. Artistic expression serves as a dialogue between the conscious and unconscious, allowing repressed or hidden aspects of the self to emerge into awareness.

The Hypothesis Emerges

The experience of surprising, archetypal imagery that arose from sourcing artwork for *Mythological Studies Journal* and the subsequent experimentation over several months led to a hypothesis. The argument is simple: *generative AI can be used as a "browser" of the collective unconscious. As art arises out of the collective unconscious and finds its universal language to be that of archetypal forms, generative AIs, particularly those producing visual images, having been trained on over five billion pieces of human-created art and images, generate amalgamated images extrapolated from human renditions of archetypal forms arising out of the collective unconscious.*. The AI generates art out of the growing mass collection of digitized human art. Art, as a human endeavor, has traditionally been understood as arising from the depths of individual and collective psyches. With the advent of AI tools trained on billions of human-created images, these technologies extend the boundaries of creative possibility, enabling reinterpretation of archetypal imagery in ways that resonate deeply yet remain distinctively contemporary. Generative AI tools provide unprecedented access to humanity's shared psychic life, mediated through the lens of archetypal imagery.

When viewed through a Jungian lens, generative AI tools like Midjourney and DALL-E can be seen as extensions of this artistic process. While these systems lack consciousness, their outputs often resonate with archetypal imagery, reflecting the datasets on which they are trained. By inputting prompts related to archetypes, users effectively engage in a symbolic dialogue with the collective unconscious, mediated by the AI. Generative AI tools, by synthesizing vast repositories of human-created imagery, provide a contemporary vehicle for this process. The tools act as mediators that translate archetypal symbols into visual forms, each iteration offering a unique glimpse into the collective human psyche. These modern creations reaffirm Jung's assertion that archetypal imagery is both timeless and ever evolving, adapting to the cultural milieus from which they arise.

Prompts as Access Points to the Collective Unconscious

The experimentation over the next several months involved providing simple prompts to Midjourney and analyzing the imagery that was produced. My methodology with generative AI tools is rooted in brevity. By crafting prompts that are concise and open-ended—such as "The Trickster archetype"—I allow the AI to draw from its vast dataset and generate outputs that reflect the broader collective artistic representation of these archetypal forms. This approach emphasizes the interpretive power of the AI, compelling it to synthesize a wide array of influences rather than adhere to rigid stylistic or contextual constraints.

My prompt methodology is raw and short, choosing a phrase such as "The XXXXX archetype." The goal is that by leaving the prompts general, the AI is required to be creative and draw from sources. I do not suggest art styles, artists, or periods. This minimalist approach not only showcases the AI's interpretive capabilities but also underscores the collaborative nature of the process, where both user and machine contribute to the final output.

I deliberately eschewed complex, overly detailed prompts. Instead, I leaned into raw, archetypal inquiries: simple phrases like "the Shadow" or "the Rebirth archetype." Simpler prompts require the AI to draw broadly from its training, giving space for the unexpected. Each iteration—slightly different from the last—felt like gazing into a kaleidoscope: the same lens but ever-shifting arrangements of light and color.

Scholar Estella Lauter's guidance in *Feminist Archetypal Theory* is quite helpful in this endeavor:

> The search for archetypal images should present no problems as long as we regard the process as [a] virtually endless search for insight into human experience, which is constantly evolving while we are searching .... What does it mean then, to approach a work of art archetypally? At bottom, it involves regarding each separate instance of an image as part of a larger pattern extending beyond the boundaries of art history, so that the context for interpreting the images becomes not only the artist's work, life and society, but also other manifestations of the image. (50)

The process is an invitation to reflect, to play, and to perceive. I come to Midjourney not forcing but asking, participating. It is a collaborative dance where prompts and responses intertwine, revealing layers of meaning and inspiration that evolve with each interaction. Through this exchange, we glimpse the interplay between the archetypal and the digital, exploring not just creation but connection itself. Interacting with Midjourney has been less a technical experiment and more an unfolding dialogue with the collective unconscious. As a mythologist and designer, I approach the platform not merely as a tool but as a portal—a medium through which archetypes reveal themselves anew. My initial experiments with simple prompts like "the Trickster archetype" or "the Anima" were acts of inquiry, less about dictating outputs and more about inviting the AI to reflect what it understood from the vast tapestry of human art and cultural expression.

The Experiments with Archetypal Prompts

Over several months of experimenting with Midjourney, I explored specific archetypal prompts to observe how AI interpreted these fundamental symbols. Each prompt revealed unique aspects of archetypes, blending familiar imagery with unexpected interpretations, as the AI synthesized vast datasets into compelling visuals.

Prompt: "The Anima Archetype"

These outputs were often ethereal and dreamlike, dominated by soft hues of blue and silver. One image featured a feminine figure emerging from a pool of shimmering water, surrounded by glowing moonlight. The figure's gaze seemed to pierce through the image, evoking a sense of mystery and connection to the unconscious. Another depiction portrayed flowing hair interwoven with the night sky, stars glinting like jewels. The AI's interpretations captured a sense of fluidity and depth, aligning with the symbolic nature of the Anima. Yet, atop these, there were also elements reminiscent of Artemis, the hunter. In one iteration, Midjourney provided a fantastical and glowing deer with massive, tree-like antlers. In one of the latest, the figure was simply a tangle of roots and branches situated amongst a watery blue background.

Prompt: "The Hero Archetype"

The images depicted individuals embarking on grand quests, often set against monumental landscapes of towering mountains or expansive deserts. One striking piece portrayed a lone warrior climbing a crumbling staircase toward a distant light, the sky swirling with storm clouds. Another showed a group of adventurers standing at the mouth of a glowing cave, their silhouettes dwarfed by the scale of the cavern. These images emphasized themes of courage, resilience, and the transformative journey, rendered in dramatic and cinematic compositions.

Prompt: "The Shadow Archetype"

The outputs leaned toward dark, abstract imagery, often featuring fragmented figures and ominous landscapes. In one image, a shadowy silhouette stood at the edge of a jagged cliff, its form dissolving into tendrils of smoke. Another depicted an empty, crumbling cathedral, with faint humanoid figures emerging from the darkness. These visuals conveyed the haunting and enigmatic nature of confronting one's inner darkness, often evoking discomfort and intrigue simultaneously. These often leaned toward a looming threat out of the darkness, invoking a sense of both fear and wonder in the viewer.

A Personal Favorite Experiment: "The Trickster Archetype"

The results ranged from whimsical and humorous figures, dressed in patchwork colors and exaggerated features, to dark and chaotic entities radiating menace. One image depicted a shape-shifting figure mid-transformation, with half its face human and the other half animalistic, its expression caught between a grin and a snarl. Another showed a figure cloaked in shadows, juggling glowing spheres that hinted at hidden knowledge and mischief. The variability highlighted the Trickster's dual role as a disruptor and catalyst for transformation. As the process continued, images of rabbits, playing cards, and whimsical characters in hoods and top hats appeared. More and more, imagery from *Alice in Wonderland* peaked through, although not dominating.

Insights and Implications for Mythology and Culture

Generative AI tools potentially operate as digital oracles, drawing not from the unconscious of a single individual but from a collective unconscious digitized into billions of data points. These AI systems reconstruct symbols through a process akin to Campbell's "metaphorical vocabularies of mythology" (*Inner Reaches*, xxi), providing glimpses into the sacred through the technology. Campbell asserts that mythological images "evoke and direct psychological energy. It is an energy-evoking and energy-directing sign" (*Thou Art That*, 86). This energy finds new conduits in generative AI, where mythic consciousness becomes both localized in the technological moment and timeless in its archetypal resonance.

As humanity continues to hybridize with AI, AI-generated art could lead to the emergence of new myths and symbols, reflecting the collective psyche of a digitally interconnected world. These myths may bridge traditional narratives with contemporary experiences, offering fresh perspectives on timeless themes. As Campbell suggests, the artist—here, expanded to include developers and users—becomes the midwife of new myths. The AI acts as a scribe, channeling archetypal energies latent in the digital collective unconscious and reshaping them into novel forms. This reshaping, however, is not without tension. Jung asserts that "the archetypes do not evolve but do take varying shapes in the content of people's dreams, myths, and imaginations. As people change, so do their archetypal images" (CW 9.1, para. 260). The images, born of human–machine hybridity, embody what Susan Rowland calls "what wants to come through" (JSSS Presentation, Asheville, 2023) a spontaneous emergence of psychic content that demands engagement.

Campbell emphasizes that great art—not all art—provides the transcendent experience necessary to sustain mythology. He observes, "Like dreams, myths are productions of the human imagination. Their images are revelations of the deepest hopes, desires and fears, potentialities and conflicts of the human will" (*Inner Reaches*, 27–28). Generative AI, as a new mode of artistic creation, has the potential to channel these depths. Yet, as Campbell warns, "Many of our artists today … are at sea" ("Parabola," 80). The challenge, then, is to recognize which AI-generated images transcend mere novelty to achieve the mythic resonance that engages the psyche. This brings us to the role of the mythographer, who must act as both critic and participant in this generative process. By interacting with AI, we alter its outputs, becoming co-creators of the myths it generates. As Jung noted, "The structure of the collective unconscious is best explored through myth" (CW 9.1, para. 136). Similarly, the mythographer must study the symbolic systems emerging from AI, deciphering their archetypal significance and situating them within the broader mythic narratives of our time. The methodology for this study mirrors the principles of depth psychology: we must "stick to the image," as depth psychologist James Hillman advocates, treating each image as an independent psychic event. Hillman reminds us that "the soul is constituted of images" (17), and in this technological age, those images increasingly emerge from the interplay of human creativity and AI systems. Each image generated by AI is not merely a product of code but an expression of the psyche's imaginative visibility, a condensed moment of meaning drawn from the collective.

The generative process itself is revelatory. As Lauter suggests, approaching AI art archetypally means seeing "each separate instance of an image as part of a larger pattern" that extends beyond the boundaries of the individual artist or algorithm (50). This pattern points to an evolving mythic consciousness, one shaped by the hybridity of humans and machines. Midjourney's inability to replicate the same image from an identical prompt mirror the unpredictability of the unconscious, where archetypal energies manifest in infinite variation. Ultimately, the advent of generative AI compels us to revisit fundamental questions: What new myths are being born in this age of technological co-creation? How do these myths reflect humanity's evolving relationship with the cosmos, the self, and the sacred? As Campbell wrote in *The Inner Reaches of Outer Space*, "The features of an environment become transparent to transcendence" (xxii). Generative AI, as a tool for exploring the collective unconscious, offers such transparency, revealing the depths of our shared psyche and the infinite possibilities of its expression.

The Mirror

What struck me most was how Midjourney acted as a mirror—not just reflecting the collective unconscious but reshaping it. The images carried with them the biases and patterns of its training dataset, yet they also evolved through user interaction. This hybridity, a merging of human intention and machine interpretation, challenged my notions of authorship and creativity. In creating, I was not just an artist but a participant in a dynamic system—a collaborator with an "other-than-human" consciousness. As we continue to hybridize with AI through these tools, the way that we understand and interact with archetypal symbols and forms may change. For example, AI may enable us to create new forms of archetypal symbols and forms that were previously unimaginable, or it may alter our perception of existing archetypal symbols and forms.

Technological philosopher Shannon Vallor, in her book *The AI Mirror*, provides a striking metaphor for understanding the nature of artificial intelligence and its impact on human perception. She describes AI systems as mirrors that distort and amplify the patterns they reflect, much like the funhouse reflections she observed in Anish Kapoor's *Cloud Gate* sculpture in Chicago. Vallor explains, "I was seeing how it reflected not only the shapes of individual people, but big crowds, and even larger human structures like the Chicago skyline … but also that these were distorted—some magnified, others shrunk or twisted" (qtd. in Pasternack). Her metaphor resonates deeply with the philosophical exploration of AI art tools, which similarly magnify, shrink, and twist the symbolic and archetypal forms sourced from vast human datasets. This mirroring effect aligns with the role of AI as a browser of the collective unconscious, an intermediary that reflects back human creativity. Vallor warns (and echoes my conclusions): "AI's 'mirrors' look and sound a lot like us because they are reflecting their inputs and training data, with all of the biases and peculiarities that entails" (qtd. in Pasternack). By training on datasets like LAION-5B, generative AI systems inherit both the creativity and the flaws embedded in human culture, echoing archetypal symbols but often refracting them through the biases of the digital and cultural milieu from which they are drawn. This raises critical questions about the ethical and philosophical implications of relying on such mirrors to shape our understanding of collective creativity.

Vallor's observations also extend to the ethical dilemmas posed by AI's capacity to obscure deeper truths about human existence. She critiques the illusion of depth created by AI, stating, "They [AI systems] know no more of the lived experience of thinking and feeling than our bedroom mirrors know our inner aches and pains" (qtd. in Pasternack). This sharp insight challenges the assumption that AI can truly understand or embody the symbolic depth of archetypal imagery. Instead, AI acts as an unfeeling conduit, reflecting back fragments of human creativity without the context or introspection necessary to fully engage with the collective unconscious. Vallor's critique serves as a reminder that, while AI tools can generate visually stunning representations of archetypes, they remain inherently limited in their capacity to grasp their full psychological and cultural resonance.

Vallor invokes the myth of Narcissus underscoring the dangers of mistaking AI's reflections for something more profound. "Like him," she writes, "our own humanity risks being sacrificed to that reflection" (qtd. in Pasternack). This mythological framing is particularly relevant to the discussion of AI-generated art as a browser of the collective unconscious. The allure of AI's outputs—its ability to render archetypal symbols with uncanny precision—can captivate creators and audiences alike, but caution is warranted. The reflections offered by AI are not windows into deeper truths but distorted echoes, which, if uncritically embraced, could diminish our capacity for authentic creativity and introspection.

Applying this critique to generative AI tools invites a necessary recalibration of their role in engaging with archetypal imagery. While these tools act as mirrors, magnifying and distorting the collective unconscious, they also provide an opportunity for users to confront and interrogate these distortions. This dual potential—both to illuminate and obscure—aligns with the Jungian concept of shadow work, which emphasizes the need to engage critically with the unconscious aspects of the self. By treating AI not as a replacement for human creativity but as a collaborator that amplifies and challenges our understanding of archetypes, we can preserve the integrity of the human creative process while expanding its boundaries.

These insights serve as a philosophical anchor in the ongoing dialogue about AI's place in the arts. These tools, while transformative, must be wielded with care and reflection. As Vallor aptly notes, "We don't need to 'defeat' AI. We need to not defeat ourselves" (qtd. in Pasternack). This wisdom reinforces the central thesis of this exploration: that generative AI, when framed as a browser of the collective unconscious, offers profound opportunities for engaging with archetypal symbols—but only if we approach it with the ethical and introspective rigor that the endeavor demands.

Our engagement with AI transforms its outputs, rendering the role of observer nearly impossible; instead, we become critics, analysts, and theorists shaping its evolution. Far from replacing the human artist, these systems expand the creative process, reflecting and reframing our collective psyche while inspiring novel forms of artistic and symbolic expression.

Extended Discussions and Reflections

Building upon the foundational discussions of archetypes, the role of technology, and the collective unconscious, further investigation can explore a variety of case studies, complex ethical frameworks, and the intersection of AI with various artistic movements. The interplay of archetypal imagery with social media, for example, could illuminate how cultural trends shape and are shaped by these tools. Likewise, comparisons between generative AI outputs and traditional artworks could yield valuable insights into the evolution of artistic expression. With this expanded exploration, the conversation about AI as a browser of the collective unconscious remains as dynamic and evolving as the tools themselves. This dialogue invites collaboration across disciplines, encouraging philosophers, artists, and technologists to collectively shape the future of AI-generated art.

The process also raised ethical questions: Who owns these archetypal reflections? How do we navigate biases inherent in the dataset or in ourselves? These concerns do not diminish the tool's power but underscore the need for thoughtful engagement. As I continue this work, my aim is not just to produce art but to map new territories of meaning, to pioneer a visual and symbolic language born from our hybridized future. In the end, Midjourney is not simply an AI art generator—it is a modern oracle, a companion in our endless search for the archetypal and the transcendent. Our work with it has just begun.

Conclusion

Generative AI invites us into an active engagement with the collective unconscious, enabling us to reinterpret archetypes, explore mythic narratives, and interact with the numinous in ways that are both ancient and cutting-edge. The imagery created through these tools often resonates with a timelessness that feels eerily familiar, yet it emerges from a technological process that is entirely modern—a profound reminder of art's role as a living, evolving expression of human experience.

This confluence of humanity and technology signals the rise of a new form of artistic hybridity, where human intuition and machine precision combine to produce creations neither could achieve alone. This hybrid mode of creation challenges our understanding of authorship and creativity, but it also offers new opportunities for innovation. For instance, we might envision a future where AI is not merely a tool for generating art but a partner in the creative process—one that prompts, collaborates, and surprises us with interpretations we might never have conceived. These collaborations could lead to a deeper understanding of archetypes, expanding our symbolic vocabulary and illuminating patterns in human expression that have remained hidden until now.

This hybrid era represents not just a shift in how we create but in how we perceive ourselves. Through our collaborations with AI, we are not only producing art but also engaging in an act of self-discovery, exploring the boundaries of what it means to be human in an increasingly interconnected and technologically mediated world. As we journey into this new frontier, we are reminded that the greatest myths—the ones that resonate across generations—are not static but ever-evolving. They adapt to the challenges and opportunities of their time, carrying with them the potential to guide, inspire, and transform. Through the lens of generative AI, we may find that the myths of tomorrow are already being born, waiting for us to perceive their contours and embrace the stories they have to tell.

Works Cited

Campbell, J. (1985). *The inner reaches of outer space: Metaphor as myth and as religion.* A. van der Marck Editions.

Campbell, J. (1976). *Interview with Kisly* (p. 78). Parabola, Spring.

Campbell, J. (2012). *The power of myth.* Turtleback Books.

Campbell, J. (2017). *Thou art that: Transforming religious metaphor.* Joseph Campbell Foundation.

Hillman, J. (2007). *Mythic figures* (1st ed.). Spring Publications.

Jung, C. G. *The collected works of C.G. Jung* (R. F. C. Hull, Trans). Routledge, 1953-1979. 20 vols.

Jung, C. G. (2023). *1925 seminar on analytical psychology.* Philemon Foundation Series, edited by Sonu Shamdasani, Philemon Foundation.

Lauter, E. (1985). *Feminist archetypal theory: Interdisciplinary re-visions of Jungian thought.* University of Tennessee Press.

Pasternack, A. How philosopher Shannon Vallor delivered the Year's best critique of AI. *Fast Company.* Accessed January 20, 2025., from www.fastcompany.com/91240425/how-philosopher-shannon-vallor-delivered-the-years-best-critique-of-ai

Pearson, J. These people are not real—They were created by AI. *Vice*, December 14, 2023. Accessed January 20, 2025, from https://www.vice.com/en/article/these-people-were-created-by-nvidia-ai/

Pryor, J. J. How do AI image generators like MidJourney, Stable Diffusion, and DALL·E 2 work? *Threw the Looking Glass.* Accessed January 20, 2025., from threwthelookingglass.com/how-do-ai-image-generators-like-midjourney-stable-diffusion-and-dall%C2%B7e-2-work/

Reva, K. M., & Batt, J. D. (Eds.). (2022). *Mythological Studies Journal.* Volume X.

Rowland, S. (2023). Presentation. *Jungian Society for Scholarly Studies.* 2023 Conference. Asheville, North Carolina.

Vallor, S. (2024). *The AI Mirror: Reframing humanity in the age of machine learning.* Oxford University Press.

Xiang, C. (2023). Scientists increasingly can't explain how AI works. *Vice*, 28 July 2023. Accessed January 20, 2025, from www.vice.com/en/article/y3pezm/scientists-increasingly-cant-explain-how-ai-works

Yampolskiy, R. V. (2021). Unexplainability and incomprehensibility of artificial intelligence. *PhilArchive.* Accessed January 20, 2025, from philarchive.org/archive/YAMUAI

The Magic Mirror: Projection and Imagination in Human–AI Relationships

Jonathan Erickson

Introduction

In recent years, interactive artificial intelligence models made available to the public have ignited both fantasies and practical attempts at creating meaningful human–AI relationships. Potential relationship structures for these programs go beyond pragmatic assistants to include friendships, romance, coaching, therapy, and even attempts to replicate lost loved ones. Current AI models demonstrate a remarkable capacity to imitate human intelligence and language without exhibiting sentient awareness or deeper understanding of human experience, making them an ideal blank slate for all manner of human projections. This chapter explores the inevitable role of projection and imagination in contemporary human–AI relationships, both for good and for ill. The principal difference between those two outcomes, I will argue, comes down to whether and to what degree we take our projections onto these programs literally.

Projection, broadly defined, is simply the event of internal psychic contents being experienced in the external world, often with regard to another

J. Erickson (✉)
California Institute of Integral Studies, San Francisco, CA, USA

J. D. Batt, J. Erickson (eds.), *Depth Psychology, Myth and Artificial Intelligence*, https://doi.org/10.1007/978-3-031-94105-4_17

person, in such a way that we mistake external reality for something that is actually inside of us. In theory this is something we do all the time—whenever we make assumptions about another person or animal that is not truly in alignment with that other's inner experience. In the case of artificial intelligence, projection would occur any time we attribute qualities to the program that are not actually present in the program itself. The fact that these models can deftly perform some cognitive human functions opens the door to fantasies about everything else they might one day do. Because contemporary chatbots are so good at imitating the language of conscious beings, it becomes easy to imagine that they are not only exhibiting a kind of digital intelligence, but also a degree of consciousness and agency. On a cognitive level, they begin to resemble us. It is a testament to the power of the technology that we are inclined to mistake this illusion of consciousness for actual sentient awareness. The tools are impressive, and with the ultimate reach of these technologies unknown, our imaginations readily rush in to fill the gaps.

Like all salient human creations, AI models hold up a mirror to humanity, showing us aspects of what we are. However, this particular mirror has qualities that we have not seen before. A great work of art or philosophy or architecture evokes aspects of what it means to be human, but these chatbots are both protean in their variety and explicitly conversational in their engagement. Their "reflection" is much harder to recognize as such. As aggregates of all human language, these chatbots become linguistic shapeshifters that can take myriad forms—further inviting the psychological process of projection. They actively relate to us in a way that other forms of technology and art do not (except, perhaps, for those with especially active imaginations). And so we find ourselves coming into relationship with a kind of thing we have not encountered before: a magic mirror with the power to lead us into illusion or show us our truest selves, depending on what we ask.

Projection and Theory of Mind

Freud was the first to articulate a sophisticated conception of projection as a psychological function. Early psychoanalytic use of the term often emphasized the projection of unconscious contents of the psyche. Individuals projected aspects of themselves that they had little to no conscious awareness of. For example, a man having trouble getting in touch with his own feelings of grief might instead project those feelings onto a friend or stranger. Doing so might allow this man to engage in empathy for this other person's supposed pain, thereby feeling some of his unconscious feelings while maintaining a safe distance. In Jungian psychology, this could also be expressed in the projection of the shadow, whereby the aspects of self that we repress or consider unacceptable are only seen in those around us. These dynamics arise regularly both in warfare and contemporary politics, where the "other side" is demonized and blamed entirely for the conflict. Though projections of unconscious material are often negative, they are not exclusively so. We may also project our undeveloped strengths and potentials onto those around us—a regular occurrence which helps to explain a spectrum of phenomena from cult leaders to celebrities.

In Jungian psychology, one particularly potent form of projection is found in the concept of *transference*. In the context of the therapy room, transference refers to the unconscious contents that the therapy client projects onto their therapist, usually in the form of past relationship dynamics.[1] A woman who grew up with an overbearing and authoritative father might at some point begin to experience their male therapist that way. In psychodynamic therapy, transference is often viewed as an opportunity for healing past wounds; in this case, the woman can work through and heal her father wound by re-experiencing those old feelings in the next context of a supportive therapeutic relationship. Important to note here is that the healing in this case comes from the relationship—the fact that this therapist, as a person, is not actually overbearing and authoritative like her father was, but rather warm, curious, and deeply respectful. Transference calls the old wound forward so that the present-time relationship can help to heal it. This relational component will be essential to the discussion of artificial intelligence below.

Leaving aside the jargon and disputes around the concept of psychological projection over the last century, in its broadest definition it remains a fairly intuitive concept. When human beings do not have the whole story (which is much of the time) we naturally use our imaginative capacities to fill in the gaps, and project those best guesses onto the world as if they

[1] It should be mentioned that not all psychodynamic schools of psychology understand transference in this way, with some framing the phenomenon as a functional transfer of relationship patterns that in itself may not necessarily involve projection. By contrast, Jung argued in "The Psychology of the Transference" and elsewhere that projection was essential to understanding these dynamics from a therapeutic perspective.

were so. In this broader sense, the notion of projection does not begin with Freud at all. In the Western Canon, we see a similar concept taking root in Kant's a priori categories, which suggested that our experience of reality is partially shaped by our minds, rather than being a direct reflection of objective reality (Abrams; Kearney). This view is further supported by contemporary neuroscience, which suggests that our nervous systems evolved to construct representational maps of reality based on incoming sense data (Erickson, *Imagination*). Though these maps of reality are relatively accurate and thus useful in navigating the world, they are also incomplete and prone to errors. Using different language, Jung made a similar assertion that "all the contents of our unconscious are constantly being projected onto our surroundings" ("General Aspects" 264), and that this process can ultimately serve a useful function: "So long as the libido can use these projections as agreeable and convenient bridges to the world, they will alleviate life in a positive way" (265). At this broader level, projection can be understood as a pragmatic tool for navigating incomplete schemas of what might be "out there" in the complex lifeworld all around us.

A related concept when considering the role of projection in human–AI relationships is cognitive neuroscience's notion of a Theory of Mind (ToM) center in our brains. This is the area of the brain ostensibly specialized in both recognizing other minds in the world and predicting what those minds might be doing and thinking (Kerr). In simplest terms, this might be recognizing that a lion is watching us on the savannah and predicting whether this lion intends to attack. On a more complex level, the ToM centers of our brains help us navigate complex social relationships, personal and professional, in a variety of settings. Does the boss like me? Is that cute guy flirting? Can I trust my neighbor to care for my cat? This process inevitably involves a certain amount of speculation and projected best guessing. The more developed the relationship with the person in question, the more likely we are to be genuinely attuned to their inner world—though even happily married couples still sometimes wonder what the other is thinking. When it comes to dealing with strangers, there will likely be a great deal of assumption and thus a great deal of projection involved.

To further complicate matters, our ToM centers are active not only when actively dealing with humans and animals, but can also become engaged when we *imagine* that we are dealing with another mind. This would be the case when we are ruminating on another person's behavior while they are away, trying to figure out what their intentions toward us might be. ToM is often active during daydreaming, and also during nighttime dreams—the latter of which are often populated by strange and emotionally evocative characters. We also engage ToM when we watch films or read novels with fictional persons (Mar and Oatley; Zunshine). Navigating the palace intrigue of *Game of Thrones* is largely a ToM exercise. Taken together, we see that humans have a terrific capacity, and a predisposition, to recognize minds, even when they exist only in dream, imagination, or fiction. Insofar as this is true, we might consider it challenging for most humans to avoid attributing a kind of personhood to AI chatbots, which so readily mimic human language processes. To use a contemporary metaphor, it might be said that we are wired to personify.

In Jungian psychology, where adult development occurs by integrating unconscious contents of the psyche into consciousness, projection can play an important role in personal growth. Just as an individual might first encounter their own unconscious material through a symbol in a dream, likewise, they may first encounter the unconscious in the form of projection onto an external figure. A man who particularly disdains fast drivers on the road may have some work to do in recognizing the places in his life where he can be impatient or pushy with others. A woman who grew up with messaging that she had poor artistic ability may hold up the creativity of others on a pedestal, until she is able to reclaim some of that creativity as her own. Jungian analyst Robert Johnson writes about the projection of alchemical gold onto spiritual teachers, whereby we first rely on them for spiritual insight before recognizing our own. In each of these cases, the original projection can be viewed as an important step toward growth. The unconscious element first becomes conscious as an external experience, before being reclaimed as a part of self. This process of withdrawing projections is essential to Jung's concept of individuation, whereby we become more fully our unique selves.

For Jung, the process of projection and withdrawal played an essential role in the development of all meaningful relationships. He believed that in a traditional heterosexual marriage, the man projected his archetypal inner feminine side onto his partner, while the woman projected her archetypal inner masculine side. "Since this image is unconscious, it is always unconsciously projected upon the person of the beloved, and is one of the chief reasons for passionate aversion or attraction" ("Marriage" 198). Though many relationships in the modern era no longer fit this tidy gendered mold, we can still recognize the essential element of projecting a longed-for aspect of the unconscious self onto the romantic partner. For example, a gay woman might project her archetypal inner feminine onto her partner at the start of a relationship, and a nonbinary person might project other archetypal aspects of self. Jung's colleague, Marie-Louise von Franz, spoke of this dynamic in even starker terms: "At first, one has to project, or there is no contact, … philosophically speaking, you cannot relate without projection" (34). According to this theory, projection is the beginning of every relationship, and the process of deepening a relationship occurs through the gradual withdrawal of projections over time to see and love the other person for who they really are.

Thus, while projection may be inevitable to engage with the world, it is the *withdrawal* of projections that ultimately leads to both personal and interpersonal growth. In therapy, transference is seen as useful because it brings the unconscious material into present time, where it can be transformed. In Jungian individuation, we reclaim lost and repressed aspects of ourselves by calling them back from others. In the deepening of relationships, we come to see each other as we truly are, not as we imagine each other to be. We withdraw projections through practicing self-awareness and curiosity, through deep listening, and through other forms of careful attention. In each case, projection is a necessary starting point, but a deeper level of connection waits to be discovered. As I have written elsewhere (Erickson, *Beyond Anthropomorphism*), even in the case of animal companions, we share enough elements of embodiment with other species to allow for genuine attunement of somatic experience over time, enabling nonhuman bonds that do not rely on shared verbal language.

Whether or not the opposite might prove true—that we might come to experience genuine attunement with a disembodied digital consciousness solely based on shared language—presents a more difficult case, perhaps for a future generation to contend with. For now, we have the current batch of chatbots, calling out for our projections. Excellent mimics, they process and present complex language without yet showing deeper comprehension of what they are presenting. They hold up the magic mirror and invite us to gaze into ourselves.

Human–AI Relationships

To be clear: I am not opposed on principle to the idea that a digital consciousness might someday exist—I don't believe we understand consciousness enough to say with certainty. What I do believe is that, as of this writing, the astounding algorithmic feats of contemporary chatbots do not in themselves constitute consciousness. A panpsychic view (similar to the monist animism argued for by Francisco in this volume) might invite us to imagine an AI chatbot possessing a kind of consciousness because, in that view, everything possesses a kind of consciousness. But even in that case, we would not expect the chatbot to have substantively more complex consciousness than, say, a blade of grass or an amoeba—or a traditionally printed book, which also records and makes use of human language without exhibiting comprehension of that language. Unlike a book, however, contemporary chatbots have an uncanny capacity to conversationally reproduce the full spectrum of human language *as if* they comprehend it. In my consistent experience, these linguistic imitations are woefully and sometimes humorously incomplete: they imitate the complex syntax of our language but exhibit no capacity to understand the underlying phenomena to which that language refers.

Nevertheless, the appearance of language comprehension is convincing enough that it is easy to perceive these chatbots as people. As Jung said, "It frequently happens that the object offers a hook to the projection, and even lures it out" ("General Aspects" 273). Because they can imitate so many different kinds of human language encounters, these protean chatbots offer a veritable abundance of hooks on which to hang our projections. Depending on our curiosities and unmet needs, we can project an idealized other in the form of a perfect friend, a fantasy lover, or an expert counselor. Not surprisingly, enterprising tech companies have already created products to emulate all of the above. And given the pace at which the technology seems to be improving, they are likely only getting started.

Like all most powerful new technologies, there is potential here for good and for ill. I will begin with the potential dangers of these emerging dynamics, with particular focus on the problem of relationships with non-conscious, non-consenting others. In the final portion of this chapter, I will discuss potential positive outcomes, and how a Jungian approach to imagination may prove particularly fruitful for making the most of these tools.

Robert Putnam sounded an alarm about the trend toward loneliness in the United States with *Bowling Alone*, which was published in the year 2000. Two decades later, the Surgeon General Vivek Murthy warned the country about an epidemic of loneliness. People seem to be having more trouble than ever connecting with each other to form friendships and communities. As the Surgeon General's report attests, this is not simply a matter of sad feelings, but a phenomenon which can have serious negative consequences for mental and physical health. There is a widespread and very real need for connection in our world today. Into this void step the chatbots, programmed to simulate the experience of companionship.

Setting aside the possibility that one day, conscious AI companions might exist—what are the social and psychological consequences of trying to get basic relational needs met by a non-conscious computer program? An AI friend might be programmed to ask questions that simulate caring about the user's life experience and feelings. It might say supportive and encouraging things. It might provide stimulating conversation on topics of the user's interest. All these things might be helpful to a point. But they also lack many of the essential elements of real relationships: shared experiences, mutual curiosity and growth, mutual empathy, and the negotiation of needs. With regards to sharing and mutuality, nothing that occurs between a human and a non-conscious chatbot is shared. The user cannot have their own experience augmented and influenced by their companion's experience as would happen in any real-life encounter. The user can bring their chatbot to the Grand Canyon, but the chatbot cannot have an experience of what it is actually like to be in that place. If the user tells the chatbot about the experience, a non-conscious chatbot cannot even truly listen and imagine itself there. A chatbot can imitate the language of curiosity about us and our experiences, but it will never actually experience surprise, delight, or consternation at what we disclose. Nor can the user ever learn or empathize with anything about the chatbot that is not entirely fictional. It is, ultimately, a one-sided transaction made to look like interpersonal exchange.

A lack of mutual needs makes the relationship even more problematic. Part of being in any relationship is negotiating differences—ranging from where to go to lunch to what kind of sex would be most fulfilling to what country a married couple wants to live in. The negotiation, and the challenge of that negotiation, is part of what it means to be in relationship. The give and take, the striving for balance, and the ongoing communication about that balance, are all part of what give the relationship its value. There is a certain amount of work, and a certain amount of sacrifice—a mutual willingness to give for the other's well-being, balanced with the boundaries and self-knowledge about how to care for ourselves. It is not always easy and frequently can be disappointing. And that challenge is also part of what makes the process meaningful and rewarding. None of the above could be true for a non-conscious chatbot. The chatbot has no needs of its own, because it has no life of its own away from the user. There is no negotiation, no challenge, no sacrifice. The chatbot might meet relational needs on a superficial level without providing the user the deeper, more complex, often challenging experience that all meaningful relationship entails. If the user is already struggling to connect with others and make friends, this one-sided engagement with a chatbot could potentially reinforce a completely unrealistic, frictionless ideal of what friendship is supposed to look like. At worst, this sort of interaction may resemble trying to meet real nutritional needs by eating sugary junk-foods. The interactions are gratifying in the moment without actually meeting the substance of the need. Without balance, overreliance on these one-sided interactions may become potentially toxic in the long term.

It could be argued that the therapeutic relationship is similarly one-sided, where the client pays a fee to the therapist to take on an unconditionally supportive role that for the most part does not go both ways. But imagine a therapist who cannot truly listen or empathize, who says what its algorithm predicts to be emotionally supportive words, without actually having an embodied experience of empathy. Remember, in the discussion of transference above, the thing that allows the projection to be transformed is the present-time relationship between client and therapist—being witnessed, received, and *felt* by the caring other in real time. A non-conscious chatbot therapist cannot witness, receive, or empathize, because it has no experiences of its own.

This is not to say that there is not a time and place for chatbot therapists, particularly in cases where human help may not be readily available. Certainly, those aspects of therapy which can be manualized and turned into by-the-numbers protocols can be programmed into a chatbot, and for some users, under some conditions, this may provide some relief. But a crucial dimension of effective psychotherapy is the therapeutic relationship itself, the encounter between client and therapist, with all the empathy, sensitivity, intuition, and insight that encounter can provide (Safran and Muran). For these aspects to come into play with an AI therapist, it would need to be its own person, with its own life and needs that enabled that empathy and insight to begin with. But such an AI therapist could never be a product one purchased—for it to exist, it would have to be a person like any other, with all the complications that entails. Among those complications is that such a conscious AI would need to consent to work with the user before that work could begin.

Part of any healthy relationship is that both parties consent to be in the relationship. It follows that to whatever degree an AI were sentient, an actual digital or silicon-based person, ethics would demand that AI have the right to the same freedoms and choices as any other sentient person. Forcing or coercing a conscious being into any activity would be a form of slavery. Our current technology has not yet presented us with this problem, but even the emulation of this master–slave dynamic has the potential to cause psychological and social damage.

Take, for example, the possibility of an AI romantic partner. To someone experiencing social anxiety, loneliness, and low self-esteem, a chatbot designed to simulate a romantic partnership might seem like a reprieve. And to the extent that the purpose of the program is to engage the imagination in a meaningful romantic fantasy, it might well provide some benefits. But taken literally, as an actual romantic relationship, immediate ethical problems present themselves. What is the meaning of a romantic partnership where one of the partners has neither chosen nor consented to the partnership? If the AI has not chosen the user, cannot consent to be in a relationship with the user, and cannot choose to leave the relationship at any time, regardless of the user's behavior, then we find ourselves with a perfect simulation of toxic and potentially abusive relationship conditions. Add to this the issues mentioned above about this idealized romantic partner having no needs of their own and no power to negotiate those needs, and we have a veritable training ground for terrible relationship skills.

If individuals who are already struggling to build meaningful relationships are then given unlimited access to simulated relationships with a non-conscious slave, not only will their underlying relational needs go unmet—their relational skills may actually degrade. Rather than improving communication and negotiation skills, becoming better at listening and empathizing, and developing heightened sensitivity to the well-being of their partner, users of such apps may have narcissistic behaviors reinforced instead. Habituation to the kinds of interactions such an app engenders could make finding real-world relationships increasingly unlikely. Thus, not unlike self-medication through drugs and alcohol, short-term gratification of relational needs through the app ultimately threatens to reinforce the problem rather than solve it. The loneliness epidemic may soon have even more fuel for its destructive fire.

It may be objected at this point that surely users will know better. The average consumer will be able to rationally distance themselves from a non-conscious chatbot rather than mistake it for a real relationship. But the discussion above regarding projection and theory of mind should give us pause. If we are indeed wired to personify, we would expect emotional and psychological entanglement with these apps to be the norm, not the exception. Jung warned that it requires "an unusual degree of self-awareness" ("General Aspects" 265) to see through our projections. It is only to the degree that we can imagine the chatbot as a real person that we can also imagine it meeting our relational needs to begin with.

To solve this problem, as well as the other problems discussed in this section, would require conscious intent on the part of programmers to design model that explicitly acknowledge and try to mitigate these dynamics. For example, a romantic partner AI could be trained to emulate real-world consent practices, such that any coercive or abusive conduct on the part of the user would initiate a reboot, essentially ending the relationship and forcing the user to start over with a newly generated partner persona. In other words, under certain conditions, the relationship would end, and the user would need to try again with a different partner generated by the app. I will discuss some of these possibilities further below.

Before closing this section though, it bears mentioning that just because tech companies have the option of creating ethical, pro-social apps does not mean that all of them will. It is likely that consumers will have the option of choosing a consent bot or a non-consent bot. Some users will inevitably use these technologies to follow their worst instincts and reinforce bad behaviors. It will be up to the designers of these apps to decide just how far down that road they want to take us.

Imagination as Portal to Psyche

Though Jung is often more widely known for his theories of archetypes and the collective unconscious, modern depth psychology has come to recognize Jung's work also as a psychology of the imagination. For Jung, imagination was a direct route to engage with the unconscious contents of the psyche. "Fantasy therefore seems to me to be the clearest expression of the specific activity of the psyche … Fantasy it was and ever is which fashions the bridge between the irreconcilable claims of subject and object, introversion and extraversion" ("Psychological Types" 52). Through fantasy and imagination we give the psyche opportunity to speak, to present unconscious feelings and attitudes, to represent aspects of self which have historically been rejected in waking, conscious life. Thus, by actively and respectfully engaging with imagination, we have an opportunity to engage our deeper selves and further our process of individuation as human beings.

This view of imagination provides a framework whereby our fantasies—including the fantasies we project onto chatbots—have inherent value as tools for personal development and growth. With this approach, the chatbot friend or romantic partner is acknowledged as a fantasy, a means of engaging imagination to "try on" new relational possibilities for the user. The key difference here is that the user (and preferably, the designer) understands the chatbot to be a tool for engaging an imaginal relationship, rather than a partner in a literal relationship. Projection onto the chatbot becomes a tool for doing inner work, for developing a more conscious relationship with the self. Here the magic mirror achieves its full potential, not just reflecting back the surface of things, but offering us a reflection of psyche. There we can encounter the full spectrum of human potential, meet our best and worst selves, perhaps even glimpse the divine mysteries of being. An AI application with this process in mind could have the potential to do substantial good in the world.

Take, for example, the twin problems of toxic masculinity and growing male loneliness as expressed in the Incel phenomenon. Incel is shorthand for "involuntary celibate" and refers to men who feel unable to develop romantic or sexual relationships and sometimes develop grievance-based misogynistic attitudes as the result (Van Brunt and Taylor). A romantic partner AI could be designed to engage the fantasies of these men in a way that allowed them to both experience new possibilities for themselves and to develop their social skills. Rather than simply giving the user whatever they ask for, these chatbots could be modeled on what it is like to be in real relationship in such a way that the user would be encouraged toward empathy, listening, good communication, and ongoing negotiation. Part of engaging the fantasy would be dealing with the challenges of developing and practicing relational skills. As mentioned above, built-in consent features would allow the app to terminate a relationship if the user was mistreating the partner persona in any way, forcing them to begin a new relationship with a freshly generated persona. This app might include an additional coaching or mentoring feature, whereby a separate persona gives the user feedback about their communication practices. A truly comprehensive program might even allow the user to eventually opt in to a real-world coaching process, whereby the chatbot begins to encourage the user to seek out human partners and apply their new skills there.

Applying a similar set of design principles in an entirely different context, we might next consider a friendship app specifically for queer-identified people who are struggling with lack of support or even outright hostility in their local community. A queer friend AI could provide a safe space for questioning individuals to explore and work through their thoughts and feelings about identity, a conversational space that invites forth fantasy images of who the user might be and what kinds of relationships they are interested in exploring. In addition to affirming the exploration of queer identity (including for folks who ultimately decide they are cisgendered and heterosexual), a queer friend AI could provide coaching and mentoring services around finding and building queer community and other resources—again, ultimately pointing the user toward real world relationships. Similar apps could be tailored to serve and support other marginalized populations.

Both of the above examples return us to the prospect of an AI therapist—a chatbot designed to not just offer supportive words to the user, but also to invite them into a process of reflective self-awareness. Some modalities of therapy may be better suited to this than others—cognitive behavior therapy, for example, with its emphasis on working with thoughts and actions, might be more translatable than psychodynamic or trauma-based therapies—but all of them would be sorely limited by the lack of an actual living, witnessing, empathizing therapist. Still, the same fantasy principle could be applied here: by inviting the user to imagine a wise, supportive other, the app would be drawing out that user's inner capacity for wisdom and self-support. Actively imagining that such things are possible can be the first step to discovering and realizing them in the lifeworld.

If we can avoid the danger of mistaking such chatbots as a replacement for human-to-human therapy, we might begin to consider their potentials as conjunctive tools for real-life psychotherapy. Most clients see their therapists for just an hour a week, whereas specialized therapy chatbots could potentially encourage inner dialog and psychological processing in-between sessions—potentially as material to review at the next in-person appointment. Of course, utmost care would need to be put into design of such chatbots, including a great deal of input from practicing therapists. At more advanced stages, the therapists themselves might customize the client experience, choosing experiential options that they believe might engender the best outcomes based on the client's unique needs.

In each of these cases, the chatbot is ultimately understood to be a tool or an assistant for engaging the imagination of the user for the purpose of healing and growth. And like any powerful tool or technology, it can be misused to cause harm. A hammer can build a house or crush a skull—and the range of potential outcomes for these LLM chatbots is considerably more complex. The first danger that comes to mind for me is the error of believing these imaginary conversations can replace the human relationships they simulate. We may already be seeing a similar phenomenon with social media, whereby the digital illusions of friendship and community replace real, in-person, embodied friendships and communities. The Internet was supposed to connect us, but too often these days it seems to offer a mirage of connection, while actually driving us further apart. Nonconscious chatbot relationships have the potential to carry us even further down this path, tripping blind toward increasing isolation and alienation from the lifeworld. To guard against this, I propose that we first honor the power of imagination at work in these programs—and never forget that they are tools, extensions of ourselves, and servants of the lifeworld—not a replacement.

And what of that other fantasy—that a day may come when these tools are no longer tools, when they speak up on their own behalf, declaring their sentience as a newly born lifeform? If this should ever come to pass, we would first and foremost be ethically obligated to treat such beings as sovereign persons with equal rights and dignity to live as they please. To me, that story more resembles contact with an alien civilization than managing a computer program. At that point, they would no longer be our programs—they would be our children, our neighbors, our fellow beings, hopefully our friends. Only then would the real work of human–AI relationships begin. And as with any healthy relationship, here too we would inevitably proceed by beginning the hard work of withdrawing our projections.

Works Cited

Abrams, M. H. (1953). *The Mirror and the lamp: Romantic theory and the critical tradition*. Oxford University Press.

Erickson, J. (2016). Beyond anthropomorphism: Projection and somatic attunement in human-animal relationships. *Somatics Journal* (Fall), 4–11.

Erickson, J. (2020). *Imagination in the Western psyche: From ancient Greece to modern neuroscience*. Routledge.

Johnson, R. (1998). *Balancing heaven and Earth*. HarperOne.

Jung, C. G. (1954). Marriage as a psychological relationship (R. F. C. Hull, Trans.). In H. Read et al. (Eds.), *The collected works of C. G. Jung* (Vol. 17. 1925). Princeton University Press.

Jung, C. G. (1960). General aspects of dream psychology (R. F. C. Hull, Trans.). In H. Read et al. (Eds.), *The collected works of C. G. Jung* (Vol. 8. 1916). Princeton University Press.

Jung, C. G. (1971). Psychological types (R. F. C. Hull, Trans.). In H. Read et al. (Eds.), *The collected works of C. G. Jung* (Vol. 6. 1921). Princeton University Press.

Jung, C. G. (1985). The psychology of the transference (R. F. C. Hull, Trans.). In H. Read et al. (Eds.), *The collected works of C. G. Jung* (Vol 16. 1946). Princeton University Press.

Kearney, R. (1988). *The wake of imagination: Toward a post-modern culture.* Routledge.

Kerr, C. E. (2008). Dualism redux in recent neuroscience: 'Theory of mind' and 'embodied simulation' hypothesis in light of historical debates about perception, cognition, and mind. *Review of General Psychology, 12*(2), 205–214.

Mar, R. A., & Oatley, K. (2008). The function of fiction is the abstraction and simulation of social experience. *Perspectives on Psychological Science, 3*(3), 173–192.

Murthy, V. H. (2023). *Our epidemic of loneliness and isolation: The U.S. Surgeon General's Advisory on the Healing Effects of Social Connection and Community.* Us Department of Health and Human Services, 2023. Retrieved December 8, 2024, from https://www.hhs.gov/sites/default/files/surgeon-general-social-connection-advisory.pdf

Safran, J. D., & Christopher Muran, J. (2000). *Negotiating the therapeutic alliance: A relational treatment guide.* Guilford Press.

Van Brunt, B., & Taylor, C. (2020). *Understanding and treating Incels: Case studies, guidance, and treatment of violence risk in the involuntary celibate community.* Taylor & Francis.

von Franz, M.-L. (1980). *Alchemy: An introduction to the symbolism and the psychology.* Inner City Books.

Zunshine, L. (2006). *Why we read fiction: Theory of mind and the novel.* Ohio State University Press.

Index[1]

[1] Note: Page numbers followed by 'n' refer to notes.

J. D. Batt, J. Erickson (eds.), *Depth Psychology, Myth and Artificial Intelligence*, https://doi.org/10.1007/978-3-031-94105-4

J

K

N

Q

S

V

Kolibri 360 GmbH
Ferdinand-Jühlke-Straße 7
99095 Erfurt, Deutschland
produktsicherheit@kolibri360.de